The Public Speaker's
Handbook of Humor

THE PUBLIC

Baker Book House

SPEAKER'S HANDBOOK OF HUMOR

Helen and Larry Eisenberg

Grand Rapids, Michigan

Library of Congress catalog card number: 67-21142

Printed in the United States of America

DEDICATED . . .

to FRANCES EISENBERG, with her ability to
enjoy the humor in all of life . . .

to FOUR BOSTON UNIVERSITY FRIENDS whose
encouragement was invaluable: John Ward,
Sam Hedrick, Cliff Moore, and Dean Walter
Muelder . . .

and to EVAN ESAR, whose analytical insight
into humor has been a special inspiration.

Foreword

We're sure you've noted how people respond with interest when someone says, "Have you heard the one about . . .?" Americans in general love humor and use it often in communication. We personally believe that God has a marvelous sense of humor and has passed it on to people. When you use an appropriate, carefully chosen bit of humor, people will recall it long after your more abstract points have been forgotten.

In this book we have sought to include a wide variety of humor for all sorts of occasions. We've even illustrated our own points in describing humor with humor. We have selected special entries for toastmasters, masters of ceremony, and meeting chairmen. Included are sample introductions and responses to introductions, as well as humor for the body of talks and meetings, and for closings.

We felt that you would appreciate humor for welcoming people, honoring them, helping them to celebrate anniversaries, birthdays, the winning of contests, as well as humor for baby and bridal showers, and for saying kind words to those leaving communities and organizations in transfers or retirement. There's also humor here for those who must take collections.

This compilation of humor has resulted from a growing file of clippings made over a period of more than fifteen years, from such publications as the *Reader's Digest; The Saturday Evening Post; Collier's; Coronet; Sunshine Magazine and Magazet; Wall Street Journal; A. M. A. News; Time;* the journals of the *PTA, Kiwanis, Rotary,* and *Lions; Gluey Gleanings; Wild West Joke Book; Class-*

mate; *Modern Maturity;* Iowa State Traveling Men's *Accidotes; The Postage Stamp; Lookout; Guideposts; Astronomer Royal; Tid-Bits* (London); *Changing Times; Volkswagen News; Southern Planter.* If we have not properly credited anyone, we would like to know so that we can rectify the matter in the next printing.

Getting the manuscript in shape was a family affair, with Helen, Laren, Johnny, and Larry all doing typing and correcting, and Donny helping to arrange and classify material. Always we are indebted to many people for assistance. Larry thanks Dr. John Ward of Boston University School of Theology for a most useful directed study in "Humor in Communication." We want to thank also Dr. Sam Hedrick, Evan Esar, Bob Shelton, Dick Moore, Martha Stewart, Tex Evans, Ben and Ethel Bowers, Lewis Odneal, Tom Curtis, and Mildred Baker for their encouragement. In addition to credited contributions in the book we want to thank Jim Greever, Tilly Bruce, Agnes Pylant, Jeanne Hill, Mrs. Donald Mitchell, Mary Ellen Garrett, Edward Winckley, Margaret Curtis, Joe Baker, Nancy Bell Thompson, Webb Garrison, A. W. Ferriss, George Steinman, Haviland Houston, Mary Hilda Hix, Jacquelin Dunkerly, Jim Watts, Jim Flynn, Bryan Hall, Pauline Crain, Dwight Dussair, Don Houts, George Manly, Dr. Robert Ozment, Dr. John L. Casteel, and Ben Solomon for humor.

We thank these people for permission to quote: Fred Russell and the *Nashville Banner;* Abingdon Press for "Stage" from *The Fun Encyclopedia;* Crown Publishers and Nathan Ausubel for material from *A Treasury of Jewish Folklore;* Bill Adler for quotes from *The Johnson Humor;* Association Press and Carl F. Burke for two selections from *God Is For Real, Man;* Harper & Row and Dr. Eugene Nida for material from *Customs and Cultures;* and Prentice-Hall and Abigail Van Buren for material from *Dear Abby.* These books are also listed in the Selected Bibliography.

The compilers are always interested to hear how you got along, if you care to drop us a note, care of the publishers.

We close with a word of deep gratitude to Bob Elfers, Roland Burdick, and Evelyn Walters of Association Press. Without them the book wouldn't have been possible.

Helen and Larry Eisenberg

Contents

Part I.

How, When, and Where to Use Humor

At home . . . At your desk, in the study . . . As a
speaker . . . As a toastmaster, master of ceremonies, or
meeting chairman . . . Other people and groups likely
to find material and help here . . . Other uses for this
humor collection . . . How do you collect material?

What does humor do? . . . Some basic types of humor
. . . Telling a funny story . . . The seriousness of humor
. . . Introducing humor

Part II.

For the Speechmaker and Meeting Leader

Part III.

Humor

Page

Quick Reference Index

(for the person with only a few minutes)

Using some of the most likely categories we give you some quick help. In some cases, the particular humor would need to be adapted to your particular need.

1. "Executive Express." For the speaker who wants to look up thirty-five clever ones that should click—quick! 1; 8; 76; 77; 93; 128; 133; 134; 141; 158; 179; 202; 212; 247; 279; 516; 525; 563; 571; 592; 612; 617; 647; 650; 683; 822; 831; 896; 1452; 1638; 1661; 1833; 1861; 1885; 1917.

2. "Getting Off the Hook." See 1207–1232 for jokes about diplomacy, tact, ingenuity; try also: 121; 123; 138; 160; 219; 528; 724; 1194; 1521; 1526; 1527; 1557; 1559; 1606; 1612; 1652; 1673; 1680; 1762; 1769; 1798; 1871.

3. Toastmaster/Toastmistress Responsibilities. See all of Chapter 3, and see "Eating" (1398–1438). In this index see No. 1, Executive Express; No. 11, Skits, Stunts, and Entertainment; No. 6, Coffee Break Fun. And try these: 6; 139; 291; 649; 660; 724; 727; 729; 830; 896; 922; 924; 956; 989; 1539; 1542; 1574; 1583; 1712; 1737; 1744; 1765; 1771; 1776.

4. Master/Mistress of Ceremonies. Use list No. 3, same as for toastmaster. See also No. 8, Women's Club or Group; No. 11, Skits, Stunts, and Entertainment; No. 12, Name-Dropping.

13

5. **Breathers for Meetings.** You're the chairman, and you want things to be relaxed. See especially chapters 6 and 7. In this index see No. 6, Coffee Break Fun; No. 1, "Executive Express."

6. **Coffee Break Fun.** See chapters 6 and 7, and check these: 28; 29; 156; 247; 250; 275; 279; 286; 291; 720; 737; 747; 924; 937; 949; 1300; 1371; 1372; 1648.

7. **Service Club speech** for such organizations as Rotary, Kiwanis, Lions, Optimist, Civitan, Ruritan, and Toastmaster's Club. Check "Eating" (1398–1438), "Business" (1619–1707), "Sports" 1466–1564), and any others you like. Also try these: 66; 76; 77; 152; 186; 203; 218; 286; 291; 308; 400; 514; 520; 600; 612; 642; 724; 767; 892; 1243; 1613.

8. **Women's Club or Group.** Check 1398–1428; 1098–1285; 1286–1345; 1565–1605. Here is a quick list: 12; 108; 120; 130; 138; 145; 147; 223; 231; 263; 423; 484; 505; 522; 527; 598; 726; 735; 769; 800; 825; 1031.

9. **Sermons.** See 2052–2166 and any other appealing categories. Here is your quick list: 1; 76; 148; 159; 161; 177; 180; 202; 410; 528; 655; 684; 685; 699; 717; 740; 772;. 890; 931; 956; 973; 975; 1382; 1710; 1879.

10. **School or College Assembly.** See also No. 11, Skits, Stunts, and Entertainment in this index; see "Education" (2167–2196), and any other appealing categories. Check these: 24; 80; 129; 163; 187; 190; 202; 204; 208; 212; 240; 516; 519; 650; 747; 763; 975; 1150; 1389; 1398; 1452; 1470; 1539; 1594; 1607.

11. **Skits, Stunts, and Entertainment.** See chapters 6 and 7, the Texas section (907–955), and any other appealing categories. Some of these below can be elaborated into simple skits: 21; 26; 29; 66; 120; 121; 134; 187; 231; 236; 250; 291; 296; 306; 308; 364; 566; 567; 568; 572; 630; 713; 716; 720; 1590.

12. **Name-dropping.** Sometime you like to use some well-known names. Here are twenty-five entries: Brigitte Bardot, 822; John Barrymore, 817; Bob Benchley, 217; Robert Browning, 1583; Bennett Cerf, 1047; Sir Winston Churchill, 1869; Diogenes, 1964; Queen

Elizabeth, 1034; Horace Greeley, 2040; LBJ, 692–695; King Herod, 1927; Bob Hope, 1537; Gina Lollobrigida, 869; Mozart, 340; Napoleon, 1799; Sir Isaac Newton, 1298; Rubinstein, 1565; Rin Tin Tin, 1365; Knute Rockne, 1546; Picasso, 1575; Rockefeller, 158; George Bernard Shaw, 1379; Thoreau, 282; Mark Twain, 740; Queen Victoria, 717; Whistler's father, 1574.

13. **Socials, Parties.** See No. 6, Coffee Break Fun, and No. 11, Skits, Stunts, and Entertainment. Copy out some and hand around for guests to read aloud. At meals, put under their plates to be read as conversation starters. See especially chapters 6 and 7.

14. **Making a Speech on "Humor."** You'll find Chapter 2 especially helpful, as well as chapters 5–8.

15. **Business.** See 1619–1707, and check these: 7; 16; 58; 161; 195; 202; 236; 256; 269; 274; 304; 515; 523; 531; 670; 703; 706; 1018; 1036; 1159; 1262; 1414.

16. **Religion.** See "The World of Religion" (2052–2166); see No. 9, Sermons, in this index, and this list: 60; 102; 103; 114; 128; 137; 138; 273; 279; 296; 364; 555; 564; 683; 684; 697; 700; 704; 743; 765; 774; 892; 1531; 1685; 1905.

17. **Medicine and Health.** See 1708–1814 and this list: 147; 157; 180; 201; 696; 698; 735; 982; 1612; 1702.

18. **Men and Women (Battle of the Sexes).** See 863–906 plus: 12; 33; 120; 231; 237; 261; 266; 268; 277; 278; 341; 405; 686; 696; 728; 767; 800; 805; 830; 832; 858; 860.

19. **Home, Family, Kids.** "Home and Family" is 1286–1345; Kids, 956–1036. See also: 189; 226; 228; 237; 240; 260; 513; 723; 725; 726; 737; 742; 773; 819; 831; 1225; 1382; 1460; 1915.

20. **Politics.** See 1868–1880 plus this list (adapting to fit): 58; 68; 85; 87; 101; 111; 122; 129; 133; 157; 179; 191; 202; 211; 240; 501; 531; 612; 692; 707; 727; 896; 1386; 1451; 1532.

21. **Sports.** See "Sports" (1466–1564, including General, Boxing, Golf, Baseball, Football, Fishing) plus these: 7; 85; 93; 142; 199; 203; 240; 242; 541; 819; 910; 916; 1066; 1326; 1338; 1353; 1356; 1358; 1366; 1372; 1379; 1383; 1913; 1916; 1999.

22. **Military.** See "The Military" (1939–1975) and "Independence Day" (1447–1451). In this index see No. 6, Coffee Break Fun; No. 7, Service Club Speech; No. 1, "Executive Express"; No. 21, Sports. Also these (adapting to fit your situation): 27; 76; 96; 148; 186; 1035; 1073; 1243; 1253; 1274; 1313; 1323; 1388; 1444; 1594; 1616; 1637; 1645; 1646; 1655; 1663; 1665; 1683; 1748; 1765.

23. **Occupational Quick Reference:** Barber, 1696–1701; Boss, 1639–1647; Cannibal, 747–762; Dentist, 1776–1782; Doctor, 1730–1768; Judge, 1823–1834; Lawyer, 1835–1843; Mechanic, 1703–1704; Nurse, 1769–1774; Plumber, 1702; Police, 1844–1851; Preacher, 2077–2113; Professor, 2197–2207; Pychiatrist, 1783–1811; Salesman, 1670–1680; Stenographer/Secretary, 1648–1669; Teacher, 2208–2245; Waiter, 1412–1438; Weatherman, 1613.

24. **Quick Reference to Types of Humor:** Conundrums, 345–384; Daffynitions, 385–513; Jingles, 414–530; Nonsense, 566–585; Puns, 318–344; Signs, 604–628; 1688–1695; 2145–2160.

25. **General Quick Reference:** Advice, 1098–1101; Aged, 1072–1097; Animals, 1346–1358; Crime, 1815–1822; Eating, 1398–1407; Efficiency 1102–1108; Enthusiasm, 1114–1118; Holidays, 1439–1465; Humility 1143–1152; Ingenuity, 1155–1160; Insults/Slams, 1186–1196; International Customs and Cultures, 1881–1931; Jewish Folklore 696–705; Marriage, 850–862; Modern Life, 1976–2024; Movies, 1596–1605; Music 1565–1572; Prejudice 1180–1183; Scouts, 1037–1041; Signs, 604–628; 1688–1695; 2145–2160; Success/Failure, 1197–1206; Tact, 1207–1232; Teen-Agers, 1042–1071; Texans, 907–955; Tourists, 775–782; Trouble/Worry, 1266–1275; Writing, 1580–1582.

26. **"Short Speech" Angles:** When you want to use humor to honor people, here are some helps, together with lead-in wording: Baby Shower, 251–260; Birthday, 236–250; Bridal Shower, 261–271; Contest Winner, 212–220; General Honoring, 202–211; Good-bye Occasions, 272–280; Money-Raising, 289–305; Retirement, 281–288; Wedding Anniversary, 221–231; Welcoming, 189–201.

PART 1

How,
When, and
Where
to Use Humor

1

How to Use This Book

A little girl, asked by a visitor what her daddy did, thought a minute and said, "He sits at a desk and throws away papers."(1)*

We can just see you now—ready for a speech, trying to get it all together. You're trying to make your transitions. (Adam said to Eve as they were leaving the Garden of Eden, "This is the age of transition." [2]) If this is your condition, you may want to jump right ahead to the humorous material. But we'd like to suggest some ways you as a communicator can use this book.

AT HOME

Try it as a bedside reader, bathroom reader, and beside-the-easy-chair amuser. Or use it as a read-aloud book for friends and guests. If you're the cook, let them read to you while you're getting the meal. Other possibilities include weddings, anniversaries, recep-

---

* Bits of humor and most ideas for speakers and leaders to use are numbered consecutively throughout this book. In most cases this number precedes the joke, but in a few it follows the joke and is enclosed in parentheses. The Index is keyed to these numbers.

tions, home parties, family homecomings, and the like. **Make notes in the margins for later use. Underline.**

AT YOUR DESK, IN THE STUDY

Read a few pages a day. Underline. Jot down some favorites for wallet, pocket, or purse. Make notes in the book's margins. Use for a relaxer. Use as a reminder for jokes you know. Note them in the margins or put them on cards.

AS A SPEAKER

Become acquainted with the system of reference and cross-reference. Do all the things suggested above.

AS A TOASTMASTER, MASTER OF CEREMONIES, OR MEETING CHAIRMAN

You will find humor here that you can use for breathers, for "in-between," for greetings and good-byes, for honoring people.

OTHER PEOPLE AND GROUPS LIKELY TO FIND MATERIAL AND HELP HERE

Radio and TV personalities, hostesses, school people, salesmen, ministers, club leaders (especially for older adult clubs). Professional meetings, gatherings of church leaders and missionaries, wedding parties, receptions, community gatherings, coffee breaks, and many other types of group meetings. Editors of humor columns may find some of their favorites here. And we mustn't forget summer camps; many of the jokes here can be made into skits.

OTHER USES FOR THIS HUMOR COLLECTION

- For the little crowd at lunch.
- For speeches on the subject of humor.

- For bulletin boards. Copy some out. Change them often. Have someone draw illustrations.
- For money collections.
- For international student gatherings—as illustration of American humor.
- For showers, anniversaries, birthdays, honoring contest winners, going-away parties, retirement affairs, and the like.
- As a trip companion.
- As a stimulator for skits and stunts.
- As a gift.
- Use the Selected Bibliography to find other humor books. Make your own collection.

HOW DO YOU COLLECT MATERIAL?

- Keep a notebook handy when listening to speakers of any kind, and jot down their best ones.
- Subscribe to periodicals that feature interesting humor. Most of the men's service clubs qualify here: Rotary, Lions, Kiwanis, Civitan, etc. **Sunshine Magazine,** Litchfield, Illinois, is an excellent source. The **Reader's Digest, Coronet, The Saturday Evening Post,** as well as a number of the farm magazines have good jokes. The publications of Girl and Boy Scouts and Campfire Girls, the **PTA Magazine,** and the **Wall Street Journal** usually have some very good humor. **Quote,** 309 S. Main, Anderson, S.C. 29621 is a weekly publication especially for those speaking a great deal. It contains serious material as well as humor and is highly valuable for the "constant" speaker, especially clergy and civic leaders. In clipping these, the authors have found long envelopes handy, since they hold small clippings better than the file folders.
- Get a number of good collections of humor and get familiar with them. Our Selected Bibliography gives many. Your bookstore could furnish more, no doubt.
- Practice developing a "topical mind." This means the facility to think of some humor when you hear or use a key word.

- You might particularly want to have a few collections of short material to be read aloud to groups. **Dear Abby, People of Note, O Ye Jigs and Juleps,** and **Fun with Skits, Stunts and Stories** are examples. (See Selected Bibliography.)

The authors would be happy to hear how you've used humor in your speechmaking, if you have time to write, sometime.

2

Humor in Communicating

Two young fellows in a sports car were touring through Canada. One asked the waitress in the restaurant what was the town. "Saskatoon, Saskatchewan," she said.

"Good grief, Bill," he exclaimed, "they don't even speak English!"(3)

WHAT DOES HUMOR DO?

If you're going to speak English, and use humorous English, you might want to look into what humor is and does.

Humor Brings Laughter generally. This is a physical and psychological good. The expansiveness you feel with humor is like that of good health, good mood.

Plato said that humor is like an itch, involving both pain and pleasure at once. The emphasis, he said, is on the pleasure side. The late Adlai Stevenson, defeated in his candidacy for the White House, said, "A funny thing happened to me on the way to the White House . . . "(4) His audience roared with laughter. He had them with him immediately.

Humor Creates Sociability. We enjoy laughing together, especially when we have something in common. In a Baptist gathering a speaker was on the subject of "groupness." Looking on the negative side, he said, "When you have twenty-five people, all of different mind, what do you have?"

A voice from the rear spoke up, "A Baptist church!"(5)

Humor Gets Attention. It can help you get the attention of the audience and keep it. The speaker must be careful not to overdo it, but most audiences are ready for another "good one."

Humor Makes Points Stick. Hang your point upon humor, and hearers are more likely to remember it. Dr. J. Robert Nelson says that he discovered this when, after delivering scholarly lectures to a theology conference in Scotland, the committee asked for his notes. When the conference publication was issued, the only Nelson in it was his three humor contributions!

Humor Leavens the Lump, Lightens the Load. When Americans have meetings, they often want "a serious part," meaning a speaker. If you're it, you may find it best to punctuate your contribution with humor.

Humor Is a Leveler. It can bring speaker and audience to the same plane of existence. Often the presentation of the speaker is done with such flourish that he is actually at a disadvantage with his audience. One such speaker set aside the flourishes by saying simply, "This all sounds so exciting that I can hardly wait to hear me speak!"(6)

Humor Can Help to Prevent or to Relieve Embarrassment. A late speaker said that he was like the Scout leader on a field hike who came puffing up to a little store to ask if a group of Scouts had come by recently, explaining, "I'm their leader."(7) The speaker was off the hook, and the group forgave him.

Humor Can Be a Peacemaker, relieving tension, even showing the absurdity of contention. In one major church denomination for many years women's missionary work (that carried on primarily by single women) had been under a separate administration from the "regular" missionary work (primarily by couples and single men missionaries). The denomination decided to unite the two administrations, and naturally this reorganization was quite a complicated procedure which required many meetings, working out many details, and occasionally created animosities.

A committee had finally agreed that in the new organization personnel would be 60 per cent men and 40 per cent women. Then this question arose, which inspired heated debate: Should bishops, who were ex-officio but always men, count under the male quota? In the midst of the argument, a committee member arose and told this story:

Some American tourists were in Scotland; they had never before seen a Scotsman and knew nothing of Scottish dress. They saw a Scotsman in kilts. Was he male or female? They sent one of their number over to examine him more closely. Returning, the "delegate" said, "I didn't talk to him, but I saw the label on his garment. It said 'Middlesex'!"(8)

The animosity bubble was punctured!

Humor Can Help Deal With Enemies, whether enemies are ideas or persons. The conservative can laugh at the liberal by calling him a man with his feet firmly planted in midair.(9) The liberal may come right back with the assertion that a conservative is one who doesn't believe anything should be done for the first time!(10)

Humor Can Establish Your Wit, giving you a favored position with your hearers. A British speaker said that Robin Hood today would be no cheap crook. He would be busy with a book on **A General Theory of Wealth Distribution** and would be elected to Parliament with a good chance of being the next Chancellor of the Exchequer!(11) His Tory audience liked it very much.

Humor Can Permit a Speaker to Say What He Wouldn't Say Seriously. The clever speaker can joke about it and mean it, and the audience will take it. Clergymen know this. Teachers do too, and so do all clever speakers. In Elizabethan days Ben Jonson elaborated on the value of "moral comedy" to correct. For instance, a speaker used this story to illustrate how a certain professional group tended to theorize too much.

"I contend that the plays of Shakespeare were written by Queen Elizabeth," insisted a well-known scholar.

A listener was not sure. "I can hardly believe that a **woman** wrote those plays," he said.

"Ah, but my contention is," said the great scholar, "that Queen Elizabeth was a man!"(12)

Humor Can Soften the Blow, even when the collection is taken. In this book is a special section of humor for collection purposes. These are a dozen of the reasons that communicators—speakers, teachers, clergy, workers-with-people in general—use humor as a merry medicine.

SOME BASIC TYPES OF HUMOR

Humor is difficult to get at because it takes so many forms. Reaction to it is not always the same—some humor calls for laughter, but other brings only an appreciative smile.

We want to describe several types of humor, leaning heavily on Evan Esar, who has studied humor in great depth (and who feels that humor is so important in communication that there should be a Chair of Humorology in at least one major University).

The Incongruous. Two unrelated things, brought together, make us smile or laugh. For instance, a man walking down the street politely tips his hat to a woman. As he raises the hat, a pigeon flies out.(13) Not being what we expect, we laugh.

Spoonerisms. This form of humor is named for an Englishman who in the mid-nineteenth century enjoyed twisting syllables and letters of words to form a humorous result. "Colonel Stoopnagle," as an outstanding radio comedian, profited from this form in relating fairy tales and historical stories with such titles as "The Pea Litte Thrigs" and "Paul Revide's Rear." (Both are available in **Fun With Skits, Stunts and Stories.** See Selected Bibliography.)

Puns. Puns involve plays on the sounds of words, with humorous result. While all puns are not necessarily funny, the modern hearer would expect a pun to be either humorous or witty. Shakespeare loved puns.

Ben Jonson once offered to make a pun on any subject. Someone shouted, "The King!"

His reply was quick: "The King is not a subject!"(14)

Hyperbole. This is a form of exaggeration that brings up colorful visual imagery. "I nearly died laughing" or "I had them rolling in the aisles" are common expressions which illustrate hyperbole. It does not always bring laughter, but the hearer usually appreciates the exaggeration. We ourselves often say, "It was raining cats and dogs," but a punster added, "and I stepped in a poodle!"(15) Both are hyperbole.

Comic Definitions. Sometimes these are called "daffynitions," and actually they are more often witticisms than definitions. We moderns like to think of this as a new form. Listen to these ancient ones:

16 Anarcharsis, the Greek philosopher, in 600 B.C. defined a market place as "a space marked out for the purposes of cheating."

17 The Chinese philosopher Chuang-tzu, in the fourth century B.C. gave two definitions of an optimist. One was "A woman who expects an egg to crow in the morning." The second, "A man who hopes to shoot down a bird by looking at an arrow!"

Satire. It ridicules, usually in good nature, seeking to cure the foolishness of men by laughing at it. Evan Esar's definition of satire is itself satire: "Satire is a mirror in which beholders generally discover everybody's face but their own."(18) Sarcasm is not so good-natured. Its intention is to have a victim. "That's a lovely dress, dear. Too bad they didn't have it in your size!"(19)

Irony. Irony is a mild form of sarcasm. The meaning is usually exactly opposite the words. For instance, a sign on the newly-seeded lawn says, "Please!" It means, "Please keep off!"(20)

This patient clerk is using irony on the woman shopper who, having looked at practically every blanket in the store, finally says, "Actually, I don't want to buy one. I'm looking for a friend."

The clerk was polite. "I'll take down the last blanket, ma'am, if you think he's in it!"(21)

The Epigram. This is a witticism making a universal comment upon a class of particulars. Here are some:

22 The best way to tell a woman's age is not to.

23 **Most people** listen with their mouths.

The Stereotyped Role. This form of humor predicts that a person will act in predictable ways. The image is usually not complimentary. Many mother-in-law, henpecked-husband, traveling-salesman, and cultural and racial jokes would come in this category. It may represent rejection, animosity.

The Parody. Using the same form or meter as the original, it takes a song or poem, sometimes even prose, and substitutes other words, with humor or ridicule in mind. "Hiawatha" has often been parodied. Popular songs lend themselves to this. Here is an example, using a familiar nursery rhyme:

> Mary had a little slam
> For everyone, and so
> The leaves of her engagement book
> Were always white as snow.(24)

The Malapropism. Sheridan named one of his characters "Mrs. Malaprop" after a French term meaning "inappropriate" or "out of place." Mrs. Malaprop says such things as this: "If I apprehend anything in this world, it is the use of my oracular tongue, and a nice derangement of epitaphs,"(25) denying stoutly that she does use words she does not understand. Sam Goldwyn, the movie producer, was said to use the malapropism (some think, deliberately). When they were considering titling a movie "The Optimist," Goldwyn asked that the name be changed, for how many of the public would actually know that this was an eye doctor?(26)

The Anecdote. This is a humorous tale about a person, usually about his likable foibles. When General Hooker, one of Lincoln's officers during the Civil War, telegraphed grandly, "Headquarters in the saddle," Lincoln replied, "He has his headquarters where his hindquarters ought to be."(27)

Farce, Slapstick, Buffoonery, Mimicry. This humor is situational, visual. You know the kind: pie-throwing, Keystone Cop, clown, exaggeration. The humor is in the overdoing. The danger is that it may cease to be funny if it is overdone excessively.

The Tall Tale. A verbal form of exaggeration, celebrating the impossible. Texas is known for tall tales. This book has a special section for Texas. "Did you know, friend, that it got so hot in West Texas one time that the sun just came right down out of the sky and got under a cactus?!"(28)

The Tongue Twister. These contain syllables hard to pronounce, like "thirty-six sick theologs." But here's a twist on the twister:

29 **Two Ubangi girls** with their big lips were trying tongue twisters. One said, " 'Peter Piper picked a peck of pickled peppers.' Now you fan me for a little while."

The Freudian Slip. Freud maintained that many of our mistakes are not really accidental but come from hidden thoughts that we dare not express. When they come out, they are labeled "Freudian slips."

30 **When Anne Morrow Lindbergh** was a little girl, her mother was afraid she'd speak of Mr. Rockefeller's big nose when he visited for tea. Mother warned daughter. When the visitor came, Anne exchanged pleasantries, then went on upstairs like a little lady. Greatly relieved, the mother turned to her guest and said, "Mr. Rockefeller, would you have cream in your nose?"

TELLING A FUNNY STORY

Some people have a knack for telling humorous stories, or even for being spontaneously funny. If you are one of these, you are fortunate. For anyone there are some pointers to keep in mind.

First, you will want to decide whether or not it is appropriate to tell the story you have in mind to this particular person or audience. Having decided that it is all right, be sure that you have the details in mind. Ask yourself in advance, "What makes this funny?" Is it a pun? Is it the irony, or the incongruity? Does it have a funny punch line?

Make sure that your audience follows you all the way, and that you get the details in proper order. If the scene is a school or bakery or synagogue, see to it that the audience understands this. If the fun is based on relationships or conflict, or perhaps embarrassment, help them to feel with the person involved.

However, don't make a story too windy. You may lose your audience. Mark Twain said that a missionary speaker once had him talked into giving four hundred dollars, but continued so long that Twain finally stole ten cents from the collection plate.(31)

Particularly if your story is a pun or a punch liner so that it all hangs on the last few words, try to make sure that everything is in order when you "pull the string."

Emphasis of important words and proper pauses help people to follow you. Let us illustrate with this embarrassing experience of a TV commercial announcer. We'll give you the story as we might tell it.

"There was a TV announcer who had been doing coffee commercials for several years; then he changed sponsors. This time it was a **cigarette** company. On camera for his first new commercial, he took a long draw on his sponsor's cigarette . . . blew a big smoke ring . . . looked into the camera and said . . . 'Man . . . that's **real** coffee!' "(32)

Let's look at this one a bit. We've tried to lay it out with the fewest words necessary. Your audience must know that there was a change in sponsors, and they must have in mind what the change was. This is the reason for emphasizing **cigarette.** The word **new** before **commercial** also reminds them that this is a different experience for the announcer. The dots represent pauses, giving your audience time to visualize, as well as to get the words. Most amateurs don't make enough use of **pauses.** The silences point up what follows.

Here's another illustration. A husband and wife were talking about security. There was a brief silence, then he said, "I was just wondering. . . . If I should die . . . where would **you** be?"

She thought a minute and said, "Right **here!** But what I wonder is . . . where would **you** be?"(33)

Try this one, with the pauses. Get used to placing them before strategic words or phrases. You don't usually **drop** the voice at the beginning of the pause—you imply that something really worth listening for is coming right away.

In telling humorous stories, voice tones are important, and emphasis as well. Nonverbal communication takes place in the telling of a story too. If you anticipate that it is funny, doubtless it will show in your whole being. If your style needs improving, observe carefully how others use humor successfully. Particularly watch their timing.

Humor can be used almost anywhere, even in a funeral sermon! We remember that a sensitive speaker at a funeral was showing how warmly human was the deceased, and he used an illustration from life. Overuse of humor, or inappropriate use, may quickly rebound, hurting the speaker more than helping.

Humor can establish a point or divert attention. In a directed study on "Humor in Communication" with Dr. John Ward at Boston University, one of the authors did an experiment with a speech class. He made a prepared speech, without humor, to half of the class and checked words recalled by the audience. Then at another time he spoke for the same length of time, on the same topic, but using humor. When he checked the twenty most easily recalled words, the percentage was more than double than the first time. While this is not particularly conclusive, it did seem to indicate what most of us know—that we like a story, and particularly a funny one. If you use it properly, it can help your cause. If not, it can divert your audience from your subject.

THE SERIOUSNESS OF HUMOR

Humor can hurt as well as help. It can belittle or elevate. It can tear down or teach. In the Bible, Jesus is shown to use humor many times in his teaching. For instance he has a man straining a gnat from his drink but swallowing a camel(34); another helping a man to get a speck from his eye when he has a huge beam in his own(35); he talks of a camel going through the needle's eye(36). Humor may be a tool or a weapon. It must be handled with care.

One sensitive to persons will not use humor to degrade. Often racial or cultural jokes have sought to belittle someone else, degrade others or, to make them unacceptable. Humor can be delicate and delightful but it can also be crude and inappropriate. The sensible speaker is also sensitive. He or she keeps sensitivity antennae high enough to sense out his group. The responsible speaker uses humor with integrity. If in doubt, it's probably better **not to!**

INTRODUCING HUMOR

A speaker hard put to bring in his joke stamped his foot hard and said, "Didn't that sound like a shot? Speaking of shots . . ."(37)

If your imagination isn't too active today, perhaps these lead-ins would give you some idea about how to start your bit of humor.

1. That reminds me of . . .(38)
2. Have you heard about . . .(39)
3. There was once . . .(40)
4. At the turn of the century . . .(41)
5. This is like the woman who . . .(42)
6. Speaking of humility . . .(43)
7. On TV the other day . . .(44)
8. We all do the same thing. Like this . . .(45)
9. Here's a good way to dodge the issue . . .(46)
10. Rollin Walker makes it clear this way . . .(47)
11. My teen-ager the other day asked me . . .(48)
12. There's a folk tale that says . . .(49)
13. Psychologists tell us . . .(50)
14. Things in New England are not always what they seem . . .(51)
15. I have a friend who often says . . .(52)
16. They were having a heated discussion . . .(53)
17. My wife likes to remind me . . .(54)
18. My boss is a man who . . .(55)
19. In our building we have . . .(56)
20. When I was in school . . .(57)

PART 2

For the Speechmaker and Meeting Leader

3

You Are the Toastmaster...
Master of Ceremonies...
Meeting Chairman

These three jobs are similar in many ways. We'll look first at the individual characteristics of each before we go on to see what they have in common.

TOASTMASTER/TOASTMISTRESS

Your setting is a meal instead of a room or auditorium. Because you are going to be very busy, it may be well to eat early, or only to nibble politely at food. Depending on circumstances, you may be responsible not only for the program, but also for ventilation of the room, for relationships between group and kitchen.

Unless someone else is clearly designated to do it, you are the group's representative. You must keep things moving, lively, and cheerful. You are the one who makes changes, stops the long-winded speaker or enthusiastic performer, and so on. You are the people's clock watcher.

You are probably more likely than the master of ceremonies to have a lot of guests to recognize. This may be done with humor, but should not be done flippantly (for most groups). You have ready some expanders, which can take a bit of time or be left out entirely.

A good banquet or dinner usually has good food, good fellowship, good music, and good speaking. Be sure to read the rest of this chapter—and good luck!

MASTER/MISTRESS OF CEREMONIES

Doubtless you've been chosen because you're a nice guy or gal. They like the zippy way you do things, your personality, your sense of humor. You're a catalyst, but you're not the show.

Unless someone else is holding the reins, you're the director of the program for the time being. Often, if you're a guest, you'll have somebody in the organization to check with, but the job of keeping things moving is up to you.

You set the mood. If the occasion is formal, you must be careful in the use of humor, for humor has some tendency to bring informality. If the free use of humor is in order, have plenty committed to memory, or on cards, or perhaps in your notebook.

You are, of course, the man (or woman) to act for the group in thanking the committee, the speaker, and any other people. You are the one who watches the clock and brings the meeting to a close on time. If the occasion is mostly social, much may depend upon you to carry on.

To get the full benefit of suggestions in this book as to your responsibility, be sure to read pages 19 to 46.

MEETING CHAIRMAN/CHAIRWOMAN

We make no atempt to tell you how you should chair a meeting. This section simply gives you some pointers in using humor in your job.

Ways You as Presider Can Use Humor

Laughter brings togetherness, something often lacking in meetings. Here are a dozen ideas:

- As an attention getter. At the beginning of the meeting, tell a good one, just for fun.
- As a reliever when things get dull in the meeting.
- As a point maker, calling the group to focus attention on a phase of its work.
- To get yourself or someone else off the hook.
- To quiet the group down or correct them. It's best if they laugh about it.
- To greet, welcome, say hello or good-bye. (See especially Chapter 5 in this book.)
- To express appreciation or laugh at ideas or at the organization and its follies, in a good-natured way.
- To level yourself or others, telling funny ones on yourself or other people. When doing this to others, be careful not to belittle. The result should be "We're all good fellows, in this boat together."
- To reduce tensions and misunderstandings.
- To introduce a break in the meeting.
- To increase fellowship by having the group share fun. (If appropriate you could have each one turn to his neighbor and tell of some funny happening in his work. This would come best at the beginning or right after a coffee break.)
- To loosen the group through group starters (see "Formality Levelers" in Chapter 6).

Many chairmen like to keep notes on cards or in notebooks. Make your own file of humorous material. Write down ideas while others are speaking or chairing meetings.

Humor for the Chairman

Throughout this book are hundreds of humorous bits which any good chairman could use. We select a few and give them to you here, with brief suggested "angles" for their use.

58 Starter. On the window of a butcher shop in London was a sign, "We make sausage for Queen Elizabeth." Across the street on a rival shop was a sign, "God save the Queen!"

59 Meeting Postponed. A few years ago the San Diego **Union** announced: "A mass feeding exercise in which county Civil Defense volunteers cook meals under simulated disaster conditions has been postponed due to the muddy ground near the C.D. headquarters here."

60 Replacement Needed. The vicar's wife had just died. Wishing to be relieved of his duties, the priest wired his bishop: "I regret to inform you that my wife has just died, and I should appreciate your sending me a substitute for the weekend."—**Maturity Magazine**

61 Hurry! A customer dashed into a hardware store. "One mousetrap, please," he said. "And hurry—I've got to catch a bus."

The clerk replied, "Sorry, sir, but our traps don't come that big!"

62 Don't Understand. As the hook said to the eye on the fat lady's dress, "I don't get the connection." (When an obscure argument is used.)

63 She'll Do It. The surest way to get a job done is to give it to a busy man. He'll have his secretary do it. (When trying to get volunteers for a committee, etc.)

64 Changed Mind. Women have developed a new driving maneuver—the O-turn. This is for the U-turner who changes his mind. (As group has shifted its position on something.)

65 Unimportant. This has been an interesting discussion, but I wonder if we haven't done it, as someone said, "with the enthusiasm groups reserve for the unimportant." Could we move on, now?

66 Destination? An absent-minded executive fished for his ticket frantically as the conductor came through.

"Oh, that's all right," the conductor said. "You can give it to me later."

"Yes, I know," said the executive, "but I've got to have the ticket to know where I'm going!"

Right now I'm looking for our ticket. Where are we going?

67 Wrong Before. When caught off base, M. Leo Rippy used to say, "Well . . . I was wrong once before!" (A chairman might find this useful.)

68 You're Right Too. "Today I feel like everybody's right. It reminds me of the agreeable judge. When the defense made its case, he said, "You're right!" To the prosecution he said, "You're right!"

A man in the room called out, "But they both can't be right!"

The judge turned to him and said, "You're right, too!"

But now, we've got to sort this out . . .

69 Blows for Water. When you're in a tight spot, this might work. One kid asked another, "Why does the whistle always blow for a fire?"

The other said, "It doesn't blow for fire. It blows for water. They've already got the fire!"

So have we. Where's the water?

70 Sleepy. A Canadian railroad journal advertised for three hundred sleepers for a big excursion. A clergyman in Iowa offered them his entire congregation. I believe we could almost offer them this meeting, too. You look sleepy and tired. Let's break (or stand and stretch) . . .

WHAT THE TOASTMASTER, MASTER OF CEREMONIES, AND MEETING CHAIRMAN HAVE IN COMMON

An amateur master of ceremonies, with his own attention focused on himself, may talk too little or too much. Often the one who leads a group or an occasion, like the M.C. or toastmaster, has been chosen for personality, charm, wit, tact, discretion, popularity. (You might have been chosen because nobody else would do it!) However, having accepted the job, you have certain jobs cut out for you.

- You are the representative of the people to keep things going. There may be somebody around bigger than you are. It is good to get straight who is "responsible for the show."

- Generally you will be thought of as the program director for the occasion, or at least the front man or woman.

- You may be responsible for handling unexpected situations—unusual group or audience conditions. A sense of humor (coupled with an active stack of humor cards) may help.

- You are the expediter, but not the show. Between program features you may display your charm and sparkling wit, but chances are the people have come for the program too.

- You are responsible for transitions. Often humor helps here.

- You need to organize your material so that you can get at it easily. The most common ways are with cards or notebook.

- You will need some expander items that can either be used or not. Most programs run longer than planned.

- You should be especially ready to get anybody off the hook who gets on. Humor is a marvelous tool for just this.

- You will want to start and end with the best. People can stand a certain amount of saggy middle if you begin and end with some zip.

- During the affair, you will almost certainly want to credit those who have worked and to help everybody cheer for them.

- Little human-interest things, such as birthdays and anniversaries, help to bring a crowd together in spirit, especially if the announcement or singing is a surprise. This can be done at many different types of gatherings.

- You should work out as warm a response to the speaker as you can, conscientiously. If you know him well enough, humor may fit in here.

- You should work out a clean, clear dismissal so that people will know the program is over. This may consist of humor, prayer, or something else, but make it clear. Some gatherings may close nicely with a "signature": "What have you enjoyed today?" If the occasion is a conference, people will sometimes speak up and share ideas for a few minutes, giving the program committee a notion of what clicked. Some will end with a thought for the day or night—sometimes humorous, sometimes serious and deeply meaningful. Appropriateness is very important here.

INTRODUCING SPEAKERS

In handling introductions properly, any toastmaster, master of ceremonies, or meeting chairman knows that he faces sometimes a com-
plexity of problems. His own relationship to the group may need
to be dealt with through a bit of humor. The speaker may be known
to him, or to the group, and he may not. The audience may welcome the speaker, or it may not. You may prepare some humor
and then not use it, when you "feel" the circumstances.

Some introducers josh rather roughly with speakers and guests.
This is fine if you know what you're doing. Probably it is best to
be conservative here. The purpose of the introduction is to get
speaker and audience together for a good start. It's good for the
introducer to remember that he is **not** the speaker.

The Introducer Himself

71 New Machine.   There is a new machine that unwrinkles raisins,
blows up foods thirty-times normal size. Somebody suggested it for
toastmasters.

72 Unnecessary.   A toastmaster (or master of ceremonies or meeting chairman) is often like parsley—isn't needed really. (Introduces
somebody already known.)

73 Good Program.   We've got a good program tonight. I hope
none of you are like the old lady who refused to buy a new hearing aid. "It would cost two hundred dollars," she said, "and I don't
know of anything around here that's worth hearing that bad!"

74 Demand for Toastmasters.   Walter Towner once used this
story to quash a brash young toastmaster. "I went to see my friend,
the superintendent of the mental institution in town," he said. "I
asked him, 'How many of these people can be reclaimed for society?'

"He replied, 'About fifty per cent. The other forty per cent stay
here.'

" 'But fifty per cent and forty per cent makes only ninety per
cent!' " "Oh, yes,' said he, 'We always have a ten per cent demand
for toastmasters at banquets!' "

Well, here I am—your happy toastmaster.

75 Practicing Preaching. If a minister were in his study, reading tomorrow's sermon, would you call that "practicing what he preaches?" I guess so. I've been practicing what I'll be saying here as your master of ceremonies . . .

76 Making Good Time. Well, it's almost time to introduce the speaker. In fact, past time. Reminds me of the pilot who reported to his passengers, "We're lost—but we're making good time!" Now I want to introduce to you . . .

77 Get Self Organized. As I was preparing to be your M.C., I made a note to myself, "Get self organized." I got self organized. Talked with wife. Got self reorganized. Talked with wife. Dropped whole idea. Talked with self . . .

78 Inexperienced. Actually, I'm pretty green at this toastmaster (M.C.) business. I'm like the girl in the cooking class at school. "What are you cooking?" her mother asked.

"Oh, we're not cooking," said the girl. "We're only as far as **thawing!**"

79 "Shall We Dance?" Dr. Ken Benne, the great Boston human relations expert, was comparing attitudes of the powerful leader and those of followers under his administration. "It's like an elephant in a chicken coop saying hospitably, 'Shall we dance?' "

With this great array of talent tonight, I feel like the chickens in that coop . . .

80 Ends in Speech. When one word leads to another, it generally ends up in a quarrel, a speech, or a dictionary. Tonight it will be a speech, and my words are going to be brief, since I'm not the speaker . . .

Introductions

81 Charm! They say that "charm is the ability to make others feel you're both wonderful!" We know our speaker is wonderful. We're going to try to be charming enough to make him feel we are too! . . .

82 Couldn't Refuse. We are genuinely lucky to have our speaker today. We wrote to his organization and asked for their wittiest man, but he turned us down. We asked for the most eloquent, and he turned us down. We asked for the most brilliant; he rejected us. Then we asked for the best-looking. He couldn't refuse us **four times,** so here he is . . .

83 Informed Man. Do any of you here know where "Sam Hill" is? Do you know how many feet in a far cry? Or the altitude of "high time"? Our speaker has not planned to answer these exact questions, but here's a man who knows the answers to the questions we need answers to. May I present . . .

84 Your Side. Two women met at a dinner party. One said to the other, "I've heard so much about you, dear, that I'd now like to hear your side of the story!" Tonight we've got a speaker about whom we've heard plenty—only what we've heard is wonderful. And we're all ears to hear his side of the story. May I present . . .

85 Duel Time. There were two duelists scheduled to go into action just outside the city limits of Paris. When the appointed morning arrived, one was present when a messenger came with a note from the other. "If I'm late," it said, "just go ahead and shoot." We're late, and I won't take more of our speaker's time, but say to him right now, "Dr. _____, go ahead and shoot!"

86 Such 'Owling. Two British Cockney gentlemen, if you can say that, were in the country at night, hearing some very unfamiliar noises.

"W'ot's 'at?" one asked.

"An owl," the other one said.

"Yes," said the first one, "but w'ot's 'e 'owlin' about?"

Our speaker knows his stuff, and he's got plenty to 'owl about. Our problem will be to keep up with him, but he promises to be open for questions later, and you can do your 'owling then. I present . . .

87 Only Nationally. Two Bostonians were talking about a man known to both who had achieved a great deal in recent years. One of them said, "He has really made a name for himself!"

The other responded, "Yes, but that's only nationally!"

Our speaker tonight has made a name for himself, not only nationally but locally too . . .

88 Let's Worry. They say that 40 per cent of our worries are about things that don't happen and 30 per cent about things that are past help. Most of the rest of the worrying is needless. Now what worries me is, with all this needless worrying going on, isn't there something more serious to be worrying about?

The answer is that there is. Our speaker has plenty to tell us that will raise the concern of us all in his subject . . .

89 Gas Savers. On the old Model-T Fords they used to have patented gas savers that people would buy and install. One man said that he'd had them, but had to take them off because they wasted so much time.

"What do you mean?" his friends asked.

"Well," he said, "they saved so much gas that I had to stop every once in a while and pour out the gas they saved. It just took too much time."

Our speaker tonight is going to show us lots of things—not how to save gas, but how to . . .

90 Good Example. It is said that "a pint of example is worth a gallon of advice." I'd put the stakes even higher. The speaker we have is one who is in his own life that pint of example. He knows what he's talking about and he practices what he proclaims . . .

91 Mr. Speaks-Well. The Congolese often have special names for missionaries, which they use in the absence of the missionary, such as "Father Take-It-Easy," or "Mr. Talks-Talks," or "Mother Peace," or "Mr. Thinks-First." If I should give our speaker tonight a name, I'd call him, I think, "Mr. Speaks-Well," for that is what he does . . .

92 Busy Man (Woman). They say that some folks think they are busy when they are only confused. Our speaker tonight is certainly not a confused person. People come to him (her) for answers, and they're good ones—to the questions people **are** asking. We've asked him to come here and give us some answers on . . .

93 Big Man. Africans have a term . . . "The **Big** Man. . . ." The accent is on the **Big**. The Chief is the Big Man. In an Atlanta church the Reverend Dow Kirkpatrick was explaining to his people that when any of the several staff ministers came to a meeting or to see them, the ministry of the church was there—the minister was there! One of his leaders, in droll Georgia fashion, rose in the meeting and said, "Dow, when I go to the circus . . . I want to see the elephant!" He's the circus's "big man." Tonight we have the "big man" with us—not an underling, but the head of the whole show, and we're proud as peanuts . . .

94 Straight From the Shoulder. It is said that "some people talk straight from the shoulder, but it's more normal to talk from higher up." I'm talking straight from the shoulder, but we've got a speaker tonight who is really going to be talking from higher up . . .

95 Good Man. The little boy had been hearing his granddaddy tell war stories, with flourishes. Finally the little fellow said, "Granddaddy, there must have been one good man on the other side!" We've been hearing one side of the issue presented, and tonight we have a good man, an excellent man, from the other side to give us another slant on the problem . . .

96 Fly Like Birds. In the 1870's a bishop and the president of one of his denominational colleges were in heated discussion. The bishop claimed that everything that could be invented had been. The college president thought differently. "Why, in fifty years," he said, "men will fly like birds!"

The bishop was shocked. "That's blasphemy!" he said. "Flight is for angels!"

From this conversation Bishop Milton Wright returned home to his two little boys . . . Orville and Wilbur!

Today we have a speaker who is going to challenge us with many mind-stretching ideas. What's still to be done? He knows, and he's going to tell us . . .

97 Bless Mr. Newman. An earnest clergyman, before a visiting preacher's sermon, prayed, "O Lord, bless our speaker tonight, Mr. Newman, whom Thou doubtless knowest . . ." Our speaker is not Mr. Newman, but _____, whom the Lord knows very well indeed. He is one who has given himself unstintingly in the service . . .

98 Real Traveler. In school a kid wrote on the subject "What I Would Like To Do" that first he would like to go to the moon, and then he would like to travel. Our speaker tonight hasn't been to the moon, but he's been almost everywhere else—not as an ordinary tourist—but as an intelligent observer . . .

99 Twenty-One—Gun Salute. In a small country, to honor the president, they gave a twenty-one–gun salute.

"Is he still standing?" asked one of the natives.

"Yes," said the other. "They missed him!"

Today we have a speaker whom we wish we could honor with a twenty-one–gun salute. We wouldn't shoot—we'd salute! He has meant so much to us . . .

100 What's Cooking? Too many of us don't know what's cooking until it boils over. We have a speaker who does know what's cooking and is going to tell us, so that maybe together we can keep it from boiling over . . .

101 Conservative? Someone has said that a "good conservative" is one who tries to steal second while keeping feet firmly planted on first. Our speaker tonight is not a wild-eyed radical by any means, but he has more daring than keeping feet firmly on first. He's off to second, third, and home, day after day, in his daring activity . . .

4

The Speaker Himself

RESPONSE TO AN INTRODUCTION

A humorous remark can be an entertaining way for a speaker to respond to an introduction and move easily to the body of his speech. Here is a selection of them for a variety of situations.

102 Real Pane. In coming tonight, I recognize that you had at first expected another. It reminds me of a young preacher who substituted in a small rural church where they had placed cardboard in a broken window to keep out the cold. In his talk he likened his substitution to the cardboard's substitution for the window. He spoke well, and at the end of the service an older lady said to him, "Son, you weren't cardboard today, you were a real pane!"

103 Smell Forever. Ed Beck, the All-American basketball player, was in Korea with a group of athletes. In the name of the host village a little girl brought flowers and, struggling with her English, said, "These flowers will die, but you will smell forever!" After this speech, I hope you don't feel quite that way . . .

104 Not Best Speech. No matter how good my speech is, it won't be the world's best after-dinner speech. That speech is, "Waiter, I'll take the checks!"

105 About Twenty Minutes. I asked your chairman what I should speak about, and he replied, "About twenty minutes!"

106 Stop Boring. Today I'll try to remember the old oil driller's formula for speaking: "If you don't strike oil in twenty minutes, stop boring."

107 Good Speech. The speech professor gave a formula for a good speech that I at least have in mind today. He said, "Have a good beginning and a good ending, and keep them close together!" Here goes!

108 Lucky! Today I feel like the little boy who asked his mother, "Where were you born?"
  "In Columbus."
  "Where was Daddy born?"
  "In Memphis."
  "Where was I born?"
  "In St. Louis. Why?"
  "Oh, nothing. Only, isn't it wonderful how we three ever got together!"
  I feel that way, and I hope you do . . .

109 Seemed Long. Let me tell you about the little girl who stayed for church while her mother went home to fix dinner for the preacher. When the child and the preacher arrived, Mother asked about the sermon. "It was good—but it was a little long," said the child. Then she realized that what she said wasn't very polite, so she added, "It wasn't really so long, Mother. It just **seemed** long!" I'll try to keep it from either being long or seeming long . . .

110 Watered Windmill. After many long-winded remarks, a speaker reached for a glass of water and drank, ready to say some more. One of the audience leaned over to the other and said, "It's the first time I ever saw a windmill that ran by water!" Tonight I don't plan to drink water. If I see any of you going for a glass, I'll recognize what it means.

111 Feel Inferior. As I stand here thinking of the sparkling speeches that have been made from this platform and my own ability, I'm reminded of the man who told about seeing his friend Joe on the street. Joe passed him up, apparently, as not being worthy of recognition. He told his wife, "I guess Joe thinks I'm not his equal."

"You certainly are," his wife retorted. "He's nothing but a bluffing, conceited idiot!"

112 Three-Point Speech. For this talk I'm observing the three points for good speaking, or at least trying to: Stand up and be seen, speak up and be heard, shut up and be liked.

113 "My Friends!" Tonight I call you my friends. I think of Red Skelton in the role of San Fernando Red. "My friends!" he said, and warned them, "Don't you say you're not my friends—nobody's gonna tell me who my friends are!"

114 Diet of Worms. I do hope that tonight the thoughts I bring you are more palatable than those as seen by a schoolboy who wrote this about Martin Luther: "After a diet of worms, Luther said, 'So help me God, I can take no other course.'"

115 Back Ag'in! I'm so delighted to be invited back to speak to you. Perhaps I should be suspicious, in the light of this story. There was a very poor preacher who moved every year for seventeen years, then stayed and stayed at one church. They kept asking for him to be sent back. He asked a church member why. "To tell the truth," said the member, "these people really don't want a preacher at all, and you're the nearest nothing they've ever had."

116 Hit Me Harder. Well, here we go with what I hope is a lively speech. Did you hear of the man who was at the speaker's table and went to sleep, due to the boring talk. The speaker flew into a rage, took the gavel, and hit him over the head. The sleeper awoke, took one look at the speaker, and said, "Hit me again. I can still hear you!"

117 Dreaming Lecturer. There was once a man who dreamed he was lecturing. When he awoke, he was!

118 Old Age As I was preparing this speech, I was thinking of how the years roll along, and I came across the five sure signs of old age. I want to give them to you to check yourselves. They are bifocals, bunions, bridges, bulges, and baldness. I've still got one to go.

119 Humility Badge. As I heard this introduction I just remembered that I left my humility badge at home! After that, I need it!

120 Get My Teeth. The old couple were sitting in the swing on the front porch. She said, "Daddy . . . why don't ye bite me on the neck like ye used to do when we wuz courtin'!" The old man got up without a word and started into the house. "Daddy, I didn't go to hurt yer feelin's," she said.

"Didn't hurt my feelin's," he responded. "I'm just goin' to git my teeth!"

Let's all get our teeth ready for this subject tonight . . .

121 Galloping! This elaborate introduction tonight has made me fearful of trying to live up to such a reputation. It reminds me of the sophisticated New Yorker who was invited to a party in a high-rise apartment building where every door looks the same. He was late, and he wanted to do something clever to offset his embarrassment. When the butler opened the door our friend put his cane between his legs, took off his top hat, and galloped into the room saying, "Here I come . . . galloping . . . galloping . . . galloping!" As he did it, he realized that he was in the wrong apartment— didn't know a soul in that party—so he left in the same spirit, saying, "And here I go . . . galloping . . . galloping . . . galloping!"

122 Help Me Down. That was such a gracious introduction. But I wonder if you'd all have come had you known who was going to speak. There was an old lady outside a town hall who said to a young man, "Young man, will you kindly help me up the steps into the hall?" He said he would, and as they walked slowly, she asked, "Young man, who is speaking tonight?"

He told her, "Councilman Smith."

"Young man," she said, "will you kindly help me **down** the steps of the hall?" I used to have a politician friend who told that on himself, but it fits me too well . . .

123 Know My Stuff. As I speak tonight, I want you to know that you are listening to a man of authority. I'm like the man who was in an argument with his wife. "I may have my faults," he said, "but being wrong is not one of them!" And if you catch me, I'll say like Leo Rippy used to, "I was wrong once before!"

124 Wise Guy! As I stand here before this crowd, knowing what an intelligent group you are, I feel something like a phony. I'm reminded of the little boy whose father was in the Christmas pageant. "What part does your father have?" somebody asked him. He spoke up proudly. "He's one of the Wise Guys from the East."

125 Using Flattery. Hearing this marvelously gracious introduction tonight, I am reminding myself that flattery is like perfume—it is to be sniffed, and not swallowed!

126 Like Coffee. They say that it's what the guests say about a speaker when they're going down the hall that counts. I hope, after so fine an introduction, that you compare me to the first cup of coffee in this story: The waiter in a restaurant brought a man a fork, a piece of pie, and a cup of coffee without a spoon. The man said, "This coffee is going to be pretty hot to stir with my fingers!"

The waiter reddened and rushed back to the kitchen bringing another cup. "This coffee isn't so hot, sir!" he said.

127 Open Minded. You people here at _____ have a wonderful reputation for being openminded. That's good. I once heard of a man who was so prejudiced that he wouldn't even listen to both sides of a phonograph record . . .

128 See Land. In preparing my speech for this occasion, I felt the need for help beyond my own strength, and I sought it in prayer. I hope I was sincere. I thought of the two sailors, adrift on a raft. They had just about given up hope of rescue. One began to pray, "O Lord, I've led a worthless life. I've been unkind to my wife, and I've neglected my children, but if you'll save me, I promise . . ."

The other shouted, "Hold it. I think I see land!"

129 Space Age? I'm sorry to be a little late. Actually, I had some trouble finding a parking place. Why do they call this the Space Age, when there's so little of it when you're looking for a parking place? Maybe it's beyond us. A kid in school was recently heard singing, "O Beautiful for Space-Age Skies!"

130 Kindness and Cooperation. Today I ask you for kindness and cooperation as we approach this difficult subject—like a Wisconsin housewife who cured her husband's snoring. She said that she used cooperation, kindness, and then stuffed an old sock in his mouth.

131 Laugh! I hope you'll laugh at my jokes as they occur. But don't laugh before they're finished. An African interpreter got tired of a long funny story told by a speaker. So he just said, "He tells jokes. Laugh!" They all did.

132 Successful Speech. One speaker said that he gave a completely successful speech to an audience. It was soothing (the people slept), and moving (half of them left), and satisfying (they didn't come back). By that definition, I shall try to have a failure by keeping you awake, and keeping you here.

133 Unscrambled Egg. You've given me a wonderful reception and a wonderful introduction. But what a subject! That's a tough one! I'm reminded of a business executive who was given an impossible task of straightening out an administrative situation. He said to a friend, "As I look at this, I think to myself, 'How do you unscramble a scrambled egg?'"

134 Weekend. Thank you so much for inviting me here. I worked on my speech a bit last weekend. By the way, do you know that all the world in America revolves around the weekend? Monday you recover from the weekend. Tuesday you make arrangements for the next one. Wednesday is the midway point with a little lull. Thursday you make definite preparations, Friday you leave for the weekend. Saturday and Sunday are the weekend!

135 Opened by Mistake. When your letter of invitation arrived, it had this note on the envelope, "opened by mistake to see what was in it"! After you've heard me, you may wish that the original opener had just thrown it away!

136 Back Home. It's good to be back home. As one speaker said, "This occasion gives me the opportunity to shake hands with many old faces."

137 In Stride. You know, I do expect you to take my speech in stride. You are the kind of folks who have a good idea of where you stand. I'm thinking of the church janitor who said, "I've seen twelve preachers come and go, and still I believe in God!" I imagine your beliefs will remain reasonably intact. But I want to challenge you . . .

138 Embarrassed. A number of times as a speaker I've suffered from "foot in mouth" disease. But I haven't been quite as bad off as the young clergyman who had in his weekly congregation's announcements: "The Little Mothers' Club holds its regular meeting Tuesday evening. All those who wish to become Little Mothers, please see the pastor after the service."

139 Free of Charge. As I think of my outline, I also think of the toastmaster who prepared the audience for the speaker. In concluding his introduction he said, "And remember—he's speaking free of charge."

140 Conservative. I suppose I'd be classed as conservative. "Come weal, come woe; my status is quo!"

141 Executive! I stand before you not only as a speaker, but as one with executive ability. A boy once asked his dad what executive ability was. The father replied, "Son, executive ability is the art of getting credit for all the hard work that somebody else has done!"

142 Remember Big. As I recall some things for you tonight, please don't be too hard on me. I'm like the Texan who said, "I really don't lie—I just remember big!"

143 Worth Talking? I'm not sure whether I ought to try to make this speech or not. A speech expert says that only 60 per cent of our thoughts come out as words and the listener gets only half of that. Is it really **worth** talking?

HUMOR IN THE BODY OF THE TALK

After the speaker has responded to the introduction and gets into the body of his talk, he finds many ways to use humor.

For Illustration. If the speaker is talking about adaptability, this story would appeal. The Nobel-Prize–winning physicist, Lord Rayleigh, was asked to write an article for **Encyclopaedia Britannica**

on "Light." It didn't arrive in time for the volume of "L" topics. It was retitled, "Optics," but the "O's" were finished without it. Next was the retitling, "Undulating Theory of Light." Still it didn't arrive. Finally it came in, and the editors titled it, "Wave Theory of Light." (144)

To Liven Up the Scene. There was a little old lady whose phone was still on the "operator" system. She heard that she had won the sweepstakes, and was greatly excited. Taking down the receiver, she called excitedly into the phone, "Hello, Central! Get me anybody!" (145)

To Point Up Where You Are, or where the group is, as in the story of the timid swain who said to his girl as he had his arm around her, "Am I making any progress?"

She replied, "You're holding your own!" (146)

To Deal With a Problem or Viewpoint. There is the true story of a round of unexpected pregnancies developing among women in a Boston suburb. The cause was finally discovered—their daughters were "borrowing" their birth control pills, replacing them with saccharin tablets. "You can afford to get pregnant," they told their mothers. (147)

Another problem could be illustrated with this story: A pilot had to parachute to a South Sea island where the people were striped red, white, and green. One of the natives looked at him and said, "Funny color, isn't he?" (148)

To Keep the Audience With You ("He's still a good fellow"). You might tell about the boy in school who was told by the teacher to pay a little attention. "I'm paying as little attention as I can," he said. (149)

Or tell about the man arguing with his wife. "Are you thinking what I'm thinking?" she demanded.

"No, I'm thinking what **I'm** thinking!" he replied. (You could reverse the sexes in the story.) (150)

To Define Humorously, as in the case of the famous economist who differentiated between recession, depression, and panic. In recession you tighten your belt. In depression—no belt. In panic—no pants. (151)

Deliberately to Bring in Something Current, modern, to show that you're with it. You might give Hal Holbrook's definition of a "Brigitte Bardot sandwich": "Tomato with a little French dressing." (152)

To Show That the Speaker Is "Educated." Through humor, using names of "educated" people, the speaker can add to his image. For instance, Keynes said that classical economic doctrines work out in the long run—but in the long run we'll all be dead! (153) Therefore . . .

To Show the Audience You're Still Aware of Them. You might tell of the school kid who said the book was good, but too long in the middle. (154) "We're through the middle and headed down the home stretch," might be your response.

Let Them Feel a Little Superior Occasionally by giving humor that would obviously put them in a superior position. For example, the Library of Congress received a letter from a patron which said, "Please send me the Library of Congress. Enclosed is 25¢." (155)

Spice It Up! In London a husband called the hospital angrily to complain that they had told him his new baby was a boy when it was, in fact, a girl. To correct this a sign appeared over the switchboard: "No sex must be given out over the phone." (156)

To Handle Hecklers. It is always wise to keep in a good humor, but sometimes a speaker is justified in being a little rough. A politician who was explaining about price supports for corn and beans once handled a man who insisted on asking, "What about hay?" in this manner:

"I'm talking about human food, friend. We'll get to yours in a minute!" (157)

Name-Dropping. Many speakers want to use names of famous people to enhance their own reputation. Too much of it may get tiresome to the audience. One of the Rockefellers was trying to get a telephone number, but there was no connection. The operator wanted his name so that she could mail him a refund. "My name is . . . Oh, forget it. You'd never believe it anyway!" (158)

To Reassure the Audience that in spite of problems, you believe in the community, the organization. Professor Milton Gabrielsen, of New York University, told of the preacher who had everybody who wanted to go to heaven to stand. All but one did. "All who want to go to hell?" He still remained seated. "Where do you want to go?" the preacher asked.

"Nowhere!" said the dissenter. "I like it here!" (159)

To Correct an Overstatement. Often a speaker will overstate his point. If there is a question period, perhaps someone will catch him up on his mistake. One speaker said, "You've got me. I spoke too quickly. I'm now bleeding from the spur of the moment!" (160)

CLOSERS FOR SPEECHES AND MEETINGS

A pointed story or bit of humor can communicate tremendously at the end of a meeting or speech. Here we bring together a number of "closers," some with suggested application, and some "straight."

161 Time Has Come. The inexperienced long distance operator, asked to tell the caller when three minutes were up, broke into the conversation with these words: "Sir, your time has come!" And so it has. In conclusion, then, friends . . .

162 To the Egress. Barnum, of circus fame, had a way of getting rid of people from his museum. Over a doorway was a sign which read, "To the egress." When people went through, they found themselves on the street. I don't want to find myself there, so in conclusion . . .

163 Lost Excuse. The children at school were supposed to bring their birth certificates, but one boy lost his. He wept to the teacher, "I lost my excuse for being born." You are born to be useful . . .

164 Not Immediately. A full-winded speaker said, "Finally, but not immediately . . ." And so, finally . . .

165 All's Well. Recently I heard a slight revision of a proverb. It said: "All's well that ends."

166 Finished Speaker. The most popular kind of speaker is the one who's not polished, but through. I'm through.

167 'Tis True. "When all is said and done, there'll usually be more said than done." I've said enough. Now . . .

168 Repent. "Well, I'm about ready to repent." That means, "Sorry enough to quit."

169 Hasn't Stopped. "Is the speaker finished?"
"Yes, quite a while ago, but he hasn't given over."

170 Either Way. A. A. Rapking, in retirement, said, "I can look forward or backward. Either way it looks wonderful." And so . . .

171 Thankful. A small Michigan newspaper had this note: "We have been fortunate to have Mr. K——— visit us, and when he leaves, we will be more than thankful." In exactly three minutes . . .

172 Willing Spirit. Dr. Frank Stanger at Asbury College says: "The spirit is willing, but the metabolism is weak." Maybe what I'm saying is hard, but . . .

173 Small Estate. In his will a man left a small estate and a clock. Why the clock? It was to wind up the estate. We're about ready to wind this up, now . . .

174 Patience! A visitor was teasing a little boy about his baby brother. "What use is he?" asked the man. "Can he walk?"
"No."
"Can he talk?"
"No."
"Can he feed himself?"
"No."
"Can he dress himself?"
"No."
"What good is he, then?"
"Well for gosh sakes, Mister, give him time!"

175 Indigestion. There is no indigestion worse than that of trying to eat your own words. I've given you enough of mine . . .

176 Hope So. An author asked a reviewer, "Have you read my last book?"
"I hope so," replied the reviewer.
You're getting my last point right now . . .

177 "I'll Wait Up." The late Bishop Quayle once said he was lying awake at night, tossing and turning, worrying about the condition of the world at large and his own world, when the Lord spoke to him distinctly and said: "You go to sleep tonight, William. I'll wait up!" (It worked, so he "resigned as General Manager of the Universe.")

178 Let It Go. There is a rule of courtesy in speech that says, "When you are holding a conversation, be sure to let go of it once in a while." I'm letting go of ours right now. Any questions?

179 Details Yours. Dr. Ken Benne tells of the grasshopper who went to the owl to see how he could weather the winter better, since he was coming to feel it so much.

"Change yourself to a cricket," said the owl. That seemed reasonable.

"But how am I to do this?" asked the grasshopper.

"I've given you the principle," said the owl. "You work out the details."

Now I've given you the principle. You work out the details . . .

180 Busy Signal. Larry Lacour tells of the telephone company executive who went to a doctor. The physician listened to the heart and reported to his patient, "All I get is the busy signal." Is that all this organization gets from your heart? . . .

181 Anywhere From Elkhart. A high school boy at a conference was bragging constantly about his hometown, Elkhart. Someone asked, "All right, what's so special about Elkhart?"

The boy said immediately, with enthusiasm, "You can get anywhere in the world from Elkhart."

That's the spirit we need . . .

182 Going Ahead. They say that "you don't push yourself forward by patting yourself on the back." We've said some good things about ourselves tonight, but there is much more to be done . . .

183 She's Hollow! Two boys were watching a fat woman mount a scale, which was actually out of order. The needle went to sixty-two pounds. "Look at that!" said one. "She's hollow!" Maybe what I've said seems hollow, but . . .

184 Booted! "He that thinketh by the inch and talketh by the yard should be kicketh by the foot!" Well, I've talked a yard tonight and . . .

185 Innocent. "In times of trial," cried the lawyer, "what brings us the greatest comfort?"

"An acquittal!"

Well, we've got it. We're innocent. That is, we haven't done anything . . .

186 Why Don't We? In this story Howie Tanner loves to tell, there is a town where they make shoes, but don't wear them. One day a visitor asked why. The townsmen looked at the visitor, perplexed, and answered, "Why don't we?"

187 "I Am Shot!" In a play an actor had a line, "Help! I'm shot!" which came after a blank pistol was fired at him. In performance, fun-loving backstagers filled the barrel with catsup. When the pistol was fired this time, the actor looked down in horror at the red on his shirt and said, "Help! I am shot!" He thought it was the real thing. That's what I want to talk about in conclusion—the **real thing** . . .

188 Old-Timer: One who can remember when time was marching on instead of running out. My time is running out, and I'll say in conclusion . . .

5

Short Speech Angles

A speaker is frequently called upon to give remarks pertaining to a special occasion or event. If he can use humor with a deft and sensitive touch, he'll do much toward making the event a notable one.

WELCOMING

189 Twice Welcome. We welcome you. We want you to find friends everywhere. There was a child playing with a worm outdoors. He took his mother's paring knife and cut it in two, with each end wriggling vigorously. "There, now, you have a friend." We hope that even the worms around here seem friendly . . .

190 Been Waiting. A few years ago the class of freshmen at Harvard made a huge sign, "Harvard has been waiting 300 years for us!" We've been waiting for you to come and be with us—not three hundred years, but a long time . . .

191 Great Opportunity. We're so glad to welcome you to our most unusual community. We've got a man here who is forty-seven and says he's worked for fifty-five years. How did he do it? Overtime! You're in the land of opportunity.

192 No Saints. A traveling Anglican was trying to get in touch by telephone with the priest in a small town. He suggested that the operator look under the word **Saint** for the name of the church. "I'm sorry," said the operator, "but there are no saints in this town." Maybe you'll find that out too, but we've got some friendly and interesting folks that we hope you'll come to know . . .

193 Right People. A woman was visiting in the Boston area. She remarked that, unlike the usual reputation of New Englanders, people she had met were very friendly. "Then you haven't met the right people," said a dowager. In that sense we hope you don't meet the "right people." We hope you'll find a friendly welcome here, and will like us very much . . .

194 Conservative. We're glad you've come to join us here. Some people say we're conservative. That's defined as feeling that nothing should be done for the first time. Or, as someone else put it, "As it was in the beginning, is now, and ever shall be." But we're beginning to move a little. Here you are! Help us to see your viewpoint, and perhaps we'll get moving . . .

195 Thoughtful Place. We want to welcome you to a most thoughtful place. You'll be getting all kinds of special attention here. For instance, I ordered a dozen oranges from a store the other day and they sent only ten. I called them, and they explained, "This is part of our special service. Two of the dozen you got were bad so we threw them away for you!" Ah, we're kidding. This couldn't happen in a thousand years in generous ———— . . .

196 Fast-Growing. You're in a fast-growing place. You may think of the Californian who was visiting a friend in Florida. The Californian was bragging a little as he pointed to a certain tree. "In California we can grow a tree like that in just a year. What about Florida?"

The Floridian replied, "I can't say. All I know is that that tree wasn't there yesterday!"

We're glad you're here to help us grow . . .

197 Made It. A cute gal was driving her sports car over the speed limit. In her mirror she caught sight of a police car. She stepped on the gas, ran even faster, whipped up to the ladies' room at a filling station, stopped, and ran in. When she came out, the state trooper was waiting. Finishing powdering her nose, she looked at him and grinned. "Thought I wouldn't make it, didn't you?" she said. Then she got in her car and drove off, while he stood, openmouthed. We wondered if you would make it—we've been waiting for you. Now we're ready to watch you with openmouthed wonder as you help us . . .

198 Great Place. We're glad you've come to this great place. We want to welcome you. You know, I came to this town many years ago—no shoes on my feet, no clothes, not a penny in my pocket. Yes, I was born here. But look at me now! We're a busy place. Sometimes we're as busy as a farmer with one hoe and two snakes! But now that you're here, we know you will help us carry some of the load. Welcome . . .

199 Can Wade. We welcome you to a crowd of people who will figure it out one way or another. When we want to move, we do it some way or other. We're like the young fellow, six feet nine inches tall, who applied for a job as a lifeguard. "Can you swim?" they asked him.

"No," he said, "but I can wade to beat anything!"

Wade or swim, we're glad you're here . . .

200 Here First. In the waiting room the nurse said to an expectant father, "You have a fine boy!"

Another man stopped his pacing and said, "Say, what's the idea? I was here before he was!"

I'm glad I was here before you. That gives me a chance to welcome you . . .

201 First Aid. A woman was telling about how her first aid-course had helped her. She was at a bloody wreck. She remembered her first aid—and put her head between her knees and didn't faint! Mostly things will be good here for you, we think. But, if you're ever buffeted to a bloody situation and you see us with our heads between our knees, you'll understand . . .

HONORING IN GENERAL

In honoring someone often you'd like to have a little humor in the process. Here are ten suggestions.

202 More Said Than Done. Someone has said, "When all is said and done, there will usually be more said than done." Tonight we've gathered to honor someone who can not only say, but do . . .

203 Push Away. We know a man who says, "I lean toward blondes—but they keep pushing me away." Tonight we're here to honor a man who, if the blondes knew who he was, would move in his direction. What a man! He is . . .

204 Need Pull. A speaker once was giving a high school commencement address. On the door on the way in, he noted the word **Push** so he included it in his speech. "What you need to get through life is the word on the door of your own auditorium here!" he insisted. But as the students went out, they saw the word **Pull!**

Here's a fellow who hasn't needed pull to get by. He can make it well on his own, and we honor him for it . . .

205 Dear Sir! In Britain, a man was writing to his friend who had been newly knighted. He began his letter, "My dear Sir!" He spelled that **Sir** with a capital letter. And so do we tonight as we gather to honor . . .

206 Perfect. They were making a movie. The director called out to the cast, "Perfect! Perfect! Now let's do it over one more time —better!" The woman we're honoring tonight has done such a perfect job that we couldn't have her do it over at all. She is . . .

207 Five Senses. They say that man has five senses, but the successful person adds two more—horse and common. Tonight we honor one who has all seven!

208 Romantic. It was a moonlit night, and the boy felt a great surge of emotion for the girl, but also a little timidity. Finally he got up his courage to ask, "If I tried to kiss you, would you call for help?"

She looked at him and answered, "Do you need help?" Tonight we honor a person who doesn't need help . . .

209 Qualified. The whole school was amazed when a certain football player got to play in the big game, for they knew he was terribly dumb. Finally his chemistry prof threw light on the reason. "I decided to let him pass if he made fifty per cent," said the prof. "First I asked him what color blue vitriol was, and he said, 'pink,' and of course that was wrong. But when I asked him the chemical formula for water and he said, 'I don't know,' that was correct, so I passed him."

Tonight we're honoring a person who not only knows what the chemical formula for water is, and what color is blue vitriol, but also . . .

210 Keeps Going. It is said that light travels at an amazing speed until it hits the human mind. Tonight, we want to honor someone whose mind when hit by light, just keeps going . . .

211 Pedigree. Two snobs were boasting about pedigree. One said, "My family dates back to King John of England."

The other said, "Sorry, but mine lost their records in the Great Flood!"

Today we honor a real blueblood of accomplishment . . .

HONORING THE WINNER OF A CONTEST OR EVENT

212 Success. There is a saying, "If at first you don't succeed— you're about average." But you succeeded so well that you won the contest, so that puts you above average, and we've got the prize to prove it . . .

213 Rising to the Occasion. They say that some men rise to the occasion, where others merely hit the ceiling. In a way, you have done both in winning. You've risen to the occasion, and your prize is about the ceiling for this kind of contest . . .

214 Stripes or Checks? There was a college boy who liked suits with stripes, but when it came to letters, he preferred checks. Maybe you like stripes, but you were so good in the contest that we've got your prize-winning check . . .

215 Wishing Well. In a movie cartoon once an Arab called down into the depths of the wishing well, "O wishing well, O wishing well, I wish I had a million dollars!"

The wishing well answered, "Soooo dooooo IIIIII!"

You may not have a million dollars, but you're better off than when you came here, because we've got a wonderful prize for you . . .

216 Sound Ideas. A friend once handed me a neatly printed white card. On it were these words: "Your ideas are sound—all sound!" Maybe they are. But yours are too—only they have the kind of soundness that wins contests. So here tonight we honor you . . .

217 No Talent. Bob Benchley once said that it took him fifteen years to discover that he had no talent for writing, but then he couldn't give it up because he was too famous! It hasn't taken us that long to discover that you do have talent, and plenty of it.

218 Chemical Outfit. There was a rich Texan once who heard his boy say that he'd like to have a chemical outfit for Christmas. He knew just the outfit—Du Pont! We don't have that for you tonight, but we do have a very nice prize for winning . . .

219 Inferior? Once there was a man who had an examination for his inferiority complex. The psychologists gave him the report. "After consulting with others as a result of your testing program, we have come to the conclusion that you do not have an inferiority complex— you are inferior." With the results of the contest before us, obviously this is not your situation. You're the winner!

220 No Confetti. We don't have any confetti tonight for our hero, the winner of the contest. Confetti means honoring today's heroes with small bits of newspapers from yesterday's. So we don't honor you with shredded paper—we do it with something better than that. In describing a certain girl, a boy said, "In the pool she was a girl worth wading for." You've won the prize, and it's worth waiting for . . .

WEDDING ANNIVERSARY

221 Better Than None. A spinster was asked why she never married. "It takes a mighty good husband to be better than none," she said. Actually this would be sour grapes if one has a husband as good as _____.

222 Get Married. Another spinster was asked about marriage. "Sure I'd get married, if I had to do it over. I'd do it before I had sense not to!" You two had sense enough to get married _____ years ago, and we're glad. Happy Anniversary.

223 Divorce? Murder? Someone asked a beautiful old lady who had been married to a fine man for many years if she's ever thought of divorce? "Divorce, never. Murder, yes," she said. She was honest, but oh, how she loved him! Today we celebrate the anniversary of two who may have thought of murder, but oh, how they love each other!

224 Pain Versus Pleasure. "Marriage has many pains, but celibacy has few pleasures."—Ben Jonson

225 Ideal Wife. "An ideal wife is any woman with an ideal husband," Booth Tarkington said. We're here today to celebrate the anniversary of both of these—ideal husband, ideal wife.

226 Model Husband. He was called that, so he looked up the word. He said it meant "small imitation of the real thing."

227 Essential Telephone. The telephone company was short of equipment. A girl applied for a phone. They asked her if it were essential. "I need one to make dates and get married and have children with," she replied. Isn't it wonderful that our anniversary couple had a telephone? (Or: How did they do it without a telephone?)

228 So Warm! Not able to get attention any other way, a little seven-year-old girl said to the company in the living room, "I feel so warm in my new ring!" Our anniversary bride can't say that. Her ring isn't new. It represents many years of a happy marriage . . .

229 Solid Gold. Years ago in a county fair, a trickster was selling what he called "gold" rings. "They are not five, not six, not seven, not eight, but nine-carat solid gold," he said. We're here today to help a couple celebrate a real, solid-gold marriage. It's their anniversary again . . .

230 Good Health. They asked an older man why he was in such good health. "Well," he said, "When we were married, my wife and I agreed that if I saw an argument coming, I'd go and walk around the block three times. And you know, fifty years of constant exercise has done wonders for my health!" Maybe both of these folks we have today for our anniversary couple have done this. They have good health. Happy Anniversary from us all!

231 Home to Mother. A young bride was quite discouraged about her housekeeping. Mother lived close by. The bride said to her husband, "There's nothing to eat. I think I'm going home to mother!"

The husband reflected a minute and said, "I believe I'll go with you!" Whether our anniversary couple ever did this or not, they both look well-fed now . . .

232 Marry Me Or . . . He was such an ardent lover that the young man said, "Marry me, or I'll die!" She didn't marry him, and in forty-six years, he died!

233 Patience. The secret of patience is to do something else meanwhile.

234 Grandmas Have Changed. When Grandma was a girl, she didn't do the things girls do today. But then Grandmas didn't do the things that Grandmas do today, either!

235 Marry a Widow. "I'm going to marry a widow."
"I wouldn't be second husband to a widow."
"Rather be the second than the first."

BIRTHDAY

236 My Birthday. A tramp went to the door and asked the housewife if she had a piece of cake for a man who hasn't had a bite to eat for two days?"

She said, "Cake? Isn't bread good enough?"

The tramp said, "Ordinarily yes, but today's my birthday!" Now, we're not calling you a tramp, but we feel that cake is none too good for you. Happy Birthday.

237 Light of Age. A little boy asked his daddy why Mommy had so few candles on her cake. "Oh, she's just making light of her age, son," said dad. We don't know whether you're making light of your age or not, _____, but do it if you want to. We're glad you're here.

238 His Age. The Archbishop of Canterbury was instructing the young lads on what to call him—"Say 'My Lord' or 'Your Grace.'" During the service he asked a boy how old he was. The boy was flustered, and replied, "My God, I'm ten."

239 What Happened? The gal said, "I hate to think of my thirtieth birthday."
Another one said: "Why, Marge, what happened?"

240 Counting. A kid at Cape Kennedy said, "I can count. Ten-nine-eight-seven-six-five-four-three-two-one." Some people count birthdays that way. Maybe you do, maybe you don't. But we're glad you're having them. Happy Birthday.

241 Happy Birthday to Me. A lonely soldier went into a restaurant, ordered a cake with candles, and when it came sang, "Happy Birthday to me!" People gathered around, congratulated him, and a good time was had by all. Today we've got a cake for **you.** Here it is . . . (Bring it in.) Happy Birthday . . .

242 Helps Feel Better. You know, there was a golfer who was noted for his unearned low scores. Some of his friends told him it was cheating. He explained it. "I golf for my health," he said, "and the low score makes me feel better." Whether your age is high or low, we want you to feel good this birthday because we're glad you're here.

243 Born Young. A fellow once asked a friend, "How old are you?" He answered with his age. "You don't look it," was the reply.
"Oh," said the aged one, "I was born very young."
We understand you were born very young too. Look how far you've come. How far is it? Anyway, we want to show you our love on your birthday . . .

244 Better Move. "How old are you?"
"In the neighborhood of twenty-one."
"Well, you'd better move!"

245 Both Ends? One lady ordered twenty candles on her cake. One of the catty guests wanted to know if she was planning to burn them at both ends.

246 Age Is Different. In the old days when they came for glasses, the oldsters complained about not reading the Bible. Now they complain about not seeing the racing forms and the phone book.

247 Spectacle. Here's one you can see through. Did you hear about the lens grinder who backed into his grinding machine and soon made a spectacle of himself? We can see through your age. No matter how old you say you are, you're one of the youngest around here . . . Happy Birthday.

248 Just Turned. "How old are you?"
  "I've just turned twenty-three."
  "Ah, thirty-two, eh?"
Turn your age any way you want to—it's fine to us. We wish you a long life and happiness. Happy Birthday . . .

249 Birthday When? "I'd be twenty in October but for one thing."
  "What's that?"
  "I was born in February."
We know when you say you were born, at least, and we're helping you celebrate. Happy Birthday, and may God continue to bless you!

250 How Many Birthdays? You've had one. All the rest of what you have called "birthdays" are really anniversaries!

BABY SHOWER

251 Started Countdown. Somebody asked a young married man if he had any children. "No," he replied, "but we've started the countdown." Mary and Bob have started the countdown, and we want you to be prepared, so we've bought a few things . . .

252 Twenty Pounds. Sally, as you're looking forward to that blessed event, we know you're watching your weight, and how hard it is. There was a woman who went to the butcher and wanted him to show her twenty pounds of pork. "I don't want to buy it," she said. "I just want to see what twenty pounds is!" There was a little girl who said, "Mommy, what makes the Tower of Pisa lean?" "I don't know," said Mother, "but if I knew, I'd take some!" Good luck on your dieting for your blessed event . . .

253 Last Long. Two little children were talking about the new baby that had come to their house. "I heard a new baby costs two hundred dollars," said the little girl.

"Yes," said the little boy, but he added wisely, "think of how long they last!"

Helen, we're here to give you a few things for this two-hundred-dollar baby to show our love . . .

254 Spock Best. A nurse in the hospital saw a patient reading the book, **Doctor Zhivago** in a maternity ward. She approached the patient kindly and said, "I don't know about this doctor, but you just can't beat Doctor Spock!" Not only are we giving you Dr. Spock, but some other things too at this shower, just to show that you can't beat our affection for you and Bill . . .

255 What a Baby! A newborn baby isn't always as beautiful to others as he is to his parents. The great New England clergyman Phillips Brooks used to look at newborn babies and exclaim, "My, that is a baby!" That always made mothers happy, and he hadn't committed himself. But we know that you're going to have the most beautiful baby in the world, and we have the gifts for you to prove it!

256 Management Pains? Someone said that a minor operation is one performed on somebody else. A businessman was in the hospital for a minor operation. He asked about the anesthetic and they described it to him. "What about this 'twilight sleep'?" he asked.

"Oh," said the nurse, "that's for labor."

"Yes," he said, "but don't you have something for management?"

Today at this shower we've got both. We've got some gifts for you when you go into labor, and some for the management of the child when it comes.

257 From Stalk. Did you hear about the mama corn who told the baby corn that the stalk brought him?

258 Big Orange. An orange got into the hen's nest. One of the little chickens said, "Look at the orange marmalade!"

259 Smallest Child. In a contest to see which mother had the smallest child on an Army base, the winner was one who was seven months pregnant.

260 Not a Dozen. The mother asked how much were photos of children. The photographer said fifteen dollars a dozen. "I'll have to wait," she said. "I only have ten."

BRIDAL SHOWER

261 In Mourning. Some girls were talking about a girl they went to school with. "She's in mourning for her husband," one of them said.

"But she never had one," another responded.

"That's why she's in mourning," said the first one.

We're glad that you're getting one, Doris. Not that you've ever been in mourning for one with all the boyfriends you have. We're awfully glad for you and Tom, and we've got the presents to prove it . . .

262 Proposal? Grace, we don't know how John proposed to you. We heard of a romantic man who sent his wife an engagement ring in a "Forever Yours" candy bar! However John did it, we're glad that he did. That's why we're having this shower . . .

263 Sixteen Husbands. Today we're having fun at this bridal shower, and I just wanted to say in behalf of us all that actually the wedding ceremony says that Betty can have sixteen husbands if she wants to. You know—"Four better, four worse; four richer, four poorer." We hope that this one will do, Betty, and to help make it so we've got some wonderful loot for you!

264 Engaged. A businessman hustled up to a taxi driver and wanted to go to his destination in a hurry. "I'm sorry, sir," the driver said, "I'm engaged!"

"Oh, that's fine!" said the man, "I hope you'll be very happy!"

Gail, you're engaged, and we're happy—so happy that we went out and spent our hard-earned money to get you and George some wonderful presents. We can hardly wait to see them!

265 Takes a Woman. A Chinese proverb says, "A hundred men make an encampment, but it takes a woman to make a home." It looks like Jim has thought enough about this that he picked him a woman—Alice.

266 Hammered Slate. Dot, do you know what a man with a wooden leg does if he wants to get married? He looks for a girl with a cedar chest! We know that Bob doesn't have a wooden leg. Maybe you've got a cedar chest. But we got together and hammered out a list of little tokens of our affection that we wanted to give you (included might be bus tokens) . . .

267 Nice for Reception. We don't know what our bride-to-be has in mind for her wedding. One girl showed up for her wedding in curlers. She said, "I want to look nice for the reception." Peggy, you look nice to us all the time, and we think that you and Don are going to be so nice-looking that we want to embellish it all with our presents . . .

268 Mixed Up. The couple was being married before a judge, and the groom was very flustered. The judge said to the bride, "Do you promise to love, honor, and obey this man?"

The bride rebelled at the "obey" part and said, "Do you think I'm crazy?"

The groom was so mixed up that he thought it was his time to answer the judge's question and said, "I do."

Whether Frances and Bill get mixed up or not, we've got some nice things here for them to use after they get it untangled, if they do get mixed up . . .

269 Getting Married. It's wonderful to be getting married, isn't it! You know, after a bus strike a girl from another town wrote to the union that struck the bus company: "My sister lives in your town where you had the bus strike. She had to walk to work. She lost seven pounds and looked better. She met a driver walking. They got married. Why can't we have a strike in my town?" As nearly as we know, Martha got Doug without benefit of strike at all. Or Doug got Martha. We're here to cheer them on their way . . . and maybe to start a strike of our own, some of us . . .

270 Beautiful and Repent. Once a little girl was asked whether she'd rather be beautiful or good. "I'd rather be beautiful," she said, "and repent." We don't know whether our bride-to-be, Mary Jane, has repented or not, but we know she's beautiful. You know, the fashion note says that there will be little change in men's pockets this year. We've gathered together a few little things to help keep a little change in Paul's pockets as they start out sailing the sea of matrimony . . .

271 Happily Ever After. Once upon a time there was a man who said to a maid, "Will you marry me?"

She answered, "No."

And they lived happily ever after!

Knowing you two, we can't imagine this as your story. You belong together. And we've gathered together some mementos of our affection for you two that belongs to you—or will, as soon as we can give them to you . . .

HONORING ONE WHO IS LEAVING

It is quite common for people to move from one community to another, even across the country or halfway around the world, leaving dear friends and favorite organizations. You may often find yourself having good-byes for such friends. Here are remarks to use at the occasion.

272 Stay Away. In Africa it is customary among the MaShona people to say "Go Go Go" as you near the hut to let the people know you are close. At a camp meeting there was an unmarked latrine used by all. A woman missionary neared it, saying "Go Go Go." From inside called out the voice of another missionary, "Stay stay stay." African customs aside, we wish you could stay stay stay with us, but . . .

273 Will of God. A Scotsman was asked to give his opinion on letting another congregation use his church's building in an emergency. "It doesn't seem either rrright or rrregular," he said, "but it does seem to be the will of God." We don't want you to go. It doesn't seem either right or regular . . .

274 "We're Satisfied!" A rather ordinary worker asked for a recommendation. "Peter Piper worked for us a week. We're satisfied," was his recommendation. You've been here much longer than that. You're leaving. We're not satisfied, but we'll have to live with our pain . . .

275 Lay There. A man was run over with a steam roller. Do you know what he did? He just lay there with a **long face!** That's what we're preparing to do now as you leave us . . .

276 Well Wishing. Your going reminds us of the very inexperienced young salesman of cemetery plots. He approached a prospect who said, "I already have a plot."

The young man was a little uncertain, but he blurted out, "I hope you'll be happy there."

We hate. to lose you, but we know you must go. And all of us say, "We hope. you'll be happy there. . . ."

277 Miss Him. The insurance man was settling up with the widow. He had brought fifty thousand dollars to her. She looked up and with a little catch in her voice said, "You know, I miss him so much, I'd give twenty-five thousand of this to have him back right now!" If it was fifty, we'd give it all if you'd stay with us. But you must go, so we wish you Godspeed . . .

278 Whence the Idea? A girl once said to a boy, "Did anybody ever tell you how wonderful you are?"

"No!" he answered eagerly.

"Then where did you ever get the idea?" she replied.

We apply this to you, but we say, **we're** telling you how wonderful you are. We're saying how much we're going to miss you . . .

279 Gone to the United Kingdom. A big businessman in New York hired a classy British secretary, and soon after, he went on a trip to Britain. On long distance a friend called for the businessman.

"I'm sorry," said the secretary. "He's gone to the United Kingdom."

There was a long pause on the other end, then a serious voice said, "Is it too late to send flowers?" Now, you're not going as far away as the United Kingdom, but you're leaving us and we are sad. We're not sending flowers, but we do have a departure gift for you to show our . . .

280 Ear's Tears. Ah, friend, we're gonna miss you. We're going to be like that song about having tears in our ears as we cry over you. Somebody came to a business where Eddie had worked one time and asked for him. "He's gone," they said.

"What about his vacancy?" the boy asked.

"Eddie didn't leave no vacancy!" was the answer.

When you go, you're gonna leave plenty of vacancy. Not only in the organization here, but in our lives. After you leave, there will be one problem: "Who is the biggest guy here now?"

HONORING THE RETIREE

At the time of retirement there are usually gatherings and presentations. Here are some words that might help.

281 Reputation. They say that you don't build a reputation on what you're going to do, but on what you've done. You have a reputation with us—a wonderful one. It has been built carefully through years of steady, intelligent service . . .

282 Eternity. Thoreau said, "You can't kill time without injuring eternity!" We're coming to the time of honoring you, who has served so well that no one can say you injured eternity. You haven't killed time—you've showed us all how to use it well . . .

283 Growing Older. A riddle says, "What is everybody in the world doing at the same time?" The answer is "growing older." We all are. Recently on a application blank, where it says "Age" a woman wrote in "atomic." We don't believe that's your age, but the bookkeeper says it's "retirement." That doesn't mean that you're not going to be the most active around. Now you can get in some deserved relaxation. Thinking of the Twenty-third Psalm a little boy who loved fishing once said, "Thy rod and thy reel—they comfort me." We hope you'll be having fun, and comfort, and that you'll be back . . .

284 Retired. The records say that the time has come for your retirement. After a busy life with us, you can get some rest. But not absolute rest. In 1905, says the Canadian humorist Stephen Leacock, Einstein announced that there was no such thing as absolute rest. After that there never was. We can't imagine you in absolute rest, anyway. You'll be busier . . .

285 Unhappiness. They say that some people cause happiness wherever they go; others, whenever they go. Your retirement has come. You've caused happiness wherever you've gone amongst us. You cause unhappiness when you go. Enjoy your retirement. But come back some day and give us the happiness that always comes to us whenever you are with us . . .

286 Reincarnated. There was once a man who said, "If I believed in reincarnation, I'd want to be a mattress in my second life."

"Why?" his friends asked.

"So I could lie in bed all day."

Your retirement is here. Maybe your reincarnation. You can lie in bed all day. We envy you. But actually, active as you are, we don't really expect this kind of conduct from you. Probably you'll be more like the Scotch couple who were going to America. "Sandy," said the wife, "do you think we should have started out on this economy trip to America?"

"Shut up and keep swimming!" said Sandy.(287)

You'll be swimming a long time rather than resting, we have an idea . . .

288 Ain't Goin'. An aging hotel manager in South Africa told on himself that a young woman came to ask him for a gift of five thousand dollars for herself and family. "You're an old man, Mr. Watson," she said, "and you can't take it with you."

"I can't take it with me?" Watson asked her.

"No!" she said firmly.

He paused a minute. "Then I ain't goin'!" he replied.

We wish you weren't going. You've meant so much to us through these years here at . . .

COLLECTING MONEY

Every organization has times of needing to gather in money. Not only do churches and synagogues take collections, but many community groups as well. A little humor makes the collecting easier. Here are some aids to making a collection less painful. (You may use one or more than one in combination.)

289 "Friend in Need." That's the one you always hear from. We're your friend in need, and we need a collection of $____ from this crowd!

290 Preacher Can. A child in the family swallowed a coin. "Send for the preacher," said Dad. "He can get money out of anybody!" Well, I'm the preacher, and I don't want you to spoil my reputation . . .

291 Like It Sweet? In the diner late at night one man watched a truck driver with coffee put in one . . . two . . . three . . . four . . . five . . . six . . . seven spoonsful of sugar, but didn't stir the coffee. He reminded the driver of the omission. His reply was "Who likes it sweet?" Well, we do. We're about to give you the privilege of contributing, and, boy, do we like it sweet!

292 Doubled It. "Has Harriet been able to keep her girlish figure, all these years?"
"Keep it? She's **doubled** it!"
Now, that's about what we need to do with our offering. Inflation is on us. They say that inflation is proof that you can't keep a good price down. We need to keep ahead in our treasury . . .

293 Begs in Askit. We're asking for a combined offering. We're like the tramp who wanted a dollar for a cup of coffee—he was putting all his begs in one askit! If you pay this time we won't be bothering you over and over . . .

294 Shake Again, Brother! On a Seminary Singers trip from Boston, Professor Houghton told this story a number of times after the incident. He said: "When we were in Washington, a man shook hands with me at the concert, and when he took away his hand, there was a five-dollar bill in mine. I felt like saying, 'Shake again, brother!' "

295 Give Cash. When we look at the blessings of our lives, some of us are willing to give God credit, but not cash. If it is true, "In God We Trust," we'll give him cash—generously—and trust him to care for our needs . . .

296 Sample Cake. One of the cleverest ideas ever was that of a finance chairman in a Baptist church. He had a big chocolate cake baked and did his demonstration during the morning worship service. He stood behind his cake, representing "Family Income" (there was a sign). People would come up to him wearing signs: "Car Payments," "Rent," "Recreation," and so on; he would give them each a slice of cake, with some remark about how much he needed them. "Church" (in a white robe) would also ask for cake. "Oh, no," he'd say, "there will be a piece for you, but not just yet!" Several times this was repeated. Finally he had given out all his cake, and church was behind him, unseen. "There!" he exclaimed. "I've made it go around!"

Church came silently around again. "Oh, Church," said the chairman, "you **know** that I had you in mind. I was thinking of you. Here—take the crumbs!" So he gave the platter to Church, who took it and then paid her bills (to other people also wearing signs). The message got across in a big way.

297 Too Much Month? One family said that they usually had too much month at the end of the money! That's why we ought to give to the church early in the month before the money is gone. It is the principle of the tithe—first fruits. Give from the top of your income . . .

298 Double Money. "The way to double your money," said one wag, "is to fold it and put it in your pocket." But there is another saying to remember: "You can't take it with you, but you can send it ahead!" We're offering you a chance to take more than a passing interest in the collection . . .

299 All Kinds. "He has all kinds of money."
"Is that right?"
"Sure—he's a coin collector!"
We are too. In fact, we're bill collectors mostly, we hope. In the offering, put either or both . . .

300 Dimes Have Changed. When we were kids, ten cents was a lot of money. But dimes have changed. Remember that when we take the collection. Since it is true that "the smallest deed is better than the grandest intention," why not do a big deed here tonight? We must have a big offering . . .

301 Cattle Call. Joe Blinco used to like to quip: "God has the cattle on a thousand hills. He only needs cowboys to round them up." Will the ushers come forward for the offering?

302 And Spoil It? There was a game the grown-ups played with little Billy. They would put a nickel and a dime out in their hands and ask him to take whichever coin he wanted. He always took the nickel and they laughed. One of Billy's playmates asked him privately if he knew the difference. "Sure do," he responded, "but do you want me to spoil a good racket?" We've got no racket. We need nickels and dimes—but mostly quarters, halves, dollars . . .

303 Hollow Ring. A woman said once to a tramp, "My man, your story has such a hollow ring!"

"Yes," he replied. "That comes from speaking on an empty stomach!"

In our organization, some people are going to have empty stomachs unless we give generously . . .

304 Two Aims. Someone has said that every man should have at least two aims in life: to make a little money first and then to make a little money last. That's what we want to do in our collection. To get not a little but a lot of money first, and then make it last.

305 Poor Welcome. The minister said, "I have always welcomed the poor in this church. The treasurer tells me that, from the collection, they have come." Could we modify that reputation tonight?

PART 3

Humor

6

Types of Humor

FORMALITY LEVELERS

In a situation free enough to use these, the toastmaster, master of ceremonies, or group leader may find them very useful in breaking down the sense of formality and helping people to feel more at home. The authors have used these little gems in all sorts of situations.

306 Honoring. One of the most usable ideas is to find some way of honoring somebody by applause, standing, singing. If it's somebody's birthday, sing to them. If you want to honor the cooks, the kitchen crew, the committee, or the sponsor, have everybody sing, to the tune of "Farmer in the Dell," "We want a cooks' parade, we want a cooks' parade; We won't give up, we'll never give up, we want a cooks' parade." (Substitute the proper name.)

307 Singing together, especially songs of fellowship and fun, can ease the formality. Clapping to the rhythm of a song, or clinking glasses at the table with spoon or fork, helps everybody to join in.

308 Gags. Depending upon the situation, you may want to use a few short "gags." One is for the chairman to say, "We pause for a moment for a spot announcement." A confederate in the audience says, "Arf, arf!" The chairman responds: "Thank you, Spot!" If unexpected people "pull" this one it adds to the humor.

Another is to have someone well known to the group to wander through the room calling, "Woman the lifeboats, woman the lifeboats!" The chairman corrects him, "I think you'll find that, 'Man the lifeboats.'" The answer comes, "You fill your lifeboats and I'll fill mine. Woman the lifeboats . . ."(309)

Still another silly one is to ask everybody in the audience to say the word **wing** six times. When they finish, the chairman acts as if he has a telephone receiver to his ear and says, "Hewwo!"(310)

311 Get Acquainted. Have you ever tried "Interview by Twos"? Have two people face each other and give each an assignment. For one or two minutes, as you designate, one tells the other, "The hardest selling job I ever did," or "Why I joined the PTA (or this organization)," or "My most embarrassing moment."

At the table a similar idea is to put a joke, tongue twister, riddle, or such under the plates. Early in the meal, ask the people to share them with those nearby.

312 Fancy Handshakes. If appropriate at all to use these. They break down reserve right away. Simply have each person face someone else and shake hands as directed.

Pump-Handle Style. Join hands, pump up and down vigorously.

Model T Ford. Crank joined hands vigorously as if cranking a car.

Paul Bunyan Style. Clasp hands in regular style except that each takes his right thumb in his left hand, as if working a two-man saw. When the tree is down, yell "Timberrrr!"

Chinese (or Japanese) Style. Shake own hands, bow three times slowly.

Fisherman's Style. Each makes his hand very limp. As they shake, wiggle them back and forth.

313 Correlation Exercises. Here are three. First, have the group try grasping nose with right hand and right ear with left hand;

then change when you call "Change!" (That is, change to grasping with left hand the nose and with right hand, left ear.)

Second, have them make a circle with right arm and at same time a figure eight with the foot. Third, for a simple stretcher, have them stand and, starting with arms at sides, raise right hand, shoulder-high, then left hand. Then right hand above head, then left hand. Move hands back down in same manner.

314   Musical Stretcher.   To the tune of "Tavern in the Town" have the people all sing, and at the same time touch the part of the body mentioned in the song:

> "Head and shoulders, knees and toes
>   Knees and toes!
> Head and shoulders, knees and toes,
>   Knees and toes, and
> Eyes and ears and mouth and nose,
> Head and shoulders, knees and toes,
>   Knees and toes!"

315   Exerciser.

> "Hands on your hips, hands on your knees,
>   Put them behind you, if you please!
> Touch your shoulders, touch your nose,
>   Touch your ears, touch your toes.
>
> "Raise your hands high in the air,
>   At your sides; on your hair.
> Raise your hands high as before,
>   While you clap, 'One, Two, Three, Four!'
>
> "My hands upon my head I place,
>   On my shoulders, on my face,
> Then I raise them up on high,
> Make my fingers quickly fly,
> Put them out in front of me,
> Gently clap them—**One, Two, Three**."
>   —R. Bruce Tom, Columbus, Ohio

316   Reading Humorous Material Aloud.   Daffynitions and conundrums given in this book would fit here, as would some of the humorous material. See Bibliography for suggestions of "read-aloud" humorous material.

317 A Noisy Stunt—"Stage,"* for example. Each time the reader reads the word **cowboys**, everyone yells, "Yip! Yip!" For the word **Indians** all cover mouths to yell in Indian fashion. For the word **women**, all scream loudly. For the word **horses**, all neigh. For the word **rifles**, all aim and go "Bang." For **bows and arrows** all draw the bow, shoot the arrow, and yell, "Zip!"

The Story: It was in the days of stagecoaches and **cowboys** and **Indians**! Alkali Ike, Dippy Dick, and Pony Pete were the three courageous **cowboys**. When the stagecoach left for Gory Gulch, they were aboard, as were two **women**, Salty Sal and a doll-faced blonde. The stage was drawn by three handsome **horses** and it left Dead End exactly on time.

The most dangerous portion of the trip was the section known as Deadman's Curve. As the stage neared this spot it could be noticed that the **women** were a bit nervous and the **cowboys** were alert, fingering their **rifles** to be ready for any emergency. Even the **horses** seemed to sense the danger.

Sure enough . . . just as the stagecoach entered the curve, there sounded the blood-curdling war cry of the **Indians**. Mounted on their **horses**, they came riding wildly toward the stagecoach, aiming their **bows and arrows**. The **cowboys** took careful aim with their **rifles** and fired. The **women** screamed. The **horses** pranced nervously. The **Indians** shot their **bows and arrows**. The **cowboys** shot their **rifles** again. The leading brave fell, and the **Indians** turned their **horses** and left their **bows and arrows** behind. The **women** fainted. The **cowboys** shot one more volley from their **rifles** just for luck. The driver urged the **horses** on, and the stagecoach sped down the trail to safety. (**In reading, it is best to pause after each "noise word" to allow group to make their noises and, often, to laugh.**)

PUNS

318 Satellite. I satellite in the window so she'd come Russian home to me.

---

319   **Circuses,** I find are so emotional. You know—in tents!

320   **The Organization,** say some of its detractors, has a tendency to keep you in a conformatory.

321   **Basin Gratitude.**   On the ship she refused the meal, but called for the chambermaid—(a case of basin gratitude).

322   **Occupation?**   In New York a British prospect was asked what he had formerly done. "I was a clark (clerk)," he said.
"You mean like 'tick-tock'?" asked his prospective employer.

323   **Camera.**   Now, that's a camera that clicks with me!

324   **Which?**
"A man is as old as he feels. I feel today like a two-year-old."
"Horse or egg?"

325   **No Caddies.**   The newly rich businessman had just taken up golf. He wired ahead to a business associate to set up a game. The answer came: "No game—no caddies." He wired back: "If no caddies, get Chevvys."

326   **Safe!**   When she fell into shark-infested waters the sharks turned away. You see, they were man-eating sharks.

327   **Let's See.**
"Do you take lodgers here?"
"That depends. What lodge are you from?"

328   **Egyptian Girl.**   She lacked knowledge of sin, and became a mummy.

329   **The Key.**   To get into a cemetery at night—use a skeleton key.

330   **Bricklayer!**   What did the hen say when she saw a porcelain egg in her nest? "Wouldn't it be awful if I became a bricklayer?"

331   **Will:**   Where there's a will, there's a wait!

332   **Revolutionary.**   Did you hear of the new milking machine that is said to be udderly revolutionary?

333   **Hot Advice.**
"I'm burning up to get at that bird!"
"Don't make a fuel of yourself!"

334 Mucilage. One glue manufacturer said to another, "I like glue manufacturing."

The other said, "The feeling is mucilage!"

335 At the Tailors.
"Euripides?"
"Eumendides."

336 Fish and Chips. In England two monks had a little roadside stand near the monastery. A woman who came to buy said to one of them, "Are you the chip monk?"

"No," he replied. "I'm the fish friar!"

337 Shocking! To the electrician, tiptoeing in at two A.M., his wife said, "Wire you insulate?"

338 Glass Eye.
"How did you know that he had one?"
"Oh, it just came out in the conversation."

339 No Mynahs. At the bar the bird tried to get a drink, but the bartender said, "Sorry. We are not permitted to serve mynahs!"

340 By Handel. The organ grinder was playing a tune. A music lover stopped. "That's by Mozart, that tune, isn't it?"

"No," replied the organ grinder. "By handle."

341 Bare Feet. A woman went to the zoo while she was pregnant. A bear made a pass at her with his paw and frightened her terribly. And do you know, when that child was born, it had bare feet!

342 Chivalry.
"Where's your chivalry?"
"I traded it in on a Buick."

343 Take Roomers?
"Do you take roomers?"
"Don't know. What have you heard lately?"

344 Hazardous Work. An editor recently dropped eleven stories into a wastebasket!

CONUNDRUMS AND RIDDLES

What is the difference between a conundrum and a riddle? The answer to a conundrum is humorous, often a pun. Therefore, it is a riddle.

345 **What wood** is most highly inflammable? Chip on shoulder.

346 **What is** the occupation in which you couldn't get anywhere without kicking? Chorus-line girl.

347 **What is it** that a woman carries, a man keeps? Compact.

348 **Why did** the locomotive refuse to sit? Had a tender behind.

349 **What is it** that is filled in the morning, emptied at night; but this is reversed once a year? Stocking.

350 **What is it** that grows by the yard, dies by the foot? Grass.

351 **What is it** that we often return but never borrow? Thanks.

352 **What is** the name of the bird that, if you don't do it, you die? Swallow.

353 **What has** four legs, but only one foot? A bed.

354 **What often falls,** but never gets hurt? Rain.

355 **What is it** that no man ever saw, which never was, but always will be? Tomorrow.

356 **Name me** and you break me. Silence.

357 **What is it** that is black and white and red all over? Blushing zebra.

358 **Why is March known** as the shortest month of the year? Because the wind blows two or three days out of every week!

359 **What is it** that you couldn't hold for ten minutes, even though it's light as a feather? Your breath.

360 **In what month** do people talk the least? February.

361 **When is** a hat not a hat? When it becomes a woman.

362 How is it that a blackboard is like the earth? Because the children of men multiply on the face of it.

363 What has four legs and flies? A dead horse.

364 Why did Moses take cheese into the Ark? Don't know, but it was Noah who went into the Ark.

365 What is the best fire escape? A chimney.

366 What part of the fish weighs the most? The scales.

367 What kind of hens lay the longest? Dead hens.

368 Who was the straightest man in the Bible? Joseph. Pharaoh made a ruler of him.

369 Who was the shortest man in the Bible? Bildad, the shu-hite.

370 What never uses its teeth for chewing? A comb.

371 What letter grows in gardens? P.

372 What letter is an insect? B.

373 What letter is watery? C.

374 What letter is an exclamation? G.

375 What letter is a part of the body? I.

376 What letter is a bird? J.

377 What letter is an exclamation? O.

378 What letter do they use a lot in plays? Q.

379 What letter is most social? T.

380 What letter do I like? U.

381 What letter represents what overeating will do to you? W.

382 What letter does the farmer want? X.

383 What letter is used by four-year-olds in speech? Y.

384 What letter is punny for **small ocean**? Z.

DAFFYNITIONS

385 Admiration: Recognition of another's resemblance to ourselves.

386 Adopted County: "Step-motherland."

387 Alarm Clock: Device for waking a childless household.

388 Alimony: Husband's cash surrender value.

389 Anniversaries: When a husband may forget the past, but had better not forget the present!

390 Apiary: House to keep apes in.

391 Atheist: Man with no invisible means of support.

392 Athlete: Dignified bunch of muscle not given to shoveling snow, carrying ashes, and things like that.

393 Bacteria: Rear entrance of a cafeteria.

394 Balanced Budget: When money in the bank and the days of the month come out together.

395 Banana Peel: Food by-product that brings down the weight.

396 Bathing Suit: Device for helping girls outstrip each other at the beach.

397 Bigamist: Man who has made the same mistake twice.

398 Bill Collector: One who won't put off till tomorrow those who can be dunned today.

399 Birth Control: Evading the issue.

400 Bore: One who doesn't go without saying. One who opens his mouth and puts his feats in. One who keeps you from being lonely, but makes you wish you were!

401 Boss: Man at the office early when you're late.

402 Cemetery: Skeleton park.

403 Cereal: Stuff heroes are made of.

404 Childish Game: One in which your wife beats you.

405 Chivalry: Attitude of a man toward somebody else's wife.

406 College: Land of midnight sons.

407 Colon: Two periods, going steady.

408 Comics: "A little child shall read them."

409 Conceit: Person with I strain.

410 Conscience: Still, small voice that becomes stiller and smaller . . . Small voice you listen to after you've told it what to say.

411 Controversy: Collision of two trains of thought.

412 Cookbook: Lots of stirring chapters.

413 Corn on Cob: Vegetable played like a harmonica.

414 Cosmetics: Stuff used by teen-aged girls to make them look older sooner, and by their mothers to make them look younger longer.

415 Counterfeit Money: Pseudough.

416 Coward: When in trouble he thinks of his legs.

417 Cynic: Having cheated at solitaire, feels that all men cheat.

418 Dark Ages: Knight time.

419 Dentist: His work is a grind. Puts him down in the mouth. Is just like pulling teeth.

420 Dieting: Triumph of mind over platter. Penalty for exceeding the feed limit.

421 Dour: Help, as in "O God Dour help in ages past."

422 Duck: Chicken on snowshoes.

423 Elephant: Proof that peanuts are definitely fattening.

424 Eskimo: God's frozen people.

425 Etiquette: Knowing which hand to use when tucking napkin in collar. Noise you don't make when having soup.

426 Euphoria: Eu for me and me for Eu.

427 Expert: Someone called in at the last minute to share the blame.

428 Fame: What you get for dying at the right time.

429 Flood: River too big for its bridges.

430 Genius: Ability to turn on your thoughts instead of TV.

431 Highbrow: Person who can say "whom" without being self-conscious.

432 Historian: "It's historian he's stuck with it!"

433 Hog Raiser: Man who makes his living with his pen.

434 Home: Where you scratch anything that itches.

435 Horrible Example: Any problem in math.

436 Hug: Roundabout expression of affection.

437 Infancy: Age of change.

438 Infant Prodigy: Child with highly imaginative parents.

439 Inflation: National headache caused by "asset indigestion."

440 Insulate: What you have to explain for getting.

441 Latin Lovers: Never in high schools.

442 Leftovers: Food kept in refrigerator until old enough to throw away.

443 Limburger: Cheese with secret weapon.

444 Lisp: To call a spade a thpade.—Oliver Herford

445 Listless: What a husband should never be when shopping.

446 Lorgnette: Dirty look on a stick.

447 Mandate: Boyfriend.

448 Marriage: What is its color? Wed.

449 Middle Age: When you have that morning-after feeling without the night before. When you need two nights in for one night out.

450 Minicar: Status thimble.

451 Monopolist: Guy with an elbow on each arm of theater chair.

452 Oboe: English tramp.

453 Old Age: When it takes you longer to get over a good time than to have it.

454 Optimist: Guy at New Year's party who saves the cork.

455 Peach: Apple needing a shave.

456 Peanut: Coconut's little brother, but without whiskers.

457 Pedestrian: Survival of the flittest . . . A guy who, when the gauge said "empty" thought he still had gas.

458 Perpetual Motion: Cow drinking her own milk. (Her song: "It all comes back to me now.")

459 Pillage: What a doctor makes his living from.

460 Pink Tea: Giggle-gaggle-gobble.—Oliver W. Holmes

461 Poise: Ability to keep talking while the other guy takes the check.

462 Practical Politician: One who finds which way crowd is moving, rushes forward, and yells like the blazes.

463 Prejudice: Opinion without visible means of support.

464 Prima Donna: Often with more temper than mental.

465 Prune: Plum that has seen better days.

466 Psychiatrist: Man who will listen (for fee) as long as you don't make sense.

467 Psycho-Ceramic: Crackpot.

468 Repartee: Insult with tuxedo.

469 Rhubarb: Bloodshot celery.

470 **Rubber Diaper:** Social security.

471 **Salt:** The stuff that makes potatoes taste bad when you boil 'em and don't put any in.

472 **Sandwich Spread:** What some get from eating between meals.

473 **Sarong:** Dish towel that made good.

474 **The Sidewalk:** Heard about it? It's all over town.

475 **Skeleton:** Bones with the people off.

476 **Small Town:** Where you can chat on the phone, even to a wrong number.

477 **Snoring:** Sheet music.

478 **Soviet:** What Russians say when they finish eating.

479 **Stalemate:** When your mate is no longer interesting.

480 **Strategy:** Military term for not letting enemy know you're out of ammunition by continuing to fire.

481 **Synonym:** Word you use in place of the one you can't spell.

482 **Tangerine:** Loose-leaf orange.

483 **Tree:** Solid object that stays in same place for fifty years, then suddenly jumps in front of a motorist.

484 **True Gentleman:** When your husband holds the door while you carry in the load of groceries.

485 **Virgin Forest:** One on which the hand of man has not set foot.

486 **Well-Informed Man:** Views same as yours.

487 **Yarn:** To open the mouth wide when sleepy.

488 **Zealot:** One who, having lost sense of direction, redoubles his efforts.

489 **Zoo:** Place where animals study humans.

DAFFY DAFFYNITIONS

490 **Amazon:** First part of a sentence, like, "Amazon of a gun."

491 **Arrears:** What we listen with.

492 **Buccaneer:** What the price of corn seems in winter.

493 **Cubic:** Language of Cuba.

494 **Cynic:** Article of kitchen equipment.

495 **Deceit:** Place to sit.

496 **Deskpot:** Autocratic office manager.

497 **Divine:** Wot de grapes grow on.

498 **Flattery:** Apartment house.

499 **Forum:** What Miss America has.

500 **Hence:** Female chickens.

501 **Incongruous:** Where laws are made.

502 **Indiscreet:** Where you should not play after school.

503 **Indistinct:** Where people put dirty dishes.

504 **Indorse:** Where you go when night comes.

505 **Lemon Juice:** An introduction, as "Lemon juice you to Mrs. Long."

506 **Magazine:** Periodical for lovers of horses.

507 **Pitch:** Fruit with fuzzy skin.

508 **Pockage:** Pocket-sized package.

509 **Saddle:** City in Washington State.

510 **Sexes:** There are three—male, female, in.

511 **Stomachache:** A little boy with green apples and cucumbers.

512 **Tomestone:** Gravestone with long, poetic epitaph.

513 **Transparents:** Parents you can easily see through.

JINGLES

514 Late to Bed.
Late to bed . . . and early to rise . . .
Makes a man baggy . . . under his eyes!

515 Barber's Yell:
Cut his chin . . . slash his jaw . . .
Leave his face . . . Raw! Raw! Raw!

516 Captain.
I am the captain of my soul,
I rule it with stern joy.
But somehow I enjoyed it more
When I was cabin boy!

517 Codfish Balls?
"How much do you like codfish balls?"
I said to sister Jenny.
"Well, really, May, I couldn't say,
I've never been to any!"

518 Burma Shave:
Don't pass cars . . . on curve or hill . . .
If cops don't get you . . . mortician will!

519 Beecher's Reward
To a hen once said Henry Ward Beecher,
"Oh, my, you're a wonderful creature!"
The hen, pleased at that,
Laid an egg in his hat,
And thus did the hen reward Beecher!

520 Alive!
Breathes there a man with soul so dead
Who ne'er hath stopped, and turned his head,
And over to himself hath said,
"Hmmmmm. Not bad!"

521 Early to Rise.
Early to rise . . . early to bed . . .
Makes you healthy . . . and socially dead!

522 Husband Stuff:

A little flattery . . . now and then . . .
Makes husbands out . . . of single men!

523 Good to Boss.

The boss is a man
You should never get smart with;
You might be the one
He can easily part with.

524 Cure.

For a cure of seasickness
A reader appeals.
A plan he might try
Is to bolt down his meals.

525 Backward, Time.

Backward, turn backward
O time in thy flight!
I've thought of a comeback
I needed last night!

526 Well Enough.

Doctor Tom fell in a well,
Died without a moan.
He should have tended to the sick
And left the well alone!

527 For Dieters.

The bigger . . . the figger . . .
The quicker . . . the snicker!

528 Sinner and Saint.

It's easy to tell . . . sinner from saint . . .
Sinner is always . . . the one you ain't!

529 Old Saw.

In order to take him down a peg,
They cut a chunk from his wooden leg.

530 Poor Jokes?
The one who thinks our jokes are poor,
Would straightway change his views,
If he'd compare the jokes we have
With those we didn't use!

PUNCH LINERS

531 You Wouldn't Know.
"There are hundreds of ways of making money," said one arguer to another, "but only one honest way."
"What's that?"
"Aha! I knew you wouldn't know!"

532 No Snow.
"Tough sledding."
"How's that?"
"No snow."

533 Just Looking.
"Shopping bag?"
"No, just looking."

534 Color Blind.
"Where is the green room?"
"Sorry. I'm color-blind."

535 No Suicide.
"Something held me back from suicide."
"How's that?"
"I can't swim."

536 Don't Know Yet.
"Poor Frank. When he lost his money, he lost half of his friends."
"What about the other half?"
"They don't know he lost it yet."

537 Chance to Grow.
"How did you get that big nose of yours?"
"Well, I just kept it out of other people's business and gave it a good chance to grow."

538 Who's Going?

"Lend me ten dollars until I get back from New York."
"Sure. Here it is. When do you get back?"
"Who's going?"

539 Fast Building.

"Did you fall down that elevator shaft?"
"No, I was sitting here and they built it around me."

540 Another Mouth.

"Well, I've got another mouth to feed."
"You don't mean . . .?"
"No, not that. Tapeworm."

541 Lost Ten Pounds.

"I think I've lost ten pounds."
"Turn around. Think I've found it." (Grand Ole Oprey, Nashville.)

542 Road to Mandalay.

"Do you know 'The Road to Mandalay'?"
"Do you want me to sing it?"
"No, take it!"

543 Chilled.

"I'm chilled to the bone!"
"Why don't you put on your hat?"

544 Not Description.

"Where did Larry go?"
"He's round in front."
"I'm sorry. I wanted his whereabouts, not his description."

545 Socializing.

"I'm a little stiff from bowling."
"I'm from Sheboygan myself!"

546 Quit Zoo.

"I quit my job at the zoo. Spots before my eyes."
"What was your job?"
"Washing leopards."

547 Like Newsreels.
"What do you think of Bermuda shorts."
"I like the newsreels better!"

548 Mattress Shepherd.
"I got a job in a mattress factory. I'm a shepherd."
"How can you be a shepherd in a mattress factory?"
"I watch the flock by night."

549 Medium.
"You went to see a spiritualist. Was he good?"
"Oh, medium."

550 Wall Device.
"Did you hear about the fellow who invented a device for looking through walls?"
"What does he call it?"
"A window."

551 Heavy!
"Why are you so heavy?"
"It must be my iron constitution."

552 For Exercise.
"What do you do for exercise?"
"I read mysteries, and let my flesh creep." (When at the University of Chicago, Hutchins said that when the temptation came to exercise, he lay down until it passed away.)

553 Second Story Man.
"Mama, what is a second story man?"
"Your father, dear. That is, if the first one doesn't work."

554 Lost Your Leg. Woman to beggar, "Why, you've lost your leg."
Beggar looks down. "Well, lady," he replies, "durned if I haven't."

555 Music Medal.
"What did you get that bronze medal for?"
"For singing."
"And the gold medal?"
"For quitting."

556 The Difference.
"What is the difference between amnesia and magnesia?"
"With amnesia, you don't know where you're going."

557 Likes It.
"How does your brother like his new elevator job?"
"Oh, he's taken up with it!"

558 Take a Walk.
"For reducing, perhaps it would be good for you to take a walk on an empty stomach," said the doctor.
"Whose?" asked the patient.

559 Let's See It.
"Wash your hands."
"Both of them?"
"No, one of them. I want to see how you do it!"

560 Not Horatio.
"Quit calling me Horatio. My name is not Horatio."
"All right. I'll be seeing you, Not-Horatio."

561 Wide Repertoire.
"She certainly has a very wide repertoire!"
"Yes, but it wouldn't show so much in a different cut of dress."

562 Taking Washing.
As children we used to help Mother take in washing. We went around to other people's lines.

563 Not There.
Woman to bus driver, "Do you stop at the Palmer House?"
"Not on my salary," he replied.

564 Ghost.
A man claimed to have seen a ghost.
"Did he make sounds?"
"Sure did."
"What did he say?"
"I'm sorry, but I couldn't tell. I don't know the dead languages."

565 You Know Best.
"I wouldn't trust my own brother."
"Well, you know your own family best."

NONSENSE

566 Peanut Butter. A workman daily would open his lunch box, unwrap a sandwich, look into it, exclaim, "Ugh! Peanut butter!" and throw it away.

On the third day a fellow workman said, "Buddy, I don't want to butt in, but why don't you tell your wife you don't like peanut butter?"

"You leave my wife out of this," said the luncher. "I make my own sandwiches!"

567 Faster. On a train a man was weaving from side to side in his seat as if he were a pendulum. "What are you doing?" asked a fellow passenger.

"Keeping time," said the man.

"And what time is it?"

"Four-thirty," said the timekeeper.

His friend looked at his watch. "You're wrong. It's five o'clock."

The other man speeded up his motion. "Then I'll have to go faster," he said. (Can be acted out.)

568 Here's an Idea: Take a famous character of history and ask him a mythical question. Such as: "Hello, President Abraham Lincoln. What is your address?" "My Gettysburg address is: 'Fourscore and seven years ago . . .'"

Or: "Good morning, Mr. Benjamin Franklin. What do you say?"

"A stitch in time saves nine. Silence is golden. Haste makes waste. A watched pot never boils."

569 Just Left. Stephen Leacock, the late great Canadian humorist, used to describe a man as being the kind that, when he entered the room, you felt that something had just left.

570 Sayings.

He who hesitates is pushed.

If the shoe fits, it's out of style.

If eggs are twenty-six cents a dozen, how many can you get for a cent and a quarter?

571 Smelled. Did you hear about the man whose nose was cut off in an auto accident? When they restored it at the hospital they got it on upside down, and ever since then he's smelled to high heaven!

572 Kiddlies. The woman customer in the butcher shop said, "A pound of nice, fresh kiddlies, please."

"What's that?"

"A pound of nice, fresh kiddlies, please."

"Pardon me, madam, I'll get the other butcher."

"A pound of nice, fresh kiddlies, please!"

"You mean 'kidneys'?"

"That's what I said, diddle I?"

573 Think It Over. "When I was in England, I bought a wonderful antique Rolls Royce, but I don't know how to get it over here."

"Easy. Just sit down and **think** it over!"

574 Washed Ashore. A shipwrecked sailor, a mile offshore, was desperate. There was no wreckage to cling to, and he was about to drown. Then he got the answer. There was a bar of Ivory soap, floating in the water. He took it and simply washed himself ashore!

575 Genteel Family. It was such a high-class family. They used nothing but cultured buttermilk and refined oil.

576 Suicide?

"What are you doing?"

"Committing suicide."

"Why do you have the rope around your middle instead of your neck?"

"I tried it around my neck, and I couldn't breathe."

577 Who Were You?

"I don't believe you knew who I was when we met on the street yesterday, did you?"

"No. Who were you?"

578 Squaw on Hippopotamus. There was sort of a status contest among Indians as to how well they set up their squaws, who had a habit of bringing out animal hides, sitting on them, and conversing. One squaw had a bear hide, another a moose hide, and so on. But one enterprising Indian had got a hippopotamus hide for his woman, and she was twice as big as any of the other two. In fact, you could say that in weight the squaw on the hippopotamoos was equal to the sum of the squaws on the other two hides.

579 Sting Along. If you're stung by a bee, and at the same time bitten by a mosquito, what do you call that? Sting—along with itch!

580 Wholesale Contact. The kids were driving nails into the expensive furniture.
  "How can you afford to let them?"
  "Oh, I get the nails wholesale."

581 Hare Restorer. The barber supply salesman inadvertently hit a rabbit with his car. With him was an animal lover. The salesman went to his sample case, got out a bottle, sprinkled some on the animal, who jumped up and ran away.
  "Marvelous!" said the animal lover. "What was it?"
  "Hair restorer," replied the salesman.

582 Lot of Money. "I've got between ninety-eight and a hundred dollars."
  "That's a lot of money."
  "Oh, two dollars isn't so much!"

583 "Suicide." The coroner pronounced it suicide, because that's the way you pronounce it.

584 Worse Luck! I went into the shop for a cigar, but a man stepped on my hand.

585 Who's Kissinger? I had a friend named Kissinger. He didn't like it so he changed it to Hale, then Beck, then Lyles, then Logan. I wonder who's Kissinger now?

BRIGHT REMARKS

586 Laredo Drunk. What do they call a drunk in Laredo? Souse of the border!

587 Norse Is Norse. There was a train leaving Oslo with a Norwegian engineer bound for Stockholm. On the same track all the way ran a train from Stockholm, headed to Oslo, at the same time, and they continued their journey all the way. Why was there no wreck? Because Norse is Norse, and Souse is Souse, and never the twain shall meet.

588 Interesting Questions:
What's that in the road . . . Ahead?
What do you do if your girl drinks . . . Likker?

589 Beatle Wisdom. To the question, "Why do you wear so many rings on your fingers?" Ringo replied, "Can't get them in my nose."

"How do you like Beethoven?"
"I love his poems."

590 Not Invited.
"I came pretty near going to that party!"
"Why not?"
"Wasn't invited!"

591 Wild Oats are sown on roof gardens.

592 Split-Level is so popular in parts of Long Island that it is reported a man is riding around there in a split-level Continental.

593 Dead Town?
"How long has this town been dead?"
"Don't know exactly, but you're the first buzzard!"

594 This Medal was given to me by the pawnbrokers of Chicago for my special redeeming qualities.

595 Shine: I do most of my work sitting down. That's where I shine!

596 Phoenician Contribution. What was the principal contribution of the Phoenicians? Blinds.

597 You Can't Win. Izzy Inchcape opines that you figure out your income tax and go to the county home. Don't, and you go to jail.

598 Horn In! The driver of the truck was loud with his horn in traffic. As he drew up alongside a woman driver, she leaned out her window and said sweetly: "What **else** did you get for Christmas?"

599   Dirty!   He was carrying books in a laundry bag. Why? "To tell the truth," he said, "they're dirty."

600   Volkswagen Fan.
"This VW that you brag about so much. What will you do when it's finished—scrap it?"
"No," said the owner. "Put it in an old Volks home."

601   Road Wisdom.   The driver is safer when the roads are dry. The roads are safer when the driver is dry.

602   Directions.   Have you noticed that they sometimes give away what your starting point is? "Up North," "Back East," "Out West," "Down South."

603   Reversed Salutation.   Stephen Leacock, the late Canadian humorist, reported once that a man entered the room saying "Hello," and when he saw who was there, reversed his salutation.

SIGNS

604   "Please Keep Off This Grass.   Remember when you were struggling for recognition."

605   "America Is a Land of Untold Wealth," reminds a sign in a district office of the Bureau of Internal Revenue.

606   "Friend of the Foot" reads the sign on the back of an African bus in Rhodesia.

607   "Listen" says the sign on the display of wild shirts in a store window.

608   Be Grateful.   Seen in an expensive shop this sign: "If you don't see what you want, be grateful."

609   Language Problems.   In the window of a Paris gift shop: "Never mind your French. We speak good broken English."

610   Dig!   On a bopster's tombstone, they say, appears a sign, "Don't dig me, man. I'm gone."

611 Oops! In a Los Angeles bakery once appeared this sign: "Cakes 66¢. Upside-down Cakes, 99¢."

612 Confused. At a convention a delegate once wore a homemade badge with the letters **B.A.I.K.**
"What does this mean?" asked his friends.
" 'Brother, am I confused!' " said he.
"But you don't spell **confused** with a k."
"You don't know how confused I am," said the delegate.

613 Don't Complain. Over the entrance to traffic court in Memphis is this sign: "Don't complain. Think of the summonses you have deserved but didn't get!"

614 Mr. Hugg? An Owensboro druggist capitalizes upon his name with his sign: "Hugg the Druggist."

615 Killin' Me! Borrowing from the Duke of Paducah, of the Grand Ole Oprey, a Tennessee sign on some new grass said: "Your feet are killin' me!"

616 Please Pay First. In a New York business is the sign: "In case of atomic attack keep calm, pay bill, run like ＿＿＿＿."

617 Don't Shoot! A sign erected near the convention platform for the benefit of press and other photographers said: "Don't photograph the speakers addressing audience. Shoot them as they approach platform."

618 "Don't Walk." The policeman pointed to the sign, "Don't walk," and asked the old lady if she could read. "Certainly I can," she replied. "I didn't know that was for traffic. I thought that was put there by the bus company."

619 "Fishing Tickle." This was the sign in the window of a hardware store. People who would come in to correct the spelling remained to buy hardware.

620 Remarkable Men. A sign in a department store window proclaimed: "Wonderful bargains in shirts for men with sixteen and seventeen necks."

621 Careful! In a State Park is a sign: "Rest Rooms Ahead. Speed —15 miles per hour."

622 Pants Pressed. On a dry cleaning establishment the sign: "Pants pressed in rear during alterations."

623 Under Water. On a backwoods road appeared this sign: "When this sign is under water, road is impassible." It may have been placed there by the man who gave these directions: "You turn off five miles this side of the store."

624 Eat. A filling station with restaurant adjoined, near Leesburg, Florida, had this alternately flashing sign: "Eat here," "Get Gas."

625 Stockings. A Sacramento women's apparel shop had a sign: "Sheer stockings designed for luxury wear but so serviceable that many women wear nothing else."

626 Accurratt. "Accuracy is our watchword. We do not make misteaks."

627 Tough! In a Texas restaurant is a sign: "Steak $1.00. That's tough, but the 75¢ steak is tougher."

628 Bargains. Clothing stores have had such signs as: "Shirts 89¢ and they won't last long at this price." "Ladies' bathing suits 1/3 off." "Underwear slashed."

7

Wisdom

OUR CURIOUS WORLD

629   Home Facts.
Each year the average homemaker washes an acre of dishes, three miles of laundry, scrubs five miles of floor, washes a mile of glass. The man shaves thirty-six thousand square inches of beard.

In the garden did you know that corn can grow as much as four inches a day?

Even in America bathing must not be taken for granted. In 1842 the first bathtub was denounced as a "luxurious and democratic vanity." Boston made it unlawful to bathe, except on doctor's prescription. In 1843 Philadelphia made it illegal between November 1 and March 15.

630   Odd Accidents.   Robert Heinbaugh, of Painesville, Ohio, was shot by his lawn mower! It ran over a bullet which entered his toe.

Mrs. Jewell Norman's dog in Lincoln, Nebraska, pawed the gearshift of the car enough to back it into another car.

J. C. Lightfoot, of Memphis, was gashed on the head when a squirrel threw an ear of corn at him.

In the home of Ishmael Lynch, of Port Gibson, Mississippi, a Civil War shell recently fell from the mantle and exploded, dam-

111

aging the house severely. Probably the last shot of the Civil War!

Trucks driven by men named George Washington and Benjamin Franklin collided. Cars driven by Tom Coffey and Ben Pott did the same.

Eugene Peete, in Lakewood, California, decided to spend July 4 at home to avoid danger. He went out into his yard and was knocked flat by a piece of metal falling from a passing airplane.

631 Curious Geography. The Gulf of California does not touch the State of California at any point. Reno, Nevada, lies one hundred miles west of Los Angeles. From Detroit, Michigan, you go south to get to Windsor, Ontario, Canada.

"WISDOM"

632 Start It.
"What do you think of civilization?"
"Good. Somebody should start it."

633 Blotter Type. Some people are like blotters. They absorb everything, but get it all backwards.

634 Women faint more than men because there are more women.

635 Can't Count. Some people are no good at counting calories, and they have the figures to prove it.

636 No Heel. When leaving your footprints on the sands of time, try not to leave the mark of a heel!

637 Little Voice. The little voice inside us used to be conscience. Now it may be a pocket radio.

638 Satisfied! Be content with your lot, especially if it is a corner one.

639 Two Reasons that some people don't mind their own business: (1) no mind; (2) no business.

640 Busy? A man is never too busy to talk about how busy he is!

641 Indispensable? Remember what happened to the horse when the tractor came along! (Note: But there are more horses in the United States today than ever!)

642 **A Neck** is something that if you don't stick it out you won't get in trouble up to. (Yet remember the turtle, who never gets anyplace until she sticks her neck out."

643 **Best Tranquilizer:** A clear conscience.

644 **Add Dirt.** It isn't hard to make a mountain of a molehill. Just add a little dirt!

645 **Printed Speeches** are like dried flowers.

646 **Authority:** It's like a bank account. The more you draw on it, the less you have.

647 **Keep Smiling.** It makes people wonder what you've been up to.

648 **Thurber says:** "A new broom may sweep clean, but never trust an old saw."

649 **For Nodding.** An auction is a place where, if you're not careful, you do get something for nodding!

650 **Influence.** Kermit Long says that Fred Stone used to tell young university students, "Boys, don't use your influence until you have it!"

651 **Proverb:** Short sentence based on long experience.

652 **You Can't Win.** If some people got their rights, they'd gripe for being deprived of their wrongs.

653 **Not Dough.** Money is not dough. Dough sticks to the fingers.

654 **Fresh:** "It's the fresh egg that gets slapped in the pan."

655 **Count Your Blessings!** If you don't get everything you want, think of all the things you don't get that you don't want!—Oscar Wilde.

656 **Human Dynamo.** They called him that because everything he has on is charged.

657 **Values:** People may be judged by the things they are willing to get in line for.

658 **Impromptu Speeches** are not worth the paper they're written on.

659 **Addressee:** The last person to read his postcard.

660 **People** are like tea bags. Until they get into hot water, they don't know their own strength!

661 **Plato:** "You can discover more about a person in an hour of play than in a year of conversation."

662 **Health Note:** To cure water on the knee, wear pumps.

663 **Mouth.** Nothing is opened by mistake more than the mouth.

664 **Balding.** To avoid falling hair, jump out of the way.

665 **Start.** Very few men have learned the business from the top down.

666 **Too Far.** They arrested a fellow for stealing comic books from the newsstand. This was just carrying jokes too far.

667 **New Invention.** I'm going to invent a suit of lint that picks up blue serge.

668 **Foot Note.** When you put your best foot forward, be sure to have your pet corn covered.

669 **Car.** What the average man wants out of his car is his teen-aged son!

670 **Cost of Living.** The easiest way to figure it out personally is to take your income and add 10 per cent.

671 **Color** is odd. When it's fast, it doesn't run. It is not fast when it does!

672 **Adam Splitting.** The first Adam-splitting brought forth Eve —a force man has never been able to control since.

673 **Shindigs.** The worst kind are those under the bridge table.

674 **Perfect Peace.** In the cemetery.

675 **A Dollar** won't do as much for people as it once did because people will not do as much for a dollar as they once did!

676 Prosperity is the period when you go broke more slowly.

677 Anatole France says: "It is part of human nature to think wise things and do ridiculous ones."

678 Praise Now. "It is better to have a little taffy when you're alive than epitaphy when you're dead."—Max Lerner.

679 Difference. It's a slim margin between keeping your chin up and sticking your neck out.

680 Good Manners. How can children have them without seeing any?

681 Friends? After a man has climbed high on the ladder, his friends begin to shake it!

682 Sunny. Don't prepare so thoroughly for rainy days that you can't enjoy today's sunshine.

READ-ALOUDS

*Non-Alcoholic Cocktails**

Ever alert to new developments in the swiftly changing world, we bring you news of "New Foolproof Soup Drinks" by a promotion-minded soup company.

Their idea is to provide a non-alcoholic drink which appears to be an alcoholic drink for people who want to look as though they are drinking when they are really not. These non-alcoholic cocktails were introduced recently at a "Cocktails a la Discotheque" party in New York.

Included among the drinks were:

"Soup and Soda" (condensed beef broth and soda)
"Madhattan" (beef broth and V-8 with cherry)
"Red Eye" (tomato soup, water, lemon juice, soda)
"Slow Soup Fizz" (tomato soup, water, 7-Up with lemon twist), and numerous others such as "Soup on the Rocks," "Beef and Bitters," and "Frisky Sour."

---

* Jackson Burns, in *St. Paul's Outlook*, April 24, 1964.

This thrills one with admiration for the brilliance and ingenuity of American business. It is a humanitarian venture as well as a money-making scheme. It can help persons to be temperate without really trying. Now you can be a secret teetotaler while appearing to be a gay dog who really "lives it up."

There are possibilities for other industries too. Optical companies could make a special contact lens for making eyes appear bloodshot. Cosmetic companies could develop special make-up for simulating dark circles under the eyes and the slightly greenish pallor of morning after. . . .

Record companies could develop special sound-effect records for persons who want to appear to be giving a wild party with raucous music, laughter, screams and the occasional breaking of glass. Neighbors who liked parties would be envious at not being invited. If such persons wanted to do something just a little devilish while they were reading (while the records were playing at top volume) they might slowly sip "Soup and Sodas" or "Slow Soup Fizzes."

Well, here's mud in your eye! (683)

God Is for Real, Man*

For reading aloud as part of talks, many are discovering the freshness of Carl F. Burke's material, gathered in cooperation with inner-city adolescents from jail, camp, and detention home settings. He encouraged the youngsters to paraphrase and to use their own language as they approached the Bible scene. This writer has used some of this material to introduce to sermons, reading the same passage first from the off-beat version, then from the Bible.

IT DON'T MAKE ANY DIFFERENCE
The Parable of the Wedding Feast (Matthew 22:1–4)

The project manager's son was getting married. So his father said, "Let's throw a wild party!" So they invited all the wheels in the city. They got everything ready—beer, pretzels, pizza, 7-up, and cokes. But nobody came.

---

* Material in this section from Carl F. Burke, *God Is For Real, Man* (New York: Association Press, 1966), used by permission.

So the manager sent out some of the older kids to remind people of the party. But they still didn't come. They didn't care and told the older kids to beat it or they would call the cops.

When the manager heard this, boy, was he mad! He wanted to start a rumble right then. But he didn't. He just said, "OK, to hell with them. We'll invite the people in the project—they ain't so bad." When the people came the manager gave them new clothes to wear. There was one guy who still wore his own rags. When the manager asked him how come, he wouldn't say anything. So the manager had him thrown out.

This is only a made-up story, but if you take out the word manager, and put in, God, and take out "party," and put in "heaven"—look what you got.

So it don't make any difference if you're a city wheel or a fuz or who—it's best to do what God wants you to do. (684)

DON'T TRY TO CON GOD
Temptations of Christ (Matthew 4:1–11)

Jesus went out by the docks and the man [the devil] tried to con him.

He didn't eat for forty days—and was starved.

After that the man came and said, "OK, if you're the Son of God, let's see you make these red bricks turn into bread."

But he didn't do it. He just said, "Cool it, man, you got to have more than bread if you want to live big."

Then the man took him to the steeple of St. Joe's. The man says, "Long way down, huh? Lots of cars, too! Let's see ya jump. Don't be chicken. There's some cats with wings to catch you."

But Jesus didn't do it. He just said, "Don't try to con God, man, 'cause you can't do it."

So the man takes him to a big mountain where he could see everything and says, "Feast your pincers on that. I'll give you the whole thing if you will worship me."

But Jesus wouldn't do it. He just said, "I told you, don't try to con God. How many times have I got to tell you to cool it? You are supposed to worship God only."

So the man sees he ain't getting switched on, so he gets out of there and Jesus gets some rest. (685)

"Advice"

One of the brightest things to hit the American scene in decades is "Dear Abby," Abigail Van Buren, whose real name is Pauline Phillips. Here are some choice bits of her advice and wisdom.

686 Dear Abby: What do you think of a man who does not remove his hat when kissing a lady goodnight? **The lady.**

Dear Lady: Maybe he's looking for a kiss that will knock his hat off!

687 Dear Abby: My boyfriend is going to be 20 years old next month. I'd like to give him something nice for his birthday. What do you think he'd like? **Carole.**

Dear Carole: Never mind what he'd like. Give him a tie.

688 Dear Abby: I've been going with this man for six years, off and on. We were engaged five times and broke off. Each time he left me for another girl and then came back to me again. I took him back because I thought he could stay true to me. For the last three months he went with another girl, and now he wants me to take him back again. Do you think he comes back to me just for what he can get? **Cassandra.**

Dear Cassandra: I don't know . . . what's he getting?

689 Dear Abby: My husband has always been very close to his mother and she has never cared much for me. I asked my husband if I was drowning and his mother was drowning which one would he save? He said, "My mother, because I owe her more." I'm terribly hurt, Abby. What shall I do? **Arlene.**

Dear Arlene: Learn to swim.

690 Dear Abby: My boy friend took me out for my twenty-first birthday and wanted to show me a special good time. I usually

---

don't go in much for drinking but since it was an occasion to celebrate, I had three Martinis. During the dinner we split a bottle of
champagne. After dinner we each had two brandies. Did I do
wrong? **Blondie.**

Dear Blondie: Probably.

691 Dear Abby: I've been married for 28 years and my husband
spends money like he thinks Hoover is still in the White House.
I have to cut my own hair and make my own clothes and he makes
me account for every nickel I spend. He isn't just thrifty—he's a
miser! He rolls his own cigarettes and has a stack of Defense bonds
put away that would choke a cow. He says it's for a rainy day.
How do I get some money out of him before we are both called
to final judgment? **A Miser's Wife.**

Dear Wife: Tell him it's raining!

*L. B. Johnson Humor**

Texas style, his humor comes rolling out. He seldom thinks of
politics, he says, more than eighteen hours a day. Of Hubert
Humphrey he said, "Best Vice-President since Lyndon Johnson!"
(692)

On his handicap for golf he says it's all handicap. (693)

Of the inaugural ball he said, "Never before have so many paid
so much to dance so little." (694)

He likes to quote Magnus Johnson, former Swedish representative from Minnesota, who said that "We must take the bull by the
tail and look the situation in the face!" (695)

Jewish Folklore

This is but a sampler of Nathan Ausubel's marvelous collection
A Treasury of Jewish Folklore.† The book is loaded with colorful
stories, many of them humorous and all of them delightful.

---

* From *The Johnson Humor,* ed. Bill Adler (New York: Simon &
Schuster, 1965), used by permission.

† *A Treasury of Jewish Folklore* by Nathan Ausubel. © 1948 by Crown
Publishers, Inc. Used by permission of Crown Publishers, Inc.

696 Iron Logic. The doctor was examining the ninety-year-old Jewish woman. "Can you cure me, Doctor?" she asked.

He pointed out that when one is older all sorts of ailments occur. "A doctor is not a miracle man," he said. "He can't make an old woman grow younger."

"Who wants to be younger?" asked the patient. "What I want is to grow older!"

697 The Modest Saint. The wonder-working **tzaddik** seemed fast asleep. Nearby worshipful disciples whispered the holy man's unparalleled virtues.

"What piety!" exclaimed one disciple with rapture. "There isn't another like him in Poland!"

"Who can compare with him in charity?" murmured another, ecstatically. "He gives alms with such an open hand!"

"And what sweet temper! Has anyone ever seen him get excited?" asked another with shining eyes.

"**Ai**, what learning he's got!" chanted another. "He's a second Rashi!"

At that the disciples fell silent. Whereupon the rabbi slowly opened one eye and regarded them with injured expression.

"And about my modesty you say nothing?" he asked reproachfully.

698 Two Against One. The doctor examined the sick man and said, "My friend, you, I and your disease are three. If you will take my side the two of us will easily be able to overcome your illness, which is only one. However, if you should forsake me and not cooperate with me but hold on to your disease, then I, being alone, won't be able to overcome both of you!"

699 Spinoza? A freethinker once said mockingly to Rabbi Pinchas of Koretz, "Would you like to know what the philosopher Spinoza wrote in one of his works? He wrote that man in no way stands higher than an animal, and that man has has the same nature."

"If that is so," remarked the rabbi, "how do you explain the fact that up to now the animals haven't produced a Spinoza?"

700 Shadow and Substance. While the servant was salting and soaking three pounds of meat according to dietary custom, the cat suddenly grabbed it and carried it away and ate it. When the mistress returned she was abusive. "All you servants are liars and thieves!" she snapped.

"You accuse me?" asked the servant. "Come with me to the rabbi."

The servant told the rabbi that she saw the cat eat the meat, so they brought the cat. The rabbi placed it on the scales. It weighed exactly three pounds.

"There is your meat!" he cried to the mistress. Then, to the maid he said, perplexed, "But tell me, girl, where is the cat?"

701 Mutual Introduction. A Jew was walking on the Bismarck Platz in Berlin when unintentionally he brushed against a Prussian officer. "Swine!" roared the officer.

"Cohen!" replied the Jew with a stiff bow.

702 Innocence and Arithmetic. A young scholar of Chelm rushed to the rabbi. "My wife has just given birth, although we have been married only three months! It takes nine months for a baby to be born!"

The world-renowned sage put on his silver-rimmed spectacles and furrowed his brow. "My son, have you lived with your wife three months?"

"Yes."

"Has she lived with you three months?"

"Yes."

"Together—have you lived three months?"

"Yes."

"What's the total, then—three months plus three plus three?"

"Nine months, Rabbi."

"Then why do you come to bother me with your foolish questions?"

703 The Price of a Millionaire. When the millionaire Brodsky came to a small Ukrainian town all the inhabitants poured out to greet him. With official pomp he was led to the inn, where he ordered two eggs for breakfast. When he had finished, the innkeeper asked him for twenty rubles. Brodsky was astonished. "Are eggs so rare in these parts?" he asked.

"No," replied the innkeeper, "but Brodskys are!"

704 No Admittance! One of the synagogue's chief means of revenue is the sale of seats for high Holy Days, done in advance since handling of money on these days is forbidden to orthodox Jews. Non-Jews are employed as doorkeepers.

One **Yom Kippur** a ticket-taker at a Brooklyn house of worship was confronted by a Jew with no ticket who needed to see his partner, Liebowitz. "It's urgent!" he pleaded.

"No ticket, no admission," said the guard.

"But it's an important business matter. I'll only be a minute."

The guard weakened. "Well, if it's business, I'll let you in for a minute . . . but remember—no praying!"

705 Applied Psychology. In a prejudiced town adults encouraged the children to call the tailor "Jew." After worrying a while, he came up with a plan. As the kids gathered in front of his shop he said, "From today any boy who calls me 'Jew' will get a dime." He paid them. Next day he gave them a nickel. The third day a penny.

"Why only a penny today?"

"That's all I can afford."

"Do you think we're going to call you 'Jew' for a lousy penny?"

"So don't." And they didn't!

8

People

Nothing is funnier than people. Here's proof:

706 AC or DC. The salesman asked at the hotel desk if they had AC or DC current. After checking, the clerk apologized. "I'm sorry," he said, "neither gentleman is registered here."

707 God Is Dead? At the end of the **Time** magazine article on "God Is Dead" was quoted this quip from a sign on a wall in Europe: "God is dead.—Nietzsche."
Underneath had been added, "Nietzsche is dead.—God."

708 Man Should Reform. Mary Little says that if man is a little lower than the angels, perhaps angels should reform!

709 Find an "E." In England a musician asked for an "E" string for his guitar. The girl behind the counter gave him an assorted box. "Pick it out," she said. "I can't tell the 'es from the shes."

710 Thin Man. "You know how thin you are. You know how thin I am. Well, he's thinner than both of us put together."

711 He Has Rights! "I think people should be stopped from shooting craps. They have as much right to live as we have."

712 Real Fix! "I'm in an awful fix. I lost my glasses, and I can't look for them until I find them!"

713 Speaks English. An American woman tourist heard a German policeman say to her, as she sneezed, "Gesundheit!"

"Ah," she observed, "you speak English!"

714 New Hat! The husband asked, "What's that bandage over your eye?"

"Bandage!" His wife was indignant. "Stupid, that's my new hat!"

715 Not So Bad. Around the little tourist town went the word that an older person had died. Then word went around again: only a summer visitor.

716 Endorsement. The young bride tried to cash her husband's paycheck at the bank. "You need an endorsement," said the teller.

She thought a moment and then wrote on the back of the check, "My husband is a wonderful man. Mary Little."

717 She's Right. Queen Victoria went rowing on the river on Sunday to the consternation of a strictly religious woman. Someone reminded the woman that Jesus also went rowing on the Sabbath, on the Sea of Galilee. "Maybe so," she responded. "But two wrongs don't make a right!"

718 Me Too! On a crowded bus a woman said rather loudly, "I wish that good-looking man would give me his seat." Five men immediately stood up.

719 No Charge! Two little boys were talking. One said, "My daddy is an Elk!" The other one was impressed.

"What does it cost to see him?" he asked.

720 What Brand? The braggart always wanted to sample what his friends were drinking and identify it as a super-connoisseur. Once he grabbed a flask from an acquaintance, quickly unscrewed the lid, and took a big mouthful. Immediately he spewed it out. "That's gasoline!" he cried.

"Yes," acknowledged the friend, "but what brand?"

721 First Aid! On the bus trip for camera fans, one of the well-equipped gentlemen fainted. "Quick!" said a thoughtful shutterbug. "Loosen his camera straps!"

722   Junk Mail.   The housewife was leafing through the morning mail. "Bills, bills, bills!" she said. "I thought they were going to do something about this junk mail!"

723   Got Seasoning!   The little girl who hadn't been to the seashore went with her family. She bent down to taste the water. "My," she exclaimed, "that's got seasoning in it!"

724   Circus Fun.   "You just don't know what fun it is to go to the circus," he was telling his friends. "Why, today at the circus I met a two-headed man, face to face!"

725   New Playmate.   "Mother: "Junior, you'll have to stop using those bad words."

"But mother," said Junior, "Shakespeare used them!"

"That's no excuse," she replied. "You'll just have to stop playing with him!"

726   Not Grown Yet.   The mother was concerned that her ten-year-old daughter was growing up too quickly until she saw her wetting her hair rollers with a water pistol.

727   Nothing Done.   The energetic housewife said to her maid, "Here it is Monday, tomorrow is Tuesday, the next day Wednesday—the week half gone and nothing done!"

728   Stricter Now.   "My ancestors came over on the **Mayflower**," said she.

"You're lucky," he replied, "immigration laws are so much stricter now."

729   Appropriate Names.   Gluey Gleanings shares these:

Wayne Flowers and Martha Trees got married in Phoenix.

In Cleveland, May Dye changed her married name to May Linger.

Frank Frost in Omaha became the divorce lawyer for Dorothy Snow.

Mary Stamp was postmistress in Luppitt, England.

A. L. Milks was director of the Dairyman's League in New York.

Frank Swallow was named head of the Logan Drinking Cup Division, U. S. Envelope Company, in Rockville, Connecticut.

C. A. Deadman, in Madison, Wisconsin, belied his name by recovering from a heart ailment.

730 Dig Deeper. All the dirt wouldn't go back into the hole that the forman ordered dug. He thought it over and finally said, "We'll have to dig the hole deeper."

731 Lost Colony! After touring fertile America, an English writer said, "Damn George III."

732 Self-Restraint: Eating one peanut or one potato chip.

733 Business Purposes. A young New Englander applied for a job with a Chicago bank. One of his references, a New England bank, wrote back his pedigree: undoubtedly he was from fine stock. But Chicago asked further information from the New England bank: "We need a little more information, since we want a man for business, not breeding purposes."

734 Depression Doings. Bob Hope says that when things were bad, he dropped some money in the telephone and a voice said, "God bless you, sir."

735 Not Habit-Forming. A friend of ours told a friend of hers that perhaps phenobarbital would help her get relaxed at night. "It's not habit-forming," she said. "I know. I've been taking it for twelve years."

736 Easiest Way. He was the laziest man in the county, but not without the spirit of experimentation. His current project, in his rocking chair on the front porch, is to see whether it's easier to rock north and south with the wind, or east and west with the grain of the floor.

737 Question: The New Yorker (an excellent source of quotable humor for speeches) took a good-natured swipe at the authors' **The Family Fun Book.** From the introduction they lifted this quotation:

"They were ready for refreshments at a children's neighborhood party.

" 'Strawberry soda, please,' a little boy requested.

" 'I'll take peach ice cream if you have it,' said little Mary.

"A 3-year-old thought a minute and then ordered solemnly, 'Make mine Ranier Pale Extra Dry.'

"Can one doubt that the family exists in a different setting from that of even ten years ago?"

Then the magazine commented: "No, we don't doubt it. But our question is, 'Did he get the beer?' "

738 Wassamatta? Two cab drivers in Hawaii almost collided. One was very angry. "Wassamatta you?" he shouted.

"Wassamatta **me**?" the other yelled incredulously. "Wassamatta **you**! **You** wassamatta!"

739 Hit the Bull. When the authors were missionaries in Africa, they ran onto this one. They were trying to decide who would do a certain needed leadership job. When just the right person was suggested, one of the African men who knew some English said, "Now you have hit the bull!"

740 Scriptural Twain. Mark Twain loved to say that he was in the Bible. "And whosoever shall compel thee to go a mile, go with him Twain!"

741 We Do Too. "I enjoy just visiting my friends so that I can look at my library."

742 Real Virtue. The kid was explaining the conduct of his western hero. "He didn't go into the bar to get drunk, daddy," he said. "He just went in there to kill somebody!"

743 Forgive Them. In one of the early civil rights actions, Jim Lawson was shown in a news picture being led from a church by two policemen. The photo also showed the church bulletin board, with the sermon title: "Father, forgive them!"

744 Borrow One. It was raining, so he went to his college dorm friend who had his raincoat and said, "I want my raincoat. It's raining."

"Can't have it," said the other.

"What will I do?"

"Do like I did—borrow one."

745 Expected Crowd. In a laboriously written note to the intended speaker for a small church, were the statistics on the adults of the church: "Thirty adults, thirty-five adultresses."

746 Birth State.
"In what state were you born?"
"I guess I'd have to say—nude."

CANNIBALS

747 Butter Up Teacher. Did you hear about the cannibal child, sent home from school for trying to butter up the teacher?

748 Wonderful Wife. The cannibal said, "My wife makes wonderful soup. Surely will miss her!"

749 Cannibal Proverb: One man's meat is another man's person.

750 Didn't Eat 'Em? The cannibal was incredulous, "Did you kill all those people in a war and then not eat them?"

DID YOU HEAR ABOUT THE CANNIBAL WHO:

751 Was very fond of children?

752 Learned to take diplomats with a grain of salt?

753 Liked to stop where they serve truck drivers?

754 Enjoyed having people for dinner?

755 Was a connoisseur of friars?

756 Liked banquets, and originated the expression "Give the little lady a **hand**"?

757 Got hay fever from a grass widow?

758 Finally got fed up with people?

759 Had a book, **1,000 Ways To Serve Your Fellowman?**

760 When missionaries came to his area, got his first taste of religion?

761 Especially enjoyed the businessmen's lunch?

762 Cannibal Etiquette.
"Should fried chicken be eaten with fingers?"
"No, fingers should be eaten separately."

REAL LIFE

While many of the bits of humor in this book happened in "real life," here is a concentration of humorous experiences that the authors know about personally.

763 Certainly Not. Into a church student exchange program office came an application from a girl. In the section which asked for "sex" (meaning, "which?") she had written, "Certainly not!"

764 Thanks for Going. A plain-spoken missionary was at the good-bye picnic for the Eisenbergs when they left Rhodesia. "Thanks for coming to our good-bye picnic," they told her.
   "Thanks for going," she replied, "so we could have a picnic!"

765 Ironic: At a church conference somebody stole a copy of **Prayer Can Change Your Life.**

766 There Go I. Dr. Kermit Long, a clergyman, told us of going to the home for wayward girls and being touched by their plight growing from their intense humanity. He related his experience in his Chicago church and concluded with the humble statement: "There, but for the grace of God, go I."

767 Fun in Bed? E. O. Harbin was present in a bookstore when a lady came in and asked the clerk, "Do you have **Fun in Bed?**" She blushed and became so embarrassed that she turned and left immediately.

768 Nine-Ninety. Entertaining some dignified older missionaries in Rhodesia, young Mary Phil Higgs showed them **The Saturday Evening Post.** One wondered how much a subscription was. "I'll go check," she said, and went to another room. Meanwhile, one of the children demanded attention, and it was ten minutes before she returned. The conversation had long since shifted.
   Rather abruptly she said, "Nine-ninety, Mr. Gates." Looking completely confused, Mr. Gates blurted out: "Nighty-night, Mrs. Higgs!"

769 Dietary Supplement. At Boston University, the faculty wives were telling something on their husbands. When it was Mrs. John Ward's time, she said, "My husband, I'll bet, is the only man here who uses Metrecal as a dietary supplement!"

770 Can Methodists Dance? A lady asked Bishop Gerald Kennedy this question. Direct as he always is, he replied: "The last one I danced with couldn't."

771 All Originals. The "Celebrities' Apparel Shop" in Hollywood has second-hand clothing of the stars and others. One woman went to the desk to ask about a dress she had found. "It's near my size, but I need bigger. Do you have another?"

"Oh, no, honey," quipped the gal. "They're all originals."

772 Banana-Bible. The late Rollin Walker, beloved Bible teacher of Ohio Wesleyan, used to tell how to read the Bible. "It's like eating a banana," he would say. "Some people peel the banana. They know the banana peeling is no good, so they look at the banana and the peeling—then throw both away. Others know the banana is good. They look at both, and since the banana is good, they eat the peeling too. Now with God's help we must learn to peel the banana, eat the banana fruit, and throw away the peeling!"

773 Starts With Musk. When the authors' son Donny was about four, his daddy got back from a trip. Donny had a surprise. Guess? The family had been playing games by giving initial letters, so he went it one better. "Daddy, it starts with a musk," he said. (It was Three Musketeers candy.)

774 That'll Cure Him. Dr. John Johnnaber came from the meeting of a committee which determines the suitability of candidates to be missionaries. "The fellow in there now is a sound Christian," he said. "He's Neo-Orthodox. But when he starts explaining Neo-Orthodoxy to Bolivian Indians, I imagine it will simplify his theology."

TOURISTS

775 Strange People. "I like the scenery around here," said the vacationist, "but the people here are strange."

"That's so," said the New England farmer, "but most of 'em go home by October."

776 Like It. Tourist: "In New Hampshire, I understand you have more cows than people."

Native: "Yep, We like it better that way."

777 Hand Over. You have to hand it to these resort hotels . . . if you don't, they'll take it anyway.

778 Strong Stomach. A sympathetic ship passenger watched another at the railing making an offering to the sea. "You have a weak stomach!" said the sympathizer.

"Weak, nothing! I kin throw as far as anybody on this ship," was the answer.

779 Florida Weather. "The weather here in Florida is so wonderful," tittered a visitor. "How can you ever tell summer from winter?"

"By the cars, ma'am," said the hotel clerk. "In the winter we get Cadillacs, Continentals, and stuffed shirts. In the summer we get Fords, Chevrolets, and stuffed shorts."

780 Just Babies. Tourist: "Any big men born around here?"

Native: "Nope. Best we can do is babies."

781 Me Too, Almost. The English sailor was showing an American tourist Lord Nelson's ship, **Victory.** " 'Ere, sir," he said, "is the spot where Lord Nelson fell."

"I know," said the tourist. "Nearly tripped myself!"

782 South Wins! The guide on a sightseeing bus at Gettysburg kept telling the story in such a way that it looked like a great southern victory: "Here is where two brave boys from Georgia captured an entire regiment of Northerners. . . ."

A woman with a New England accent spoke up: "Didn't the North win a single victory here?" she asked.

"Nope," he said. "And they ain't goin' to, as long as I'm drivin' this bus!"

THE BATTLE OF THE SEXES

783 Years Off. When a man has a birthday, he may take the day off. When a woman has a birthday she may take as much as five years off!

784 Mistake. The man who brags that he never made a mistake has a wife who did!

785 One for Each. For every girl who's got the curves there is a man who's got the angles.

786 Spic or Span? Some girls would look more spic if they had less span.

787 Definition: Slacks: something the back of a fat woman's aren't.

788 Matches: They're made in heaven, we understand. What would they do with them in the other place?

789 Father's Eyes. He has eyes like his father—pop-eyes.

790 Too Late. By the time a man understands women, he's no longer interested.

791 It Is! "A word to the wives is sufficient."

792 They're Close. "Boys will be boys, but girls are running them a clothes second."

793 Ageless. "Boys will be boys—and so will a lot of middle-aged men!"

794 Most Dangerous. A man's most dangerous age is his wife's.

795 Not Head. A wise woman makes her husband feel he's head of the house, when he's only chairman of the entertainment committee.

796 Mending Women. The trouble with women is that they'd rather mend your ways than your socks.

797 Observant. The most observant guy in history noted that Lady Godiva was riding a horse.

798 Stronger? The weaker sex is the stronger sex because of the weakness of the stronger sex for the weaker sex.

799 For Girls: "A ring on the hand is worth two in the voice."

800 Seven Ages. The seven ages of woman are baby, child, girl, young woman, young woman, young woman, and poised social leader.

801 Often Shy. In telling her age, a woman is often shy.

802 Tricky. Her problem: to get a dress tight enough to show she's a woman, loose enough to show she's a lady.

803 Usually. A woman seen stroking a man's hair is after his scalp.

804 Fashion: Fashion is what a her does to a hem to get a him.

805 Bachelor's Degree? A bachelor's degree is fine, but many college gals would rather have the bachelor!

806 Hard Reduction. Women are such hard losers. If you don't believe it, try living with one who is trying to reduce.

807 She'll Try. Give a woman an inch and she'll try to park a car in it.

808 No Excuse. To call your wife "relative by marriage" is no excuse.

809 Corral No. 5. Have you heard of the masculine men's cologne —Corral No. 5?

810 Smart German! Have you heard of the German who made his living by the sweat of his frau?

811 Which Is Worse? A wife driving from the back seat—or a husband cooking from the dining table?

812 News Item: "Overcome by gas while taking a bath, the young lady owes her life to the watchfulness of the custodian."

813 Greek Wisdom. In ancient Greece, a man getting a divorce couldn't marry a woman younger than his first wife.

814 Which One? Marriage is the institution that makes two, one. The lifelong struggle is to find out which is the one.

815 One Master. In Sunday school a youngster justified monogamy by quoting from the Bible: "No man can serve two masters."

816 Scare Her! Try praising your wife occasionally, even though it may frighten her at first.

817 Grab and Run. "Fight a woman with your hat," said John Barrymore. "Grab it and run."

818 Mirage? A young boy asked his father if "mirage" spelled "marriage."

819 Sounds Like Fun.
"Mother, can Freddie and I go out and listen to Daddy fix the flat tire?"

820 Costly. Mary had a little lamb. And her escort at the restaurant paid plenty for it.

821 Bowed. You couldn't exactly say that her legs were without equal, but you could say that they were without parallel.

822 Still Students. Outside a movie house in Rio de Janeiro students yelled, "Brigitte Bardot isn't worth thirty cents," which is one reason they're still students.

823 Monotony. An elementary schooler wrote: "In some countries a man can have only one wife. This is called monotony."

824 Mistake. "Many a man in love with a dimple makes the mistake of marrying the whole girl!" said Ring Lardner.

825 Cancelled. In England the play **World Without Men** was cancelled. All seven women in the cast, as well as the cat, were pregnant.

Courtship

826 The Difference. Men look for opportunity to knock. Women usually prefer a ring.

827 Would Do It. She's lovely . . . she's engaged . . . she uses jujitsu!

828 "Glass." She returned his engagement ring in a box marked "Handle With Care."

829 So Sudden. He: "Let's wander along the bridle path."
She (with artificially lowered eyes): "Oh, Jack, this is so sudden!"

830 Won't Be Long. The young woman looked back to smile sweetly at the waiting line at the telephone booth. "I won't be long," she said. "I just want to hang up on him."

831 Eight-Year Wishes. Of all the letters received when she announced her engagement, a pretty young school teacher cherished most a carefully written one from an eight-year-old girl. "Dear Miss Smith, I hope that you have a happy and sexful married life. Your friend, Shirley."

832 "Let's Get Married," she said to her boyfriend, who hadn't mentioned it in the twenty years they had been going together.
He answered. "Aw, who'd have us?"

833 Lead Me!
"You should see the new altar at our church," he said.
Said she, "Lead me to it!"

834 Ideal Woman. After years and years of search, he finally found the ideal woman. Eagerly, he proposed. She refused him. You see, she was looking for the ideal man!

835 Speak for Yourself. John Alden: "They say that kisses are the language of love."
"Speak for yourself, John," said Priscilla.

836 Someone Else? "Why won't you marry me?" he demanded. "Is there someone else?"
"Oh, Edgar," she responded, "there **must** be!"

837 Kiss? He said, "What do you say to a little kiss?"
She replied, "I don't know. I never spoke to one."

838 Kiss?
He: "May I kiss you?" There was silence.
He: "May I please kiss you?" More silence.
He: "Are you deaf?"
She: "No. Are you paralyzed?"

839 Kiss
He: "Will you give me a kiss?"
She (affronted): "What cheek!"
He: "Either one."

840 Fractional Appeal. That platinum package of pulchritude who provides palpitation for the office male population admits that sex appeal consists of 25 per cent of what a girl has, and 75 per cent of what men imagine she has.—Iowa State Traveling Men's **Bulletin.**

841 Stiff Neck. "Oh, boy, but I have a stiff neck and a sore arm this morning!"

"How come?"

"My boyfriend and I were at the drive-in movie last night."

"And you were necking, no doubt. But how could that give you a stiff neck and a sore arm?"

"We were in different cars."

842 Your Happiest Day.

"This is the happiest day of your life!"

"But it's **tomorrow** that I'm getting married."

"Yes, I know!"

843 A Prize! Father: "Whoever marries my daughter will get a prize!"

Young man: "May I see it, please?"

844 Stop Running.

"Ronald makes me tired!"

"Then why don't you stop running after him, dear?"

845 New Address. They had quarreled the night before. She telephoned. "Is that you, George?"

"Yes."

"You know I told you never to set your foot in this house again?"

"Yes."

"Well, we're moving and I just wanted to tell you our new address."

846 Wasn't You? "What would you have said if I had kissed you as we went through that long tunnel?" asked he as the courting couple were traveling by train.

"Oh," she exclaimed, "wasn't that you?"

847 Short Story. He: "Will you marry me?"

She: "No."

And they lived happily ever after!

848 Yours Forever. The English prof, emphasizing repetition in learning vocabulary, said to the class: "If you keep repeating a word over and over, ten or a dozen times, it will be yours forever."

A cute little coed in the back closed her eyes and began: "Johnny, Johnny, Johnny. . . ."

849 Taken Out. He tried to call her, but got no answer. The operator told him: "That number has been taken out!"

"By whom?" he asked.

Marriage

850 No Robbery. The three men planned to rob the house, and the job for making the entry fell to one whose boots squeaked. As he went up the steps he heard a feminine voice demanding, "You go right downstairs and take those boots off! I'm tired of having to clean up this mud and dirt! March right down and take them off!" He came outside and told his friends, "I just couldn't rob that house. It's too much like home!"

851 Beats Wife Up. He is a man who beats his wife up every morning. He gets up at seven thirty and she gets up at eight o'clock.

852 Hopping Mad. She's married to a man with a wooden leg and a terrible temper. She says it takes very little to make him hopping mad!

853 Right Is Seamless.
"How are my stockings?" she asked hubby.
"The left seam is OK. The right one is seamless," he replied.

854 See That Letter. The suspicious wife said, "Let me see that letter you've just opened. The handwriting is a woman's and you looked shocked when you read it."

"Here," said hubby. "It's a bill from your dressmaker."

855 Words. He and his wife had words, but they were all hers.

856 No Reform. She married him to reform him and then was disappointed that he didn't need it.

857 Good Husband.

"Is she making him a good wife?"

"Not exactly, but she's making him a good husband!"

858 How Much? She: "I got this girdle today for a ridiculous figure!"

He: "I know. But how much did it cost?"

859 Period Furniture. The fancy interior decorator was prepared to help the young wife. "What kind do you now have?" he asked. "What is the motif—Modern, Oriental, Early American?"

She thought, and answered. "I'd say that it's more like Early Matrimony," she said.

860 All the Breaks. "You men get all the breaks. Here I slave all day over this hot stove, while you get to work down in that nice cool sewer!"

861 Aim's Improved.

"When I was first married, my wife often sang to me 'Oh, How I Miss You Tonight.'"

"She doesn't sing it now?"

"No. Her aim's improved!"

862 Strange Look. "Your wife has a strange look on her face lately."

"Yes, she's trying to resemble her latest photograph."

She

863 Nice Compliment. He: "Doesn't the biggest idiot always marry the prettiest woman?"

She: "My. You handled that compliment so nicely!"

864 My Brains. He: "Don't you think our boy has really gotten his intelligence from me?"

She: "Must be. I've still got mine!"

865 Blow Brains Out. He: "Refuse me and I'll blow my brains out!"

She: "How could you?"

866 Expensive Thumb: She wanted five thousand dollars from the insurance company for the loss of her thumb. That, said she, was the one she kept her husband under.

867 Good for Nothing. Johnny insisted on money for being good. "Certainly not," said his mother. "Be like your father—be good for nothing!"

868 Not Dead. "Chivalry is not dead. Today as I got off the bus with some packages I fell down. The man behind me didn't step on me—he stepped over me!"

869 That Dish. They were ordering in an exclusive restaurant. "Dear," he said to his wife. "How do you pronounce that Italian dish I'm so crazy about?"
"I think it's 'Gina Lollobrigida,' " she replied.

870 Just Ordinary. "Is your husband a bookworm?"
"No, just an ordinary one."

871 Short Business. "Shopping bag?"
"No, just looking."

872 Easy, Now! The passerby helped the woman motorist change a tire. "Let the car down easy," she warned. "My husband is sleeping in the back seat!"

873 Clouded Vision. He was advised to get firm with his henpecking wife. He decided to try. "Shut up!" he said to her at the top of his voice. Well, he didn't see that woman for four days. And then he could see her just a little out of one eye.—Tex Evans

874 To Maternity. Girl (to cab driver): "Maternity Hospital. And you don't have to rush. I work there!"

875 He Asked. "Why did you ever marry such a homely man?"
"He asked me, dearie!"

876 50–50. As they split up the house, they decided that 50–50 would be fair. So she took the inside, he took the outside.

877 Just Her Luck. "Tex" Evans, sometimes called Texas' Will Rogers, tells on himself that one of his kids asked his wife, "Mamma, if Daddy should die, do you reckon there's another man in the world like him?"

She said, "Maybe there is. And it'd just be my luck to get him!"

878 It's a Wig. "What have you done to your hair?"

"To tell the truth, I'm wearing a wig."

"Well, well. If you hadn't said it, I'd never have known it."

879 His Size. "I don't know exactly what my husband's size is," she told the shirt counter clerk. "But I can just get my fingers around his throat."

880 Domesticated. The experienced wife said, "I have my husband trained so that he eats out of my hand."

"Does save a lot of dishwashing," said the young bride.

881 She's Flipped! At the psychiatrist's the woman said, "I can't stand it any longer. My husband tells me **everything** that happens at the office."

882 No Fists! The henpecking wife was giving him a good tongue-lashing. He sat in dejected silence. "And," she added with a final flourish, "don't sit there and make fists at me in your pockets, either!"

883 Somebody Else. "If you really loved me," she said, "you'd have married somebody else."

884 New Furs.

"How did you happen to get your new fur coat?"

"We had a stroke of luck. We couldn't afford it, and then John fell and broke his collarbone and we got five hundred dollars insurance."

885 Pretty, Isn't It. The husband asked the paperhanger, "Who told you to put that awful paper on the wall?"

"Your wife."

"Pretty, isn't it?"

He

886   An Angel.
"My wife's an angel, that's what she is!" he said in a burst of emotion.
His friend replied, "Mine's still livin'."

887   Man or Mouse?   The friend was counseling with the henpecked husband. "Are you man or are you mouse?" asked the friend.
"I must be a man," said the husband. "She's afraid of a mouse."

888   She's Better.   "How's your wife?"
"She's better. But the way she carries on when she's better, I think she's better when she's worse!"

889   Demanding Wife.
"My wife keeps wanting money."
"And how much have you given her?"
"None." (This might be used as a collection story.)

890   Modest Man.
"I may have my faults," said the humble husband, "but being wrong is not one of them."

891   Yawning Woman.
"If that woman yawned once, she yawned a dozen times," she told her husband.
"Maybe she wanted to say something, dear," he replied.

892   Wrong Answer.
"Since I saw you last," said one male friend to another on the street, "my wife has died and gone to heaven."
"I'm sorry," said the friend. Then as he reflected on heaven, he added, "I'm glad." But that didn't seem totally right either, so he added, "I'm surprised!"

893   She Needs Something.   The farmer told the doctor that his wife was ailing. She got up at the regular time, about four o'clock, milked the cows, got breakfast for the hands, did her housework, churned. About ten o'clock last night she said she felt a bit tired. "What would you recommend for a tonic, Doc?"

894 Don't Know Her. A young bride was training her husband. "Now that couple across the street are so devoted. Every morning he kisses her good-bye. Why don't you do that?"

"I haven't even been introduced to her," he said.

895 Suicide.

"I've considered shooting the man who married my wife."

"That would be murder."

"No—suicide."

896 That's a Lie!

"There's the most beautiful woman I ever saw," he said to a friend in her hearing.

"I wish I could say the same for you," she retorted sharply.

"You could," he said with a courtly smile, "if you could lie like I can."

897 Even-Tempered. He had a wife who was even-tempered. That is, she was always mad.

898 Three and Three. Killing flies in the house, he reported to his wife that so far he'd gotten three males and three females. "How can you tell?" she asked. "Easy. The females were on the mirror, the males on the pie."

899 Finished! "Our quarrel was finished," said he, "when we admitted that I was wrong!"

900 Below Wife. He was filling out a blank that called for "marital status." On it he wrote "below wife."

901 Got One! Two Irishmen met on the street. "Let me present me wife to ye," said one to the other.

"No, thanks," was the reply. "I've got one of me own."

902 Garden of Eden. The feminist speaker said, "Where would man be but for woman?" "In the Garden of Eden," piped up a man, "picking strawberries."

903 Tit for Tatting. To hint, she got out the hammer and began to beat around the house. He responded by getting her sewing kit, sewing on some buttons.

904 Interesting Idea. He received a sinister note: "$1,000 or we kidnap your wife!"

"I don't have the money," he replied, "but your proposition interests me!"

905 Not Cure It.

"Doctor, my wife has an inferiority complex."

"And you want me to cure it?" "No, be sure she keeps it!"

906 Leaving Axe.

"Here you are going away from this house for three whole days and not a stick of wood for the stove."

"Well, what are you gripin' about, woman. I'm not takin' the axe, am I?"

TEXANS

907 Texas—State of Mind.

"Son, don't ask a man where he's from. If he's from Texas, he'll tell you. If not, there ain't no need to embarrass him!"

908 This Is Texas. John William Rogers, Dallas journalist, says, "The big thing in Texas is the simplicity of the people in comparison to the elaborateness of the wealth of many."

909 Small Map of Texas? An innocent tourist asked for one. There isn't any.

910 The Oil of Texas. Texas has been described as an oiligarchy, with the theme song "Oil Folks at Home." One oil tycoon got up in the Cotton Bowl to invite everybody to dinner and was disappointed when only two thousand showed up!

911 Insufficient Funds. Across a check written by a Texan, they say, the words "Insufficient Funds" were stamped, and then handwritten: "Not yours—ours!"

912 Bird of Paradise. In dry hot West Texas a tourist stopped at a filling station and in the course of conversation asked about a bird he saw. "Bird of paradise," answered the Texan.

"Long way from home, eh?" said the tourist.

913 Texas Shortage. Bushels, for people to hide their light under.

914 Raise a Ton! They were playing cards and the Englishman in the game bid a pound. The Texan responded quickly, Texas style. "I don't know how you figure your money, but I'll raise you a ton," he answered.

915 Layover. Did you hear about the Texan who had to lay over between trains—stock trains?

916 Texas Contest. The **Houston Post** reports that there is really no truth to the rumor that a merchant in Oklahoma City has started a contest, offering as first prize a week of vacation in Texas, and as second prize a two-week vacation in Texas.

917 Health Reasons. A preacher moved to New Mexico "for health reasons."
"They were sick of me in Texas," he said.

918 "Baked Texas." This is the name of the new dessert being offered in Alaska hotels.

919 Alaska Split? There is the rumor going around that Alaska may split its territory in two and make Texas the third largest state instead of the second.

WEST TEXAS:

920 It's so flat that you can see forty-eight hours ahead! So dry that when a man faints they have to throw sand in his face!

921 Gets so dry that crows have to kneel down to eat corn, and the churches have to change their methods: Baptists sprinkle, Methodists use a moist towel, and Presbyterians give a promissory note!

922 In fact, a West Texan died and went to the hereafter. "I never knowed heaven was like Texas," he said.
"Son," replied the inmate, "this ain't heaven!"

923 Horse Influence in Texas. Sometimes people get a disease called "broncho pneumonia." They mark their rest rooms "Heifer" and "Steer."
When a cowboy falls off his horse and hurts himself, he has his

horse trained to go for a doctor. Just one thing—they can't break the horse from bringing a horse doctor.

924 Biggest Lamb Dyer. Forgot to tell you about the rancher in West Texas during the drought who sold off most of his cattle and his sheep but had a few lambs left. One day his wife was doing laundry outdoors when a lamb fell into a pot of bluing.

The next day it was prancing near the fence. A Cadillac drove up and a woman asked, "That a blue lamb?"

"Shore is."

"How much do you want for it?"

"Twenty-five dollars."

She bought it.

Well, he recognized the possibilities and so he would dye a couple of the lambs and let them run and people would buy them. Then he began to buy up large quantities of lambs and dye them, and before long he came to be known as the "biggest lamb dyer in Texas."

925 Healthy in Texas! The air alone is so wonderful that people stay health. A Texan rushed up East to see his mother, who was grievously ill. Realizing what she needed, he went out and got his spare tire and let the Texas air loose in her room. She got so well that she lived for another sixty-five years! And when he came back home he refilled his tires and said to his wife, "See how much better the car rides on that good Texas air!"

WEALTH IN TEXAS:

926 It's true that some poor people in Texas have to wash their own Cadillacs.

927 A Texas oil man gave his girlfriend a sports car for each day of the week.

928 Actually, there's a city named Dollars, Taxes.

929 Valuable Property. Yes, there was a Texan who made his wealth on only thirty acres. "They call it 'Downtown Dallas,'" he says.

930 How Much? And then there was the cute little blonde gal who said to the wealthy Texan, "How much did you say your name was?"

931 Good Boy! Did you hear about the Texas kid who pledged one hundred dollars a week to the church? The pastor came to inquire if it were in error. "Oh, no," said his daddy. "I'm glad he did it. I'm teaching him to tithe."

932 Dry in Texas. In the Panhandle a visitor asked a rancher, "What is the longest that you remember that you went without rain?"

The rancher scratched his head a minute and replied, "Well, I remember **one time** [there was a distant look on his face] when it **never did** rain!"

933 Dry. Another visitor remarked that it looked like rain, and the rancher said, "I hope it does rain. Not so much fer me as fer m'boy. Ye see, I've **seen** rain!"

934 Call the Continents. Should have told you about the wealthy Texan touring the world in his private jet plane. The pilot called to him on the intercom, "That's Brussels down below, sir!"

He replied, "Never mind the details. Just call the continents!"

935 You Go, Shorty! In a western movie about Texas they were shooting at the villians who were holed up in the ranch house. At the barn one of the brave cowboys said, "We'll stay here, Shorty, and you go and surround the house."

936 Healthy Liver! You know, there was a Texan who took a certain kind of liver pills all his life. When he finally died, his liver had become so healthy that they had to operate, take his liver out, and beat it to death!

937 Yes, Who? A man from Louisiana said you were to call him "Tex."

"How do you get that?" asked his companion.

"And who wants to be called 'Louise'? "

938 What Is Fort Worth? Dallas and Fort Worth argue, you know, about which is superior. Two Texans had been doing it for years when suddenly the Dallas antagonist said, "I'll have to admit that Fort Worth has something Dallas hasn't got!"

"Ah," said the Forth Worthian, "and what is that?"

"A great big beautiful, prosperous metropolitan city thirty-five miles from its borders."

939 One Hundred Texans? Back in DC3 days of plane travel, a pilot radioed to the tower at LaGuardia that he had a load of one hundred passengers in a plane that carried, at the most, twenty-eight. They were curious, so they let it in ahead of bigger planes. Sure enough, a hundred little people got out. The pilot explained that these were just Texans with wind removed. In the airport they found a ten-gallon hat clear down over a set of boots, and this proved to be one of them who had had the air completely let out of him.

940 Texan First. At the Notre Dame-SMU football game in the Cotton Bowl three priests yelled for Notre Dame, but one was yelling for SMU. People nearby asked the loner why. He replied, "It's simple. I was a Texan before I was a priest."

941 Chilled Dallas. There was a big semi-truck down from Denver that had its tires slashed on the north side of Dallas. This let loose some of that cold Colorado air which cooled the hot Texas air so much that there was only a 32 per cent bragging level for the next seventy-two hours.

942 Accidents? The cowboy applied for insurance. "Any accidents?"

"Wal, steer once broke most of my ribs and a sidewinder set his fangs in me."

"Don't you call those accidents?" asked the examiner.

"Heck no," replied the cowboy. "They done it a-purpose!"

943 Triple Pun. The **Reader's Digest,** several years ago, told of the sons of a Texas rancher who renamed the spread "Focus," that is, "Where the sons raise meat." They call it the only triple pun in the language.

944 Words for Texas A and M A reprobate died in Texas, and they were trying to get somebody to say some good words for him at the burial, in the absence of a preacher. Nobody could. Finally a Texan stepped forward and said, "If nobody has anything to say for old Joe here, I'd like to say a few words for Texas A and M."

945 Seat Seven. The gracious Texas lady was known for her entertaining. She was describing her new home to a friend. "What about bedrooms?" asked the friend.

"I can sleep twelve," she replied.

"And baths?" "I can seat seven."

946 Apostle Paul a Texan? No, this is impossible. He said, "I have found that in whatever state I am I can be content."

947 Texas Burials. Let me tell you two stories. There was a Texas lady known for her explosive ways. Finally she died and they buried her. As the last Texas soil was placed into the grave a tremendous clap of thunder came. One of the mourners said devoutly, "She made it!"

948 But there's another one about the fellow buried in a black Cadillac, sitting at the wheel. They lowered the whole contraption into a big hole. One of his friends looked on and said to another indoctrinated Texas friend, "Man, that's livin'."

949 Plain Texas Clubs. An easterner did a favor for a Texan, who insisted on giving him a gift. "Oh, a few golf clubs maybe," said the easterner.

A few days later a telegram arrived in the office of the eastern friend: "Have six golf clubs for you but not all with swimming pools."

950 His Deal. The easterner watching the Texas card game noticed that the dealer gave himself four aces from the bottom of the deck. He whispered this to another onlooker. The native son smiled and said, "Well—it's **his** deal!"

951 Local Call. A Texan complained about the price of a telephone call. "Why, in Texas we could call to hell and back for that!" he insisted.

"Yes," replied the operator sweetly, "but isn't that in your city limits?"

952 Too Much for Shark. An Oklahoman fell into shark-infested ocean waters. What must he do? He remembered that as a young and foolish lad he had had some tattooing done in Texas. So he reached up, pulled off his clothes. Across his chest was tattooed "Texas is God's paradise." The sharks all turned away. You see, even a shark couldn't swallow that!

953 Dry and Windy. A Texas preacher's wife got a barometer instead of a thermometer by mistake at the drugstore. She put it in her husband's mouth and then took it out to read, to her surprise, "Dry but windy."

954 Good Judgment. An old Texan was being quizzed about how he had lived so long. "Good judgment," he said.
   "How do you get good judgment?"
   "From usin' bad judgment."

955 Last One Wins. The Texan and the Californian had a running argument about superiority. The Texan touched a watermelon in California and said, "Was this Texas avocado shipped in?"
   "Look out!" replied the Californian. "Take your hand off that California olive!"

KIDS . . .

. . . *In Church*

They see it all through kid eyes, and they don't always hear it right. For instance:

956 The Lord's Prayer.
   "How did you know my name?"
   or "Harold be thy name."
   "Give us this day our jelly bread."
   "Lead us not into Penn Station."
   "And deliver us from people."

957 Crazy! One hard-of-hearing child thought they were singing, "Crazy, crazy, all ye little children, God is love . . ."

958 A Bear? A child came home saying that they had sung about a bear at Sunday school. It was the "consecrated cross-eyed bear."

959 Dirty Socks. Also "While shepherds washed their socks by night" instead of "watched their flocks."

960 "Born." The name of the king of Israel was "Born." Don't you know—"Born is the King of Israel"?

961 Drawings of the Christmas scene have included Round John Virgin and even Pontius, the Pilot (flying the holy family), or an unnamed baby-sitter.

962 "Holy Catholic Church" for one little fellow became "Holy Cats in Church," and for another it ran the "Holy Castor Oil Church."

963 You'll Get It. Another said that in church they learned "Don't worry—you'll get your quilt." Mama discovered it was "Fear not—the comforter will come."

964 And With a Broom? Another thought it was "Jesus swept." (Jesus wept). At the end of prayers, a number of children say "AM" and some add "FM."

965 Bang It Again! A little boy was upstairs during a thunderstorm. His mother, thinking he might be afraid, found him instead with the window up, watching the lightning and hearing the thunder and saying, "Bang it again, God!"

966 Grace at Meals? A little boy, accustomed to grace before meals was eating with friends. "Don't you pray before you eat?" he asked.

"No, we don't."

He laughed. "You're just like my dog. Start in eating!"

967 More Fun. A little boy said, "Mother, if you ever go to the circus, you'll never go to church again!"

968 Then They'll Know. A little boy was drawing a picture.

"What is it?" asked his mother.

"God," he said.

"But nobody has seen God," she reminded him.

"Then they will when I get through," he said.

969 Notable Ambition. Asked what he wanted to be when he grew up, a little boy told his minister that he wanted to be a "returned missionary."

970 Down the River. The Sunday school teacher in Pennsylvania was asking the children where Jesus was born. (There is a Bethlehem, Pennsylvania.)

"Williamsport?" one guessed.

"No," she said.

"Mauch Chunk?"

"No," she replied. "It was in Bethlehem, Tommy."

"Oh, yes, I remember!" he said. "I knew it was one of these river towns."

971 Faith in Prayer. The congregation of a rural church prayed for rain. But they noted that a little girl was the only one with faith enough to bring an umbrella.

972 Church Service. Children love church service, but also have their opinions about it. One liked the music but thought the commercial too long.

973 Kid Prayers. To the question "Do you pray every night?" a little boy replied, "No—some nights I don't need anything."

974 Left-Handed God. A little boy, corrected for doing things with his left hand, said he was only doing like God had to do. How could God do otherwise when Jesus was, as the Bible says, "sitting on his right hand."

975 New Prodigal Son. A little boy told the story of the Prodigal Son for his Sunday school class:

"He sold his coat to buy food.

He sold his shirt to buy food.

He sold his undershirt to buy food,

and then he came to himself."

976 Sins of Omission.

"What are sins of omission?" was the Sunday school question.

One answered, "Those you should have committed and didn't."

977 Sacrifice for Lent. One little boy indicated he was giving up soap.

978 Note From God. After punishing an eight-year-old, the mother found a note addressed to her, pinned to her pillow. It said, "Be kind to your children and they will be kind to you.—God."

979 Missionary There! A Boston resident, visiting in Salt Lake City, was telling a Mormon child about her town.

"Do you know where Boston is?" she asked.

"Oh, yes," replied the little girl. "Our church has a missionary there."

980 God Spoke! A four-year-old climbed onto the roof of the house and would not get down. His father used his two-way radio in his car. On the telephone he told the mother to turn up the radio so he could talk with Billy. He shouted, "Billy, get down from that roof this minute."

When Billy came down his face reflected real awe. "God told me to come down from the roof, Mother."

981 Can a Child? Billy, aged four, came home from church weeping. It took his mother (who had done some canning that day) fifteen minutes to discover that they had sung the children's song, "Can a little child like me / Thank the Father fittingly?" The imagery was too much! He was taking the first line personally.

982 New Samaritan. The Sunday school teacher was telling the story of the Good Samaritan, with some gory details. "Now if you saw a man there, lying on the roadside, wounded and bleeding, what would you do?"

A little girl volunteered, "I'd throw up!"

983 Not to You. A little boy was saying his prayers in a very low voice. His mother said, "Dear, I can't hear you."

"I wasn't talking to you," he replied.

984 God Help Us. The four-year-old had been saying "Thank you for this food, Amen." He took advantage of his parents' encouragement to say a bit more on the night they had chili, which he didn't like. "Thank you for this food—and help us to get it down all right. Amen."

985 Wish Daddy Worked. Bryan Hall's young daughter came home from school wanting some fancy shoes like Alice, the only daughter of a businessman, had. Mother explained that they didn't have the money, that Dad's salary as a clergyman wasn't large. Accepting the explanation reluctantly, she said, "I wish my daddy worked for a living!"

986 Not a Preacher! A three-year-old chanted during the Christmas season "Not a preacher was stirring, not even a mouse!"

987 Christmas Ride. It was December 26 in a Catholic church in San Francisco. The "infant Jesus" was missing from the manger scene. The priest finally found him outside, riding in the wagon of a little boy who explained, "A week before Christmas I prayed to the little Lord Jesus and I told him if he would send me a red wagon for Christmas I'd give him a ride."

988 Presbyterians? A four-year-old heard a radio sermon saying that it would be good if even little children could be Christians. He turned to his mother and said, "Wouldn't it be good if we weren't Presbyterians so we could be Christians?"

989 Change Him. The Sunday school teacher asked the class what they'd do if they were in the situation with Pharaoh's daughter, hearing the baby crying in the bullrushes. A little girl's hand went up.

"I'd change him," she said.

Kids in General

990 Mixed-Up Sounds. At school, kids get the sounds of things mixed up.

One thought the pledge of allegiance included these words: "One nation . . . in a vegetable . . . with liberty just as far off."

A little boy said, "Bring up a child and **away he goes!**"

991 It Was Open. Mother was aghast that five-year-old Peter had to stand in the corner for putting mud in a girl's mouth at kindergarten.

"Why did you do it?" she asked.

"Well . . . " he replied, "it was **open!**"

992 Exciting! The mother was afraid that the house fire would have a lasting bad psychological effect on Junior. She was relieved when the next week he wrote on "The Most Exciting Thing in My Life," and used as his subject "The Cub Scout Meeting."

993 Short Circus. A rural five-year-old described a farm incident. "A piggy backed into the electric fence," he said, "and caused a short circus."

994 Play Pen. A four-year-old told his mother excitedly on TV there were some men fighting in their playpen.

995 It Gurgles. Janet had some stomach trouble, which she reported to her mother. "It hurts," she hold her, "but the worst is . . . it gurgles!"

996 No Operation. Mother insisted that her eight-year-old wash his hands before the meal. He resisted stoutly.
"I'm only gonna eat," he said, "not operate on somebody's brain."

997 Resisting. Grocer to the little boy: "Are you taking an apple?"
Boy: "I'm trying not to take one."

998 Instant Tomorrow. Seeing the sunlight as the train emerged from the tunnel, little Bobby exclaimed: "Look, Mommy. Instant tomorrow!"

999 Short Count. They were playing hide and seek, and four-year-old Sue was "It."
"You'd better hurry and hide," she warned the children, "cause I can only count up to seven."

1000 Seafood. There was the clever little boy who assured his mother that he loved seafood—saltwater taffy.

1001 They Helped.
Father: Did you help Mother today?
Mary: Yes, Daddy. I washed dishes.
Bobby: I dried.
Timmy: I picked up the pieces.

1002 Trade-In. He was the little son of an automobile dealer, and he had heard that a new baby was coming. This put him in tears. "I guess I'll get traded in on him," he said.

1003 The Jiffies? Using a clock with a second hand, a mother was teaching her little girl which were the seconds and which were the minutes. The child was puzzled. "But Mother," she asked, where are the jiffies?"

1004 Strong Arm. The violin teacher was reasoning with young Johnny. "Look at it this way," he said, "the more you practice, the stronger your bowling arm will get."

1005 No Electricity. Returning excited from school, little Larry said to his daddy, "We've got the most wonderful record player at school, Daddy. It doesn't take an electricity at all. You just wind it up!"

1006 Another Playmate. On the first day of school a little girl told her mother, "You'll have to find another playmate now that I'll be in school all day."

1007 Upsy-Daisy! A four-year-old fell down and skinned his knee painfully. A helpful lady said, "Upsy-daisy, little man."
"Upsy-daisy yourself!" he replied. "Can't you see I'm hurt?"

1008 A Pig. The father told his little boy not to eat so much. "You'll make a pig of yourself. Do you know what a pig is?"
"Yes, Daddy. It's a hog's little boy."

1009 Disorderly House. A girl of eleven suddenly began straightening up her room immaculately. Her mother discovered that it had frightened her to read that a woman was fined for running a disorderly house.

1010 Help! Running to her mother in tears, little Joanie said, "I can't fasten my dress, Mommy. It buttons in the back, but I'm in the front."

1011 Good Deed. Mother asked her new Scout if he had done his good deed. "Sure!," he replied. "I taught a smart aleck down the street not to stick out her tongue at Boy Scouts."

1012 Only Whole One! A little girl was asking a new friend about relatives. "I have two half-brothers and a half-sister," she said.
"My!" replied little Martha, amazed. "Are you the only whole one in your family?"

1013 You're Four. Two little boys were talking. "How old are you?"

"I don't know."

"Do girls bother you?"

"No."

"Then you're four."

1014 Just Like TV. Mother had just finished the cake. "Mother," said her little girl, "your cake would look just like the pictures on TV if you'd cut a piece out of it!"

1015 Won't Grow. The child of the cook solemnly watched the camp director bury a dead bird as an example of camp cleanliness. "Do you know what I'm doing?" he asked the child.

"Yes," replied the kid, "but it won't do any good. It won't grow."

1016 Judging a Day. Little Sally prayed, thanking God for the beautiful day, though it was raining. Her mother asked why she said such a thing.

She replied, "Mother, never judge a day by its weather."

1017 He Turned. Mother: "Why did you kick your little brother in the stomach?"

Willie: "He turned around."

1018 Doing It Right. As a joke the businessman put on his desk a dollar bill and a dime for the little girl to choose from.

"I have learned to take the smallest piece," she said, picking up the dime, "but so I won't lose it, I'll wrap it in this piece of paper."

1019 What Channel? The teacher asked the class about the English Channel.

"I don't know," said Bobby. "It certainly is not on our TV set."

1020 Wrong Side. Grandma was visiting for the first time. Little Doris asked, "Who are you?"

"I'm your granny on your father's side," she said.

"All right," Doris said, "But you're on the wrong side."

1021 His Fault.
"Billy broke my dolly."
"When?"
"When I hit him over the head with it."

1022 Sin. Two little boys were fighting. Johnny warned Billy to stop fighting because it was a sin.
"What is sin? Does it have claws?"
"No," admitted Johnny.
"Then I'm not afraid," said Billy, and kept on whacking.

1023 Beginner. Little Barbara, in the first grade, told a friendly policeman, "This is my boyfriend."
"A pretty girl like you with only one boyfriend?" he joked.
"Well," she said, "I'm only in the first grade."

1024 Choking Her. Two eleven-year-old boys had just seen a love movie. One thought it was awful, but the other said he had gotten through the kissing scenes by closing his eyes and imagining that the screen Romeo was choking her.

1025 Good Questions! "Mommy, how can a saleslady smell a yard?"
"How it is that just enough things happen in a day to fill a newspaper?"

1026 Off Standard. Mother (to baby-sitter): "Did you have any trouble with Junior? He's usually good as gold!"
Sitter: "About an hour ago he went off the gold standard!"

1027 Age Question.
"I'm six," said the proud little boy.
"Six!" teased the adult. "You're not as tall as my umbrella."
"And how old is your umbrella?" asked the little boy.

1028 Didn't Work. Bobby watched Mother put cream on her face before bed.
"Why?"
"To make me pretty," she said, wiping it off.
"Didn't work, did it?" said Bobby.

1029 She Won. At the ballet the six-year-old girl was enthralled, especially with the flowers given to the ballerina. "Oh, Mother," she exclaimed, "she won!"

1030 Why?

"Pa."

"Now what, son?"

"Why didn't Noah swat both flies when he had such a good chance?"

1031 Like a Lady. Little daughter was in the habit of fighting with the boy next door. "Don't hit him back," said her mother. "Remember that you're a lady. Out-talk him."

1032 Hot! Child calling to Mother, as Daddy snores: "Hurry, Mommy! Daddy's boiling over!"

1033 Noise Out. Little Lulu liked carrots. She was having her first experience with cooked ones. "Mother," she said, "how did you get the noise out?"

1034 Proper Source. An eight-year-old asked, "How did Queen Elizabeth know she was going to have a baby?"

Her seven-year-old friend was disgusted with such ignorance. "She can read the papers," she replied.

1035 Which? "Little boy, if you had a large apple and a small apple, which would you give to your brother?"

"Do you mean my little brother or my big brother?"

1036 Good Question. Daddy was tired of being questioned by his four-year-old.

"Daddy . . . ?"

"Yes?"

"What do you do at the office?"

Daddy screamed, "NOTHING!"

The little one thought a minute and then said, "But Daddy, how do you know when you're through?"

Scouts

1037 Went Home. They were staging a mock air raid. Scouts were to act as wounded people. One Scout lay there for over an hour. Nobody came. He left. When they finally arrived, they found a note in his spot: "I bled to death and went home."

1038 What Is a Scout? "A scout is a fiend to all, and a bother to every other Scout," wrote a misspelling Boy Scout.

1039 Little Scouts. A cartoon in **The Saturday Evening Post** showed the Scoutmaster and the Scouts fleeing a vast forest fire. "That's how it is, men," said the Scoutmaster as they all ran for safety. "You just rub two sticks together."

1040 But Good. Their agreement on the camping trip was that the cooking staff would continue until there was complaint. The cooks got tired and doctored the food, especially with salt. The other boys struggled valiantly. "The food's awfully salty," said one, but remembering that complaint would put him on the cooking staff, added: "But it's good!"

1041 Speak the Language. Some little Brownie Scouts asked a visitor from England if he would "speak a little of the language."

TEEN-AGERS

1042 What's Cooking. The modern miss may not know exactly how to cook, but she surely knows what's cooking.

1043 Not Even Here. Elderly flirt: "Where have you been all my life?"

"For the first forty years," replied the modern miss, "I wasn't even born."

1044 Me Too. "I'd like to have a date with _____ (use name of very popular, well-known female) again!"

"How's that?"

"Yes. Once before I felt like I'd like to."

1045 Love Gift. With the orchid he sent his girl, the young man wrote a short note: "With all my love and most of my allowance."

1046 Got the Jump. "The dance was progressing by leaps and bounds."

1047 Chicken? Bennett Cerf tells of a game reported by Billy Gray which some roosters play near a state highway. They wait for a car to come along, then dash across the road almost under the wheels. Any chicken losing his nerve is called "teen-ager."

1048 Hairstyle. "How do you like your new hairstyle?"

"Well, it keeps the sun out of my eyes, but I'm getting a little tired of having people whisper in my nose."

1049 Holiday Note: They say that mistletoe is bad for trees, but anybody know it's fun for twos.

1050 Your Choice. The love-smitten farm boy was taking his new city girlfriend for a stroll when they saw a cow and calf rubbing noses affectionately. "That makes we want to do the same," said he.

"Go ahead," she replied. "It's your cow, isn't it?"

1051 See Operation. "Would you like to see where I was operated on?" she said to her boyfriend.

"Yes," he said eagerly.

"Well, it's down the street here just three more blocks!"

1052 Boy to Teacher: "Good morning, sir—spelled 'C-U-R.' "

1053 Good-Bye. Two boys, at the close of a conference, came to say good-bye to each other. One said, "It's been . . . "

The other replied, "Sure has."

And they parted happily.

1054 Songs. Have you heard . . . ?

Girl's version: "I Dream of Harry With the Light Blue Jeans."

The Horror Songs: "With a Prong in My Heart," and "Singing in the Drain."

1055 Typical. She was a typical college freshman. And when she was a junior, she was still a typical college freshman.

1056 Shrink?

"Do you shrink from kissing?"

"If I did, I'd be skin and bones!"

1057 To Elders: If you want to stay young, associate with youth. If you want to get old quickly, try to keep up with them.

1058 Famous.

"What's your name?"

"Caesar."

"First name?"

"Julius."

"My, you're pretty famous."

"Ought to be. I've been working in this same filling station for three years now!"

1059 Love's Strategy: "She spurned him on."

1060 Only a Glass. "And what to drink?"

"Ginger ale."

"Pale?"

"Oh no, a glass will do!"

1061 Language Barrier. The young gal said to the mother for whom she had finished baby-sitting, "If I were younger, maybe I could understand what your baby was talking about."

1062 Cops and Teen-Agers. In the old days the kids played "Cowboy and Indian" or "Cops and Robbers." Now they play "Cops and Teen-Agers."

1063 Wrong Vegetable! The young man was sitting next to a glamorous gal at a big banquet. In the course of the meal, without warning, although their conversation had been very friendly, he took a bowl of vegetables and turned it upside down on top of her head. "How dare you put those turnip greens on my head!" she exclaimed, highly indignant.

"Turnip greens?" he asked, astounded. "I thought it was spinach!"

1064 Generous!

"I spent sixteen dollars on my girl."

"Boy, that's a lot!"

"Sure—but it was all she had."

1065 Nobody Home. The teen-aged gals arranged a slumber party and set themselves up by the telephone. Then one of them wailed, "We're all here! There's nobody to phone."

1066 Spare the Rod. Junior to hot-rodding Daddy: "Can you spare the rod, Dad? I've got an errand in mind."

1067 Different Now. "Marcia, I wonder if a nice girl would be holding that boy's hand?"

"Mother, nowadays a nice girl has to!"

1068 Wisdom: Do as the Romans do—and get your face slapped!

1069 So Hungry!
He: Going to have dinner anywhere tonight?
She (eagerly): Why no, not that I know of.
He: "Gee, you'll get awfully hungry by morning."

1070 God Loves You. They were a part of a group on a sleigh ride and it was cold. She was romantic. "Nobody loves me," she said, "and my hands are so cold!"
"God loves you," said the boy, "and you can sit on your hands."

1071 No Light.
"I told him not to see me anymore."
"What did he do then?"
"Turned out the lights."

AGED

1072 So Old: He remembers when the big dipper was a drinking cup . . . And at his birthday party the guests were overcome with the heat of the candles.

1073 No Fool. "There's no fool like an old fool. You just can't beat experience."

1074 Gilded. "Golden Age" turns out to be gilded on examination.

1075 Defiant. Some men defy old age. They believe that they are as good as they never were!

1076 Not Yet.
"Lived around here all your life?"
"Not yet!"

1077 Ag'in 'Em.
"How long have you lived around here?"
"Eighty-five years."
"Seen a lot of changes, haven't you?"
"Yep. And I've been ag'in all of 'em."

1078 Not Gallant. Her husband didn't help her on the bus. "You're not as gallant as you were when I was a gal," said she playfully.

"And I'm not as buoyant as I was when I was a boy," he retorted.

1079 No Enemies. "Yessir. Ninety tomorrow. Not an enemy in the world."

"What a beautiful thought."

"Yep. I've outlived them all!"

1080 Younger Generation. There's only one big thing wrong with the younger generation. A lot of us don't belong to it any more.

1081 Another Excuse. You're young only once. After that you need some other excuse.

1082 Knees the Same. To the doctor an old man of eighty-four complained of trouble with his left knee. "Perhaps it's just getting old," said the doctor.

"No older than my right knee," he replied.

1083 Old Age Coming. When a man starts making excuses to stay at home instead of to get out, old age is about to overtake him. In other words, old age is when you don't care where your wife goes, so long as you don't have to go too.

1084 Wrinkles: A sign of old age in everything except prunes, pants, nutmegs, and automobile fenders.

1085 Back Next Year. Reporter (to a man of ninety-nine): "Hope I can see you next year."

Old Man: "Wal, son, you look healthy enough to me!"

1086 World Cares? At twenty we don't care what the world thinks of us. At forty we are concerned about it. At sixty we discover that it wasn't thinking of us at all!

1087 Worser! "How are you today, Grandma?"

"Oh, not so good. Yesterday I could get my hand 'way up there [demonstrates] but today I can only get it up to here [demonstrates a lower level]."

1088   Stronger Now.   "How old are you?"
"A hundred."
"Doubt that you'll see another hundred."
"Well, I'm stronger now than I was when I started the first hundred."

1089   Old Timer: One who can remember when the village square was a place instead of a person.

1090   Growing Institution.   They tell this of the retired old gentleman who had established a college and returned to speak on the occasion of the twenty-fifth anniversary of its founding. Hooking his thumbs in his vest pockets, he patted his bulbous tummy and said, "Young gentlemen, I have watched this institution grow for twenty-five years. It is very near and dear to my heart."

1091   Who Says?   At ninety-eight the old man lived on the side of the mountain. His son, seventy-eight, wanted him to move down. The older man told the grandson, fifty-seven: "It's not that I mind movin'. It's jest that I hate to have a young upstart tellin' me what to do."

1092   Broke Him.
"I broke my husband of biting his nails."
"How?"
"I hid his teeth!"

1093   How Old?   Two old ladies insisted they were the same age. It was therefore a New Year's Day ritual with them for one to come to the other and ask, "How old are we to be this year?"

1094   Young.   "You're young as you feel, they say, but seldom as important."

1095   Don't Know Yet.   They were interviewing him on his hundredth birthday. "To what do you attribute your long life?" they asked.
"Don't know yet," "I'm dickering with a couple of cereal companies right now!"

1096   Can Climb Now.   An old lady who lived on the second floor of a rooming house was warned by the doctor, as he placed a cast on her broken leg, not to climb stairs. After several months he took off the cast.

"Can I climb stairs now?" she asked.

"Yes," he replied.

"Good. I'm sick and tired of shinnying up and down that drain-pipe!"

1097   Smart Woman!

"Good heavens. Your hair is full of gray."

"Thank heavens, you noticed it. I was afraid you were color-blind."

9

Qualities and Foibles

ADVICE

1098 **To profit** from good advice requires more wisdom than to give it.

1099 **A good scare** is often worth more to a man than good advice.

1100 **Most** of us would get along well if we used the advice we give to others.

1101 **Kind Words.** A man in a restaurant ordered "ham and eggs and a few kind words."

The waitress brought the ham and eggs. "And now the kind words—'don't eat 'em.'"

ECONOMY AND EFFICIENCY

1102 **Economy:** That's a way of spending money without having any fun in the process.

1103 **Energy Economy.** They thought he was lazy, but the doctor called it "voluntary inertia."

1104 Walking Beside. In Rhodesia, the residents joke about the railway system, which runs mostly local trains. The theme song, they say, is "I'm Walking Beside You."

1105 Efficient Insurance. "My insurance company is so efficient that when I was sick recently I got my check in three days."

"That's nothing. A man jumped out of the seventeenth floor of an office building the other day and Mr. Johnson handed him his check as he passed the third-story window!"

1106 Do It Today. Never put off until tomorrow what you can do today. There may be a law against it by then.

1107 Do It Tomorrow. Sometimes it is better to put off until tomorrow what you are likely to botch today.

1108 Cheap Phones. In an African country two visitors were discussing the national telephone service. "The phones are wonderfully cheap," said one. "Just one thing—you can't hear!"

EMBARRASSMENT

1109 Two R's. The college boy asked how to spell "financially." His roommate told him and then added, "There are two r's in 'embarrassed.'"

1110 Height of Embarrassment: Two eyes meeting at the same keyhole.

1111 Red Teacher. A schoolteacher spoke in friendly fashion to a man on a bus, then realized that she had made a mistake. "Pardon me," she said, blushing, "I thought you were the father of one of my children."

1112 Listen! A clergyman, speaking to a rural congregation, was being very dramatic. "Listen!" he shouted, and waited. There was dead silence. Just as he was about to make his punchy point, a bull bellowed loudly outside.

1113 Grant It! Dr. Ned Wiley loves to tell of preaching during his seminary days in a small rural church on Mother's Day. An old lady, very hard of hearing, was encouraging him along audibly, with such expressions as "That's right." Near the end, to dramatize mother love, he made a cross of himself and said, "If I were hanged on the highest hill, Mother of mine, Mother of mine . . ." The old lady, not hearing too well, croaked out, "Lord, grant it!"

ENTHUSIASM

1114 Good Thing. It would be wonderful if it were as easy to arouse enthusiasm as it is suspicion. They say people will believe anything if you whisper it.

1115 Guaranteed.
"Is this hair restorer guaranteed?"
"Sir, we give you a comb with every bottle!"

1116 Parking Space.
"There are not many buildings in this new town of yours here."
"True," replied the enthusiastic realtor, "but look at the parking space!"

1117 New Blood. In this town things are moving. Even the fencing club is looking for new blood.

1118 Don't Need None.
"I suppose you don't know of nobody who don't want to hire nobody to do nothin', don't you?"
"Yes, I don't."

FLATTERY

1119 Flattery, like perfume, is supposed to be sniffed, not swallowed.

1120 Spray Some. You can't spray perfume around without getting some on yourself.

1121 My Story.
"You are looking marvelously beautiful tonight."
"Oh, you flatterer!"
"No. That's my story, and I'll stick to it!"

GRUDGES AND GROUCHES

1122 Grudge: A place to keep your automobile.

1123 Grouch: A man always dissatisfied, especially when he gets what he deserves.

1124 Limited Service. A fox should not be on the jury at a goose's trial.

HAPPINESS

1125 Never miss an opportunity to make others happy, even if you have to leave them to do it.

1126 Enjoyment Counts. It isn't how much you've got, but how much enjoyment you get from what you've got that counts.

1127 Happiest People: These are the ones too busy to notice whether they are or not.

1128 Happiness. Some cause it where they go, others when they go.

1129 Happy Hours. The hours that make us happy make us wise.

1130 Dog Tired? Maybe you've been growling too much lately.

1131 Free Cheese. There's always free cheese in mousetraps. But did you ever see a happy mouse there?

HONESTY

1132 No, Daddy. Magician, to small boy called up on the stage to assist: "Now, my boy, you've never seen me before, have you?" "No, Daddy."

1133 Lying. What you're doing when you're not standing or sitting.

1134 Truth. "That's the truth if I ever told one."

1135 Wrong Number. The dialer got a wrong number. "Are you sure that is the wrong number?"

"Certainly. Have I ever lied to you before?"

1136 About Half. Someone asked the elevator operator how many people work in the building. "About half of 'em," he said.

1137 My Father. The school principal received a telephone call. "Tommy Thompson won't be in school today."

"Who is speaking?"

"This is my father speaking."

1138 Pay Up. The college boy said to his roommate, "I just got a check from home."

"Then pay me the five dollars you owe me."

"Let me tell you the rest of my dream!"

1139 You Know. Manager: "Sorry, but I wouldn't cash a check for my own brother."

"Guess you know your family best."

1140 Ethical Problem. Two brothers were in the coal business. One joined the church and urged the other to do so.

"If I join the church," said the second, "who'll weigh the coal?"

1141 Ethics.

"Dad, what is ethics?"

"It's like if I go to the bank and they give me twenty dollars, but I find that two new bills have stuck together. Now that raises the question, 'Shall I tell your mother?' "

1142 Lick System. The customer in the bakery shop asked the little girl who was helping if she ever ate a cake. "Oh, no," replied the child. "That would be stealing. I just lick them!"

HUMILITY

1143 Most Humble. When it comes to my humility, I take off my hat to no man.

1144 Best People. It's not hard to pick them out. They'll even help you do it.

1145 Nice Guy. The sophomore said, "When I came here to school I guess at first I was conceited, but that got knocked out of me and now I'm one of the nicest fellows in the whole school."

1146 Not Conceited. They say most geniuses (or "handsome men" or "beautiful girls") are conceited, but I'm not.

1147 Elusive. Humility: when you know you've got it, you've lost it.

1148 Poor Judge. The man who thinks too highly of himself proves to be a poor judge of human nature.

1149 Modesty: (1) The feeling that others will discover how really wonderful you are. (2) The art of enhancing your charm by pretending not to be aware of it.—Oliver Herford

1150 Exceed All Others. Members of three religious orders were discussing the relative merits of their contributions to mankind. The first group said that their scholarship had been most useful. The second group insisted on their service as superior. A spokesman for the third had the last word: "Certainly ours is the greatest contribution, for we exceed all others in humility."

1151 Full Knowledge. Two kids had just finished elementary school. One said to the other, "Isn't it wonderful to know all there is to know?"

1152 Honest, Now! If you had it to do all over, would you fall in love with yourself again?

IGNORANCE

1153 Dedicated Ignorance will get you nowhere.

1154 Too Bad. It's a pity that things were not arranged so that an empty head, like an empty stomach, would not let its owner rest until he put something into it.

INGENUITY

1155 Smart Boy. A boy of ten found a purse containing a ten-dollar bill. Before returning it to the owner, he had the bill changed into ten ones.

1156 Mother's Hands. In his boyhood Sir Thomas Lipton suggested in their little country store that his father let Mother sell the eggs. "In her hands they look so much bigger," he said.

1157 Snowbound. The salesman wired the office: "Snowbound." The office replied: "Start summer vacation at once."

1158 New Invention. This is a combination of shoe polish and toothpaste for people inclined to put their feet into their mouths.

1159 Straight Scoop. A firm selling oil burners gave away 250 shovels. On the handle was a notice: "If you had one of our oil burners you'd be upstairs watching TV instead of down here!"

1160 Right Back. The ingenious jack-of-all-trades in the small town ran a store, which he had to leave occasionally. He made a sign: "Back in 15 minutes. Already gone 10."

MISTAKES

1161 "Absolutely Positive": Being wrong at the top of your voice.

1162 Ouch! The class yell from the school of experience is "Ouch!"

1163 Business Sense. He was asking the editor of a small-town weekly paper how they ever kept in business. Subscriptions, job printing, and advertising helped some, admitted the editor, but the thing that kept them in the black was selling their typographical errors to the humor departments of big city dailies.

1164 Careful! Don't cross any bridge until you're sure one is there.

1165 Educated Selling. One salesman told another that he couldn't sell Mr. Jones and encyclopedia. "That guy already knows all there is to know."

"Then in that case, he'll enjoy checking through and finding the errors!"

1166 Foolish Virgin? They were discussing the "wise virgin" and "foolish virgin" story in the Bible and decided that these days there is no such thing as "foolish virgin."

MONEY

1167 Money Talks. Sure it does. It says, "Good-bye!"

1168 Imagination: What makes you think you are having a wonderful time when you are only spending money.

1169 Poorest Man. The poorest man I know is the man who has nothing but money.

1170 No Interruptions. When money talks, there are few interruptions.

1171 "Keep Florida Green—BRING MONEY," says a sign.

1172 Minor Matter. A miner is about the only one who can make money by going into the hole.

1173 Just Enough. He counted out the money for the grocer. "Seventy-two, seventy-three, seventy-four, seventy-five." That was the amount of the bill.

The merchant looked up. "That's just barely enough!" he said.

1174 Cheap? Most of the things you get for nothing are actually pretty expensive.

1175 Making Money. How to make money: invent a fad.

PERSEVERANCE

1176 Plodders, Thinkers. Douglas Sargent, in **The Making of a Missionary,** says that there are two kinds of missionaries—the plodders and the thinkers. The plodders keep plodding on and the thinkers keep thinking up ways to get home.

1177 Patience: The ability to idle your motor when you feel like stripping your gears.

1178 Right Train. The right train of thought can take you to a better station in life.

1179 Persevere: Getting on is largely a matter of getting up each time you get down.

PREJUDICE

1180 Prejudice: Being down on the thing you're not up on.

1181 Won't Listen. Some people are so prejudiced that they wouldn't even listen to both sides of a phonograph record.

1182 Wise Man. It's a wise man who knows whether he's fighting for a principle or defending a prejudice.

1183 They Do?
"All Indians in South America walk single file," said Cyril Eric Bryant.
"They do?" asked a friend.
"At least the one I saw did," he replied.

RESPONSIBILITY

1184 Do It Right. It usually takes less time to do a thing right than to explain why you did it wrong.

1185 Follow Through. To **look** is one thing. To **see** what you look at is another. To **understand** what you see is a third. To **learn** from what you understand is still something else. But to **act responsibly** on what you learn is what really matters.—**Educator's Dispatch**

SLAMS—INSULTS—SQUELCHES

1186 Which Way? "Eggs sunny-side up, or to match your disposition?"

1187 Dumb Clerk!
"Isn't there a smarter clerk to wait on me?"
"No, madam, the smarter ones saw you coming."

1188 Better Neighborhood.
"We're going to be living in a better neighborhood soon."
"We are too."
"You moving too?"
"No. We're staying here!"

1189 Spelled Wrong.
"What horrible words written on our community sidewalks! What will ousiders think? Some of them aren't even spelled right!"

1190 Yard of Pork. The joker ordered this in the butcher shop.
"Give that man three pig's feet," said the ingenious butcher.

1191 All Knowing. George Bernard Shaw was bored with his visitor. "Between us we know everything in the world. You know all except that you're a bore, and I know that."

1192 "Good Morning, Doctor," a businessman greeted another in the elevator. (He was not a doctor.)
"Same to you," replied the other, evenly.

1193 Not a Doctor. Ernie Logan, when called "doctor," says, "I'm not a doctor. In fact, I'm not even a nurse."

1194 Rats! A guest clergyman was preaching to a congregation in the inner city. Members had been pouring out into suburbia, leaving the church forlorn. "When a ship is sinking," said the clergyman, "the rats leave it. They don't leave because the ship is sinking—they leave because they're rats!" The exodus slowed to a trickle!

1195 Childhood Ambition. The businessman said, "As a boy I had a great ambition to be a pirate."
Replied a friend, "That's interesting. It isn't everybody who gets a chance to realize his childhood ambition."

1196 Leaked Out. A clergyman serving as an area executive, who enjoys a laugh on himself, tells of calling a young pastor to get his people together for a conference, but the young man forgot to announce it. Almost nobody showed up. "Did you tell them I was coming?" asked the superior.

"No, sir, I didn't," admitted the young man. "It must have leaked out."

SUCCESS-FAILURE

1197 For Success: Think up something that costs ten cents, sells for a dollar, and is habit-forming.

1198 To Succeed: Keep your head up and your overhead down.

1199 Discouraging. There is one discouraging thing about the rules of success—they won't work unless you do.

1200 Opportunity? The reason some of us don't hear her knock is that we're over at the neighbor's pouring out a hard-luck story. And if we did hear her knock, we'd complain of the noise!

1201 Success? Failure? No man is a failure who is enjoying life. No man is a success who isn't.

1202 Failure: The path of least persistence.

1203 Communist: A man who has given up all hope of becoming a capitalist.

1204 Too Successful. What on earth will today's younger generation tell their children they had to do without?

1205 Right Idea. When someone in the group came up with a sparkling idea, he was told: "Now you have hit the nail on the finger."

1206 Successful Sale. A store actually put out an item, 14 cents each, two for 29 cents, and sales increased 84 per cent.

TACT AND CONSIDERATION

1207 May Be Something. One of the world's most successful executives, listening to the viewpoint of another, tells him, "There may be something in what you say!"

TACT:

1208 The art of making a point without making an enemy.—Newton.

1209 Lying about others as you would like them to lie about you!
—The Postage Stamp

1210 The ability to shut your mouth before someone else wants to.

1211 Whale Advice. The mother whale, wise in the ways of the world, said to her baby, "The less spouting off you do, the safer you are!"

1212 Shave or Haircut? A customer sat down in a swanky restaurant, tucked his napkin in his shirt collar, and began to examine the menu. The tactful headwaiter came over to his table and inquired politely, "Shave or haircut, sir?"

1213 Boy or Girl.
"Quick, tell me," said the young father, "Is it a boy?"
The nurse was tactful. "The middle one is," she said.

1214 Tactful Remedy. When a person has a chip on his shoulder, let him bow once in a while.

1215 Sit Where? Mother was entirely disgusted with little Bobbie. "If you don't behave," she said, "I'll spank you right out here on the street."
"But Mother," he reminded her, "where would you sit?"

1216 Hospitality: The art of making one feel at home when you wish they were.

1217 Height of Politeness: To listen with interest to things you know about, from someone who doesn't.

1218 Diplomatic Phraseology.
"Dad, what does that mean?"
"If you said to an ugly girl, 'Your face would stop a clock,' that would be stupidity, but if you said to her, 'When I look into your eyes, time stands still,' **that** would be diplomatic phraseology."

1219 Where Will I Be? The boss told his secretary: "I've forgotten where I'm supposed to meet my wife at one o'clock. Call her up and ask her where you can reach me at that time.

1220 Fifty Pennies, Then.
"Daddy, will you give me fifty cents?"
"When I was you age I asked for pennies."
"OK then, Daddy, give me fifty pennies."

1221 Too Close. Roy Short tells of a local ballgame with a great big batter, a big catcher, and a small umpire. The first ball came over. The umpire called out, "Strike one!" The big batter turned and glared darkly. For the next ball he called out, "Ball one!" The big catcher glared. On the third ball he called out, "Two!" Both catcher and batter looked at him intently.
They both said, "Two what?"
The umpire shrank into his padding and said, "Too close to call!"

1222 Pardon Me, Sir. One of the world's quick-thinking diplomats found himself unintentionally in the ladies' room. He bowed and said to the woman there, "Pardon me, sir!" and departed quickly.

1223 Real Opportunity. The employer said to the young man, "I think I can use a man with your strength and leadership. I'd like to have you on my team."
"That sounds good. What is your business?"
"Borax. I have a team of twenty!"

1224 A Smile: The magic language of diplomacy that even a baby understands.

1225 When It Started. Hearing exciting noises in the children's room, father went to investigate. "Tommy, now who started all this?"
"Well, it all started when Billy hit me back."

1226 French Diplomacy. To end the trouble they were having from carriages driven by women, Louis XV ordered his minister to issue an edict: "Ladies under thirty are forbidden to drive carriages." That did it!

1227 Count Silver.
"Little man, what do you do in the house?"
"I count the silver when company's gone home."

1228 Sensitive Child Diplomacy. The mother brought her little dear the first day of school and said to the teacher, "My child is quite sensitive. If he misbehaves, just slap the child next to him. That will frighten him and he will stop."

1229 Consideration. That's like the wife shooting her husband with a bow and arrow so as not to wake the children.

1230 Be kind to your friends. If it weren't for them, you'd be a total stranger.

1231 Do Anything. A shoe shop had a sign, "We'll save your sole and gladly dye for you."

1232 Consideration (or tolerance) is the ability to listen enthusiastically to somebody telling your favorite story.

TALKINESS AND GOSSIP

Closed-Mouth Wisdom

1233 Nothing is opened by mistake more than the mouth.

1234 To get a reputation for being wise, keep your mouth shut.

1235 Usually the first screw loose in a person's head is the one that controls the tongue.

1236 Did you ever get your tang all tongueled up?

1237 A lot of trouble in this world is caused by combining a narrow mind with a wide mouth.

1238 The man of few words doesn't have to take so many of them back.

1239 **Why is it** that the man who has nothing to say says it, while the man who does doesn't?

1240 **Silence** is one of the most beautiful, impressive, and inspiring things known to man. Don't break it unless you can improve on it.

1241 **People,** like boats, make the loudest noise when they're in a fog.

1242 **One Tongue.** We have two eyes and one tongue. This means that we're supposed to see twice as much as we say.

1243 **Spade a Spade.** Every man should call a spade a spade— even the man who trips over one.

1244 **Hard To Do.** Harder than breaking a bad habit (or "dieting")—not telling how you did it.

1245 **No Words.** "I had some words, but I didn't get to use them."

1246 **Certificate:** "This is to certify that I am not a member of the Society for the Discussion of the Affairs of Others.

$$\text{Signed, \_\_\_\_\_."}$$

1247 **Keep a Secret?**
"Can you keep a secret?"
"Yes."
"So can I."

1248 **No Gossip.**
"Sarah, I wouldn't gossip for the world, but I want to tell you about this so you can pray about it!"

1249 **Connections!** Does she like to gossip? Well she's the kind of gal that, what she says, goes!

1250 **It's Good!** "I wouldn't say anything about her unless it was good—and boy, is this good!"

1251 **No Details.** "I won't bore you with more details. In fact, I've already told you more than I heard myself!"

1252 No Repeats. "She told me not to repeat, so I'll tell it only once."

1253 Unimpeachable Source: The one who started the rumor.

1254 Don't Like Him. "There goes a guy I don't like, and from all the things I've said about him, I never will!"

1255 What a Fright!
"Did you hear about the terrible fright Milton got on his wedding day?"
"I was there. I saw her!"

1256 Sweet Girl. "She is one of those sweet, shy, unassuming girls. You know—a **real** phony!"

1257 No Idea. "Do you know what she said about you?"
"I don't have an idea in the world."
"That's exactly right!"

1258 Most Are Some. "You have to be little to belittle."

1259 Terrible. She said it was terrible to tell her the things I told her, but to please go ahead.

1260 Conversationalist. A gossip talks about others. A bore talks about himself. A brilliant conversationalist talks about me.

1261 Exercise. The only exercise some people get is from jumping at conclusions (or sometimes, sidestepping issues).

1262 Minds Business. Village gossip: "And what does your husband do for a living?"
"He has his own business, and actually spends most of his time minding it!"

1263 Polished Conversation. That is, it was casting reflections on others.

1264 Mark Twain said that nothing needs reforming so much as other people's habits.

1265 Gossip is like an egg. When it is hatched, it has wings.

TROUBLE—WORRY

1266 Dig! Dig someone out of his trouble, and you'll make a hole for burying your own!

1267 Search Warrant? A man looking for trouble usually doesn't need a search warrant!

1268 Trouble is usually produced by somebody who doesn't produce very much else.

1269 Desert. "All sunshine makes a desert."

1270 Worry: A circle of inefficient thoughts whirling about a pivot of fear.

1271 Worry is as useless as whispering in a boiler factory.

1272 Not So Bad. Today is the tomorrow you worried about yesterday.

1273 Remember? Test your memory. Try to recall the things you worried about this day last week.

1274 History Accurate? If you want to worry about the accuracy of history, just listen to two eyewitnesses describing the same auto accident.

1275 Booked Ahead!
"You look worried."
"I'm so worried that if anything happens to me today it will be two weeks before I can worry about it."

WORKING

1276 Five-Day Weekend. What I'm waiting for is the five-day weekend.

1277 Day Off: You can take the day off, but you can't pay it back.

1278 Manana. The greatest labor saver of today is tomorrow.

1279 Is It Work? What you're doing is really not work unless you'd rather be doing something else.

1280 Making Ends Meet. The easiest way to make ends meet is to get off your own.

1281 Well-Heeled. To be well-heeled, get on your feet and keep on your toes.

1282 Dollars. They are not readily made if you habitually deposit your quarters in an easy chair.

1283 Labor Saver. Some of us will work day and night to buy a labor-saving device.

1284 Turn Up? Looking for something to turn up? Maybe it's your sleeves!

1285 Greener Grass? Sometimes the grass looks greener over there because they take better care of it!

10

The World of Everyday

HOME AND FAMILY

1286 Precaution. We never give the baby a sharp object to play with—it might cut its teeth.

1287 Relatives. If the knocking at the door is loud and long, it isn't opportunity—it's relatives!

1288 New Toy. Parent: "Isn't this toy a bit complicated for a small child?"

Clerk: "It's an educational toy, designed to adjust the child to today's world. Any way he puts it together it's wrong."

1289 Joy of Motherhood: What a woman experiences when all the kids are in bed.

1290 When? Sam Levenson says that when he was a boy he used to have to do what his father wanted, and now he has to do what his boy wants. When can he get to do what **he** wants?

1291 Bathtub Music.
"Why do you sing in the bathtub?"
"The door won't lock."

1292 Kid Wisdom: "Be it ever so humble, there's nobody home."

1293 Good Cook. "My daughter is a good cook. She can prepare the best meal you ever thaw!"

1294 Good Morning! The guest had slept on a couch overnight. The hostess asked if he had a good night.

"Fairly," he replied. "I got up from time to time and rested."

1295 Try It. The best way for a housewife to have a few minutes to herself at the close of the day is to start doing the dishes.

1296 Odd Vision. It is funny that a wife who can see right through a man can't notice a missing button!

1297 Can't Afford It. The maid did the family bookkeeping. When the father suggested a raise for her she figured carefully and said, "We can't afford it this month!"

1298 What Channel? The seven-year-old daughter heard that her daddy used to work on the ranch.

"Were you a cowboy, Daddy?" she asked.

"I certainly was," said Daddy.

"What channel were you on?" she wanted to know.

1299 Fined! When Daddy came home he found his tricycle-riding youngster unusually quiet. "What's the matter, little one?" he asked.

"I've been fined for speeding," replied the child.

1300 Wrong Egg! He was horribly hard to please. On his birthday his wife wanted especially to please him. "What for breakfast?" she asked.

"Two eggs—one scrambled and one fried," he ordered. She worked hard at it and placed them before him, hoping for a nice comment. He looked at the eggs and at her and responded, "Well, if you didn't go and scramble the wrong egg!"

1301 Only a Nose. Mother called softly to young daughter: "Is Daddy asleep?"

"Yes," came back the reply, "all except his nose."

1302 Why Not Pretend? The little girl asked, "Daddy, why is Mommy singing?"

"To get the baby to go to sleep."

"Will she stop when baby goes to sleep?"

"Yes, dear."

"Then I wonder," said the little girl, "why baby doesn't just pretend to be asleep."

1303 Like Little Girl? The saleswoman at Christmas was showing a doll to a daddy. "This one is just like a little girl. When you lay her down, she closes her eyes and goes to sleep."

The father looked a bit skeptical. "I guess," he responded, "that you've never had a little girl."

1304 Making Light. The eight-year-old asked, "Why did Mother have just sixteen candles on her cake, Daddy?"

"Oh, son," his father replied, "she's just making light of her age."

1305 Lower Learning. At college the professor congratulated the father on the daughter's brilliant paper on the influence of science on the principles of government.

"Good," said the father. "Next I want her to begin to work on the influence of the vacuum cleaner on the modern rug."

1306 Likes Nothing Better.

"Does your wife like housework?" asked one man of another.

"She likes **nothing** better," was his reply.

1307 He Bites. In the crowded elevator a woman was concerned about the four-year-old boy who was with his father. "Aren't you afraid he'll be crushed?" she asked.

"Not at all," he replied. "He bites."

1308 Not Even a Dog. Junior was rushing to the door, the rain coming down in torrents outside, to do an errand.

"Where are you going?" his mother asked.

"Out to put my bicycle in," said Junior.

"I wouldn't let a dog out on a night like this," said Mama. "Henry," she called to her husband, "go out and put Alvin's bicycle away!"

1309 Her Name. "Bob, what did you call your mother-in-law after you were married?"

"I didn't know quite what to call her," admitted Bob. "The first year I just used the term 'Say' and after that we called her 'Grandma.'"

1310 Easily Waked.
"How do you get your son up in the morning?"
"Just toss the cat on his bed."
"How does that wake him?"
"He sleeps with the dog."

1311 Stop Them! "John, find out what the kids are doing and tell them to stop it!"

1312 Still Have Mine. Dad, trying to bolster his ego a bit, asked Mom if she thought Junior got his intelligence from the male side of the family.
"I believe so," replied Mom. "I've still got mine!"

1313 Not Too Late. The frowsy-looking housewife, hair in curlers, wearing faded bathrobe and sloppy slippers, appeared at the door early one morning and called out to the garbage man, "Yoohooo! Am I too late for the garbage?"
"No, ma'am," called back the garbage man politely. "Jump right in."

1314 One To Go. Mother came in where the family was gathered and announced, "I've just been working on the family budget. One of us will have to go."

1315 Not Lately. The visiting clergyman asked the young bride if she had ever cast her bread upon the waters.
"Not since my first batch," she said proudly.

1316 Sapping Cereal? A mother of three boys went to the manager of her grocery store and pleaded, "Isn't there some cereal that will **sap** their energy?"

1317 On Solids Now. The young mother was telling the visitor about her child. "He's eating solids now. You know—keys, bits of newspapers, crayons, pencils."

1318 Until Son-Down. The young mother wrote to her mother that she worked without stopping from son-up to son-down.

1319 Out Together. The Kansas cyclone took off the roof, picked up the bed with man and wife sleeping in it, and gently set it down in the barnyard. The wife was weeping softly.

"Don't be scared," soothed the husband.

"I'm not," she replied. "I'm just so happy. It's the first time in twenty-five years that we've been out together."

1320 Station? The family were traveling together by train. One of the kids said, "Mother, what was the name of the last station?"

"I don't know," she replied, disinterested. "Why?"

"Well," said the nine-year-old, "Sister got off there."

1321 More Dishes? There was a horrible crash in the kitchen. The mistress called out to the maid, "More dishes, Matilda?"

"No ma'am," was the reply. "Less."

1322 Real Modesty. "It's all right for you to come in now," called the maid to the mistress of the house. "The canary's had his bath."

1323 Closed Mouthed. The mistress was instructing the maid for the evening's formal dinner: "Now, Mary, when you are serving tonight, be careful and don't spill anything."

Mary: "Don't you worry, ma'am. I never talk much."

1324 No Dust. To encourage thorough housecleaning, the mistress was urging the maid to move the furniture and sweep under the bed so that the ladies coming for dinner wouldn't see dust under the bed.

The maid contemplated it all for a moment and said, "You know —if these women coming are ladies, it doesn't seem to me they'd be looking under the bed!"

1325 Horse. A friend came upon another who was pushing a live horse into his house, up the steps, and into the bathroom. Why? "My lousy brother-in-law lives with me here. He knows everything. Tomorrow is my day. When he goes into the bathroom, he'll holler, 'There's a horse in the bathroom,' and I'll holler back, 'You're tellin' me!' "

1326 Tough Beard. The wife heard the voice of her husband muttering from the bathroom that his razor wouldn't cut at all this morning.

"That's silly, John," she said. "Your beard just couldn't be as tough as the kitchen linoleum."

1327 No More Baths. The mother told her little boy he must never do anything he wouldn't be willing for the whole world to see him do. His reply was, "Whooppee! No more baths!"

1328 Hello, Father. The daughter got in very late from a date. Stern, self-righteous Father greeted her, "Hello, daughter of Satan!"

She responded quietly and meekly, "Hello, Father!"

1329 No Den. Two little ones were discussing their fathers.

"Does your daddy have a den?" asked one.

"No, he just growls all over the house," was the reply.

1330 Answers. What does your father do? Kids give different answers. One said, "Whatever Mother tells him." A more sophisticated version is, "What Mother tells him, after consultation with us children."

1331 Who's That Man? Daddy and Mother had been up late the night before and had not gotten up yet. Young daughter and a neighbor girl were discussing a picture of Daddy, taken many years before, when he was very much younger.

"Who's that?" asked the neighbor girl.

"My daddy," said the daughter.

"Then who," wanted to know the neighbor, "is that in bed with your mommy?"

1332 Mother Is Loaded. The five-year-old daughter felt that she must explain to the bus driver why she was putting in the fare for her mother, who followed her, weighted down with packages. "I'm doing this," said she, "because my mother is loaded."

1333 Good Dreams Here? Little daughter came into her parents' room and said, "In my room there aren't any good dreams. May I sleep here?"

1334 Light From a Bulb. The kindergartener came home, demonstrating the song they sang called "God Bless America" ending with ". . . guide her through the night with the light from a bulb."

1335 Bum Party. The small boy didn't really like the party, he said, because his mother told him he could eat as much as he wanted to, but he couldn't.

1336 Pretty Far. Son bummed a dollar off Dad, who said, "Make it go as far as you can."

"I'll make it go so far you'll never see any of it again," he promised.

1337 Self-Made Man. "Yes," said Dad modestly, "I'm what you'd call a self-made man."

"That's what I like about you, Pop," responded his son. "You're always willing to take the blame for anything!"

1338 Can't Throw. Mother was being very severe with Bobby, who had been throwing rocks at a neighbor boy. "When he throws rocks at you," she told the neighbor, "you come and tell me," she insisted.

"That wouldn't do any good," said Bobby, disgusted. "You couldn't hit the broad side of a barn!"

1339 Without Consent. Junior protested being sent to bed without supper, on the grounds that the Declaration of Independence insists on no governing without the consent of the governed.

1340 Music Lover? The small son said that he didn't believe their neighbor knew much about music because he suggested cutting open the drum to see what was inside it.

1341 Grand Child. When I was born, my grandmother said something wonderful about me. She said I was a grand child!

1342 Talk To It. A little girl, who loved grandmother's reading of stories, brought her favorite book and said, "Talk to it!"

1343 More Welcome. "Why haven't you been to see your son and daughter-in-law? You can afford it, and with planes so fast, it doesn't take much time."

"Oh, it isn't that. I'm waiting for the first baby. You know, grandmothers are a lot more likely to be welcome than mothers-in-law."

1344 Night Out. The grandparents called their children to ask if they could leave the grandchildren with their own parents that night. "We're invited out for the evening," they said.

1345 Motherly Wisdom. "Don't line your pantry shelves with newspapers," Mother advised her newly-wed daughter. "If you do, everybody will know when you last cleaned your shelves."

ANIMALS

1346 Skunk! One skunk said to another, "so do you."

1347 Udderly Dependable. That's what the farmer called his cow, who gave milk every time he milked her.

1348 Whale Luck! When they began to use kerosene instead of whale oil for lamps, an old New England lady was perturbed. "What will the poor whales do now?" she wondered.

1349 Get to Work! A conscientious motorist went up to the farmhouse and confessed that he had run over their cat.

"I want to replace him," he said.

"Good," replied the farmer's wife. "Get busy. There's a mouse in the pantry right now."

1350 You Feel Inferior. The two cows were visiting when a milk truck went by, bearing a sign which proclaimed its milk to be pasteurized, homogenized, and standardized, with Vitamin D added. One cow said to the other, "Doesn't that make you feel inferior?"

1351 No Rabbits. The American was bragging in Australia. Everything the Aussy showed him reminded of something bigger in the States. Finally a kangaroo came hopping by. "What's that?" asked the American, startled.

"No jackrabbits in America?" asked the Aussie.—Gloster Udy

1352 Don't Feel Jumpy. A kangaroo went to the doctor. "What's the matter?" asked the doctor.

"I don't know," replied the kangaroo. "I just don't feel jumpy!"

1353 Bear Logic. The two hunters for bear came upon some huge tracks, showing that they were near pay dirt. One of them was scared nearly to death. "I tell you," he said to his friend, "you go and see where he went, and I'll go back and check where he came from!"

1354 Pets' Kids. It's very nice for the children to have pets until the pets start having children.

1355 Wrong Straw. At the circus a man stood studying a camel for a long time. As the camel came near him, he bent over, got a straw, put it on the camel's back, and waited. Nothing seemed to happen. "Wrong straw," he said, and left.

1356 No Runner. There was a horse that played baseball. Yes, it's true. He devised a way of holding the bat, and he could slug 'em. Finally they let him play, and he laced out a hot grounder, headed for center field. "Run, blast you, run," said a hometown rooter when the horse just stood there.

"Run?" exclaimed his owner. "If he could run, he'd be at Hialeah!"

1357 Elephant or Flea? What's the difference between fleas and elephants? Elephants can have fleas, but fleas can't have elephants.

1358 Donkey Doings. A man sold another a donkey. "He'll do anything you want if you'll be kind and courteous to him," said the seller. Soon the buyer brought him back, saying that all the donkey would do is stand, even though he had been treated with kindness and courtesy. The seller picked up a stick and hit the donkey hard right over the head.

"What did you do that for?"

"Well, you've got to get his attention first!"

Dogs

1359 Not for Sale. One thing that money alone cannot buy—the wag of a dog's tail.

1360 He Started It. The doting mother asked her child, "Why are you making faces at the bulldog?"

"Well," said the kid, "he started it!"

1361 Melon Collie. Tex Evans says that he has at home a collie that eats cantaloupes. They think of him as a melon collie.

1362 Has Plenty. To the question "Has your dog a license?" the answer was "Sure, he's got a lot of them things."

1363 Down the Aisle. When the dog show patron asked for the location of the Labradors, the usher said, "Right down the aisle, second door to the right."

1364 To the Races. The fleas were planning to leave the kennel and go to the dog races. One said, "Shall we walk or catch a greyhound?"

1365 Fan Mail. The dog star Rin Tin Tin once received a letter saying "Dear Mr. Tin . . . "

1366 Association. The owner of a dog without papers entered him in a dog show. "It isn't that I expect him to win," he said. "I just want him to associate with all these big dogs."

1367 Frenchy. The poodles were comparing names and pedigrees. There were Henri, Andre, Suzette. A mongrel poodle said his name was "Fido."
"But wait till you hear me spell it," said he, "P-H-I-D-E-A-U-X."

1368 Obliged To. The rabbit was chased by a dog up a tree.
"Rabbits don't climb trees," said another. "Why did you do it?"
"To tell the truth," replied the rabbit, "I was **obliged** to!"

1369 We Hope Not. There was once an ill-tempered lap dog who often took pieces from legs of visitors. Seeing him set his teeth into the flesh of a male visitor, the mistress said to the dog: "Poor little dear creature! I hope it will not make you sick!"

1370 Smart Dog. In school a little girl insisted that she had a dog who could say his own name.
"And what is his name?" asked the teacher.
"His name is 'Woof,'" replied the little girl.

1371 Out of Gas. There was a little dog who loved to smell the gasoline as it came from the pumps in the filling station where he frequently stayed. One day he sniffed deeply, ran and ran around in circles, behind and in front of the filling station, and fell over on the ground. His master rushed to see if he were dead. But he wasn't—he just ran out of gas.

1372 Remarkable Pointer. There was a pointer who was known throughout Virginia for his accuracy, and for his complete loyalty to his master. Actually, you may not believe this, but he would run birds into an animal hole and then let them out one at a time for his master to shoot.

Once this same dog was pointing at the water. In the water was a fish. Although some were skeptical, the owner got the fish out and cut him open, knowing that the dog never missed. In the stomach of that fish, sure enough, was a **bird!**

The Cat Family

1373 Cat's Name. We had a cat named Ben Hur. We called him "Ben" until he had kittens.

1374 Bruce Tom. He said that half the cats in his state of Ohio were named for him personally.

1375 We Have Too. "Say, have you ever seen the Catskill Mountains?"
"No, but I've seen 'em kill mice."

1376 Good Neighbor. The family was called away suddenly. They left a note at the neighbor's: "Would you please feed our cat, Hercules. But don't put yourself out."

1377 Seeing Spots. A leopard was once consulting a specialist.
"When I look at my wife, I see spots. I'm worried, Doc."
"Yes," said the specialist, "but that's natural. You're a leopard, and leopards have spots."
"True," answered the leopard, "But my wife is a zebra."

1378 Wrong Expression. The guide asked the hunter why he didn't shoot the tiger nearby.
"I would have," said the hunter, "but he didn't have the right expression for a rug."

1379 Two Views. G. B. Shaw once said that when a man goes out to murder a tiger, the man calls it sport. When a tiger wants to murder him, he calls it ferocity.

1380 Preventing Lions. A not-too-balanced individual was making some peculiar motions. People asked him, "Why are you doing that?"
"To keep lions away," he said.
"But there are no lions in thousands of miles," they told him.
"See how effective it is," he replied.

1381 Thankful Animal. A hunter once found himself face to face with a lion, which was ready to leap. Suddenly the lion stopped and lowered his head, crossed his paws. The hunter breathed a sigh of relief, until he heard the lion giving thanks for the coming meal.

1382 Way Home? Little Emily was at the zoo with Daddy, having a wonderful time until they came to the lions. There she became fearful. Daddy asked her why.

"I was wondering, Daddy," she said. "If a lion broke loose and ate you up, how would I know what bus to take home?"

Winged Creatures

1383 New Bird Species. Some "ornerythologists" have discovered a number of hitherto unrevealed birds: Tufted Dowager; Double-breasted Tiddledewink; No-left Turn; Hairy-chester Back-slapper; Restless Bed-thrasher; Perma-prest Seersucker; Scarlet-hued Teenager; Quick Gander; Extramarital Lark ("Kinsey-Kinsey-Kinsey" is his call.)

1384 A Duck: A bird that walks like it had been on its first horseback ride.

1385 Nest Egg? What good is one, if you only sit on it?

1386 Laid An Egg! One of the late Dukes of Norfolk liked owls. He raised so many that he had a man to look after them. One owl was called Lord Thurlow. One day a lawyer was in the Duke's study. The owl-keeper came by to announce, "Please you, my Lord, Lord Thurlow's laid an egg!"

1387 Singer? The canary he bought was crippled. He took it back to the pet store to complain. The manager said, "I knew the bird's leg wasn't right, but I thought you wanted a singer, not a dancer!"

1388 Tail on Fire? Two birds saw a jet streaking through the air. "Is that bird fast!" said one.

"You'd be too," answered the other, "if your tail were on fire!"

1389 Where Is Everybody? All the ostriches but one had their heads in the sand. He looked around and said, "Where is everybody?"

1390 Robinson. He named his rooster "Robinson" because he Crusoe.

1391 People-Pimples. Did you hear of the goose, headed south, who flew over an outdoor movie showing a horror picture and got people-pimples?

1392 To Hatchet. Did you hear of the hen who kept sitting on an axe? She was trying to hatchet.

1393 Nightingale. They asked the retired vocalist to sing for the gathering. "I'm now a nightingale," she replied, looking over at her wealthy new husband. "It does not sing after it has made its nest."

Insects

1394 Mosquito. It's like a kid. When silent, it's up to something!

1395 Religious Insect: The mosquito. It sings over you, then preys on you. But it also bites the hand that feeds it.

1396 Modern Mosquito. A salesman recently saw a modern mosquito. Its habit is to check the hotel register to see what rooms the guests are in.

1397 Millennium:
"Pop, what a millennium?"
"It's like a centennial, only it's got more legs."

EATING

1398 Noblest. There is no more noble animal than the dog. There is no more noble dog than the hot dog, which feeds the hand that bites it.

1399 Etiquette: That's the noise you don't make having soup. In fact, never break bread or roll in your soup.

1400 True. Everything comes to him who orders hash.

1401 Sick.
"Ed got food poisoning from eating salmon."
"Croquette?"
"Naw, but he's mighty sick."

1402 Interiority Complex. That's what he said he had after a tremendous meal.

1403 Still Alive. Mother: "Eat your Jello, Son!"
"Can't. It's not dead yet!"

1404 You Again? A camper looked at some soggy French toast a moment and finally said to it, "I thought I ate you yesterday!"

1405 More Signs. Down by the railroad the restaurant named itself "Chew Chew." Nearby is a butcher: "Headquarters for hindquarters."

1406 Perfect Marriage. "I married the woman of my dreams. She is as beautiful as the day I met her, and her hands are white and soft, her coiffure the latest, and her dresses always perfect. No, I don't regret it. But there is one little thing—I'm getting a little tired of eating in restaurants."

1407 Leftover Leftovers. The farmer said, "I don't mind eating leftovers and leftover leftovers, but leftover leftover leftovers is going too far."

Maid—Cook

1408 Prepared. The mistress told the cook that her husband was bringing some of his friends home for dinner tonight and asked if she were prepared.
"Yes, ma'am," said the cook. "I've already packed!"

1409 Delicious. Mistress: "Did you clean out the refrigerator like I told you?"
Maid: "Yes, and everything was delicious!"

1410 Undressed. The mistress told the cook to serve the salad without dressing. She came in, clad only in her slip, carrying the salad bowl. "You said to serve it undressed," she said, "but this is as far as I go!"

1411 More Soup? The mistress instructed her maid carefully that before removing the soup bowl, she was to ask the guest if he wanted more. The next day the maid asked a guest, "Would the gentleman like more soup?"

"Yes, please," was his reply.

"Well, there isn't any left," she told him.

Waiter

1412 From Brazil. Slow waiter: "This coffee is from Brazil."

Customer: "Wonderful! And it's still warm!"

1413 Which Way? Customer: "Mutton chops and french fries. And make the chops lean."

"Yes, sir," said the waiter. "Which way, sir?"

1414 The Backstroke?

"Waiter, what's this fly doing in my soup?"

"I'm not certain, sir, but I think it's a backstroke."

1415 Not a Meadow.

"Waiter, I'd like some raw carrots, some raw beans, and some raw cauliflower."

"Madame, this is a **restaurant,** not a **meadow!**"

1416 From Dressing. I found a button in my salad, but I just decided it came from the dressing.

1417 Mad Over Nothing: A waiter expecting a good tip.

1418 Like Dishwater.

"Waiter, this soup tastes like dishwater."

"Pardon me, sir, but how do you know?"

1419 Well Done.

"Waiter, didn't you hear me say, 'Well done'?"

"Yes, sir [ignoring pink steak], thank you, sir. It's seldom that we get nice appreciation like that."

1420 Wheel It In! ·

"Yessir, the specialty of the house is sirloin steak à la carte," enthused the waiter.

"Fine!" exclaimed the customer. "Wheel it in."

1421 Couldn't Wait.
"Waiter, why didn't you bring the soup before the fish?" inquired a diner.
"To tell the truth, sir," said the waiter, "that fish couldn't wait any longer."

1422 Rare Indeed. The waiter brought the steak to the diner.
"Is it **rare** now?" asked the diner.
"Only one of its kind," said the waiter.

1423 No Soup. Customer: "There's no soup on the menu."
Waiter: "Well, there was, sir, but I wiped it off."

1424 It's Apple.
"Waiter, is the pie peach or apple?"
"What does it taste like?"
"Glue."
"That's apple. Peach tastes like plaster."

1425 Slow Turtle. "Waiter, I ordered turtle soup a half hour ago."
"Yes, sir. I'm sorry sir. You know how turtles are!"

1426 Muddy Coffee.
"This coffee tastes like mud."
"Yes, that's because it was ground this morning."

Waitress

1427 Burger and Cuppa. Waitress: "I have calf brains, spareribs, hog liver, cooked tongue . . . "
Truck driver: "You've got your problems, kid, but all I want is a burger and a hot cuppa coffee."

1428 Relief Coming. Impatient diner: "Waitress, must I sit here and starve?"
"Oh no, sir, we close at six o'clock!"

1429 Which Way? The waitress at the truck stop said: "I can heat your soup so you can eat it, or so you can stay a while."

1430 Tipping?
"I see tips are forbidden here," said a customer in an English restaurant.

"Lor' bless you, sor," replied the waitress, "so was apples in the Garden of Eden."

1431 Ram Steak. He was thoroughly angry about the steak. "Take this back and ram it down the chef's throat," he muttered. She came back shortly. "You'll have to wait, sir," she said. "There are several others ahead of you."

1432 Mabel OK? The very particular customer gave his order: "Toast—not too brown, not too light. Coffee hot but not boiling. A white egg cooked exactly two and a half minutes, and in an egg cup if possible. And hurry."

"Just one question," said the waitress. "Our hen's name is Mabel. Will that be all right?"

1433 Raise Salary. She had already broken more dishes than her week's wages. When the boss talked it over, the only solution she could think of was that he raise her salary.

1434 Homesick. The traveler told the waitress: "Two eggs fried so hard they're black at the edges, two slices of burnt toast, cup of cold coffee. Bring it and then sit down and nag me—I'm homesick!"

1435 Stuffed Tomato.
"Waitress, have you forgotten me?"
"Oh, no, ma'am. You're the stuffed tomato."

1436 Chicken Salad. The restaurant offered two chicken salad sandwiches. The fifty-cent one was made of veal and pork, and the seventy-five-cent one of tuna.

1437 Hard Job. The boss asked the new waitress if she'd filled the salt shakers. She said, "Not yet. It's hard, pushing salt through the little holes."

1438 Smoke Here! The timid male customer, embarrassed, asked the waitress where the smoking room was. "Oh, you can smoke right here at the table," she replied.

HOLIDAYS

New Year's

1439 Good Resolutions. Resolutions are like babies crying in church. They must be carried out to be good.

1440 Weak Resolutions. The weakness of most New Year's resolutions is that they're allowed simply to go in one year and out the other.

1441 Good Time? At a New Year's party, a woman looked at the waiter and with uncertain voice croaked out, "Waiter, am I having a good time?"

Washington's Birthday

1442 No Lie!

> That Washington never told a lie,
> Of course is very true.
> But he went into politics
> When the country still was new!

1443 Why Close Banks? A little girl asked, "If George Washington is so honest, why do they close all the banks on his birthday?"

1444 Washington a Texan? Texans, some of them, claim that Washington was originally a Texan. His father asked him about his hatchet work on a tree. "I cannot tell a lie. I did it with my little hatchet."

His father was disgusted. "If you can't tell a better story than that, let's get out of Texas!"

1445 Good Husband. The teacher really laid it on about how the Father of Our Country was brave, resourceful, honest, sincere, kind, a man of perseverance. The little second-graders listened intently. "And now, children," she said in conclusion, "for what high position do you think a man like this would be fitted?"

A little girl raised her hand. "Miss Thomas, I think he would make a nice husband!"

1446 New England Sign. In many places in New England accommodations in private homes are expensive because "George

Washington slept here." One enterprising home-owner with rooms for rent had a sign: "George Washington did not sleep here. Beds $3.00."

Independence Day (July 4)

1447 My Country. In kindergarten they were getting tuned up for the Fourth of July. Each child had a part in the informal presentation. One little girl said, "This is the flag of my country."

"What is your country?" asked a visiting adult.

"'Tis of thee," she replied.

1448 American! He was so American that he had his wife starch the flag with red, white, and blue starch to keep it flying when there wasn't any wind!

1449 Great Celebration. Ah, he was a great citizen. He had been married three times, and now in July he will celebrate the Fourth.

1450 Why Do It? Why do people travel a thousand miles on their July 4 vacation to have their pictures taken by their cars?

1451 Fourth-Graders on "The Flag." Mrs. Donald Mitchell, Delray Beach, Florida, got these responses from fourth-grade pupils: "When a person has a flag he should be loyal, not like Benedict Arnold." . . . "I love the flag because it is used for many things like it is put on top of the coffen." . . . "The flag means to me to trust and have faith and be kind and not get into fights and praise God and be kind to parents and teachers." . . . "It means natune under God in deveable with liberty and jutise and all." . . . "It means that my country is well being and God is the nature of it." . . . "The flag stands for our Nation of 52 states." . . . "It means a flag of freedom and of war and of peace and of the president of the United states and of God and Liberty and Truth and of Abraham Lincoln who set free the slaves." . . . "It means that young boys fighted long ago so that we could have a free land and not communisom." . . . "Treat the flag like the most precious thing you own and never call it names." . . . "It means that we should invite people from other lands to come and join us. These people from other lands will also help make our country a strong country."

Halloween

1452 Retail Spirits. Last Halloween there was a little ghost who lost his tail. He worried about it. Then he had an idea. He just started looking for a store where they retail spirits!

1453 Trick or Treat. The children were "Trick or Treating." A little girl came by a home with her bag. In bringing a contribution, the mother of the household noted that her Halloween mask was in the bottom of her bag. "Why don't you have it on, honey?" the kindly woman asked.

"I'm afraid of it," said the shy little one.

Thanksgiving

1454 Pilgrim Mothers. The lecturer spent a long time on the Pilgrim Fathers. A woman in the audience wanted to know about the Pilgrim Mothers. The lecturer said, "Well, what about them?"

"Why, they endured all the Pilgrim Fathers did," said the woman, "and the Pilgrim Fathers besides!"

Christmas

1455 Christmas Shopping. People are not being held back in their Christmas shopping. They're charging right ahead.

1456 Christmas Custom. To the question in school, "Name a Christmas custom" a kid wrote, "Getting into debt."

1457 Christmas Spirit. If your husband complains about the tie you gave him for Christmas, give him a sock.

1458 Poem:

> Under the hanging mistletoe
> The homely coed stands.
> And stands and stands and stands and stands
> And stands and stands and stands!

1459 Arrested for Christmas. One of the most interesting bits of Christmas humor is O. Henry's tramp who tries to get arrested to be in a warm jail for Christmas; he does several illegal things but is always "let go." Finally he hears music from the church, becomes mellow, starts in to worship, and is picked up for loitering.

1460   Horse of Horse.   At Christmas the little boy wanted a real horse. They offered him a stick horse. "No." A rocking horse? "No." A riding vehicle that looked like a horse. "No!" He began to cry. "I want a horse made of **horse!**" he said.

1461   Love That Book.   The child wrote an aunt, "I love the book you sent me for Christmas. I have been reading day and night and am on page 10."

1462   Merry Christmas!   On an examination a student wrote, "God knows. Merry Christmas." The answer came back: "God gets 100 —you get 0. Happy New Year."

1463   Wanted Present.   "Dear Aunt _____: The present you sent for Christmas was almost as good as the one I really wanted!"

1464   Christmas Star.   Timmy was the three-year-old brother of seven-year-old Sally, who in the Christmas pageant was Mary, the mother of Jesus. He wanted to be the baby Jesus. Knowing his reputation, the director was hesitant. Finally she gave in. During rehearsal Timmy was wonderful, lying in the manger without motion or sound. But during performance he could just **feel** that audience. He raised one experimental eye over the side of the manger. A titter went across the audience. This encouraged him so much that he sat up full, aimed both fingers at the audience like machine guns, and went "A-a-a-a-a-a-a-a-a!" That was the end of the pageant for that particular year.

1465   Kid View of Christmas.   Children see modern life, as well as certain confusions, in the Christmas scene. For example, a four-year-old thought Mary and Joseph took Jesus to Jerusalem with them because they didn't have a sitter.

SPORTS

1466   Foiled Again!   We've just heard that our fencing team has lost another contest. Foiled again!

1467 World's Record? The athlete was being attended by the doctor. "What's my temperature, Doc?" he asked.

"A hundred and two degrees," replied the doctor.

"What's the world's record, Doc?" he asked.

1468 Can You Ski? Well, I thought I might take up skiing, but then I decided to let it slide.

1469 Handsome Athlete. The athlete got a marvelous mash note several pages long. He was really thrilled until he read the last line: "Please excuse the crayon. They won't let me use anything sharp in here."

1470 Hot Words. Did you hear about the athlete who got into an argument with his wife while they were eating alphabet soup? Eventually they threw soup at each other. In fact, hot words passed between them!

1471 Heat Faster. On a long trip the athletes were killing time. "Which is faster—heat or cold?" asked one.

Another replied, "Heat is faster. You can catch cold!"

1472 Scratch Him! The socialite was helping in a charity horse race. An owner came to report. "You'll have to scratch my horse," he said.

"Where?" asked the volunteer.

1473 Better Off. Your first horseback ride makes you feel better off.

1474 Fast! He was so fast that he could turn out the light and then go twenty feet to bed before the room got dark!

1475 Runs In Family? The ones who say that fat runs in the family probably never did much running.

1476 Both Loaded. Every hunting season accidents happen because both hunter and gun are loaded.

1477 Lost Hunters.

"We're lost," cried a hunter to his companion. They'd been trying to get back to camp for several hours.

"Take it easy," said the friend. "Shoot an extra deer and the game warden will be here in a minute and a half."

1478 "Don't Shoot." Every year before hunting season a New England farmer paints on the sides of his herd the word "COW" in huge letters. "What about the other sex?" asked a friend.

"Use the same on both," he said. "No use confusin' them New York hunters with the dee-tails!"

1479 Who, Me? The tennis fan, a bit overweight, told how he felt. "When I play, my opponent hits the ball to me. My brain says, 'Race up to the net, slam a blistering drive to the far corner of the court, and jump back into position.' But my body says, 'Who, me?'"

1480 Two Old Sports. The school quiz asked for the class to name two ancient sports. One answer was, "Anthony and Cleopatra."

1481 New Sport. "Let's go to Lake Louise and Banff."
"OK, but how do you Banff?"

1482 Office Sport: In Australia. From the cigarette machine, will the coin (change) be heads or tails?

1483 Scrub Teams. "What is the purpose of the scrub teams?"
"Don't you know, silly? To get the other teams clean!"

1484 Predictions. When better predictions are made, they won't be by sportswriters.

1485 Pro or Amateur. One of the big differences between the professional and the amateur athlete: the pro is paid by check.

Boxing

1486 Keep Swinging. The boxer asked, "Have I done him any damage?"
"No," replied the manager, "but keep swinging. The draft might give him a cold."

1487 No Good. Manager to boxer in ring: "Remember—if he were any good he wouldn't be fighting you."

1488 "I'll Fix You!" You lowdown, sneaking, spineless jellyfish. I'll break every bone in your body.

1489 Who Did It? "Say, what a black eye! Who did it?"
"Mike."
"That little shrimp did that to you?"
"Don't speak disrespectfully of the dead."

Golf

1490 Golf Irony. By the time you don't worry about the number of golf balls you lose, you find you can't hit 'em that far!

1491 Lucky Discovery. The golfer took two enthusiastic swings at the ball and missed cleanly both times. He looked up at his companions and said, "It's a lucky thing I found this out. This course is two inches lower than the one where I usually play!"

1492 How to Win at Golf: Cheat.

1493 Two Lookouts. A threesome of pros saw an old duffer waiting around. "Want to make a fourth?" they said.
"Sure," said he.
"We want to warn you. We're pros, and we play for a dollar a hole."
"That's all right, if you'll give me two lookouts," he said. Not knowing what that was, but thinking it innocent they agreed. As the first man teed off, the old man screamed at the top of his voice, "Loookkkout!" He never used the second one, of course, but won all eighteen holes!

1494 To Put. The dictionary says that "to put" means to place a thing where you want it. In golf, to putt is a vain effort to do the same thing.

1495 Scots Good. They say that the Scots are good at golf, because it makes the ball last longer.

1496 Play Through? The man in the electric golf cart said, "May I play through? My batteries are low!"

1497 Funny Game!
"Funny game, golf!" said the player.
"'Tain't meant to be," responded the caddy.

1498 Coincidence.
"You are the world's worst caddy," said the furious golfer.
"Might be," said the caddy. "But that would just be too much of a coincidence!"

1499 Medical Advice. The big executive went to his doctor, who examined him carefully. "I'd say," said the doctor, "to give up golf, and spend more time at the office!"

1500 Heavenly Golf. St. Peter drove off, made a hole in one. St. Thomas drove off, made a hole in one. "Now," said Peter, "let's cut out the miracles and start playing golf!"

1501 Homing Iron?
"Will this iron get me home?" the golfer asked his caddy.
"I can't say," replied the boy. "I don't know where you live."

1502 Suburbanite: A man who hires someone to mow his lawn so that he can play golf for exercise.

1503 Name It! The best club griper bearded the secretary of the golf club in the clubhouse on the subject of wormholes in the greens. "Isn't this the time of year you treat worms?"
"Certainly," replied the secretary, motioning to the refreshment center. "What'll you have?"

1504 Novice? The "expert" instructed the novice. "Knock the ball as near that flag as you can." It landed within a foot of the hole.
"What do I do next?"
"Knock it into the hole."
"Into the hole? Why didn't you tell me that in the first place?"

1505 Average Golfer: Forty around the chest, thirty-eight around the waist, ninety-six around the course, nuisance around the house.

1506 3.98. When "Fore" shouted twice didn't move the women on the green ahead, a fellow golfer suggested trying "3.98."

1507 How to Golf. Yell "Fore." Take six. Put down five.

1508 Third Stroke. He was driving about a foot ahead of the teeing mark in the home tournament. The club secretary said, "That'll disqualify you."

"Go back to your clubhouse," retorted the home-talent golfer. "I'm playing my third stroke!"

Baseball

1509 Hates Umpires. Do you know about the guy who is such a baseball fan that he even hates umpires in winter?

1510 You're Out. An old umpire baiter, Dick Cooley, was once vanquished by Joe Cantillion, said Doug Moore in **Collier's.** Dick drove a high, deep fly to center. The ump ran right alongside him and made him carefully touch first, second, third, home, which he readily did, thinking it was a homer. After he touched home, Cantillion said, "You're out. Fly ball to center field."

1511 Miss My Turn? The patient was a tremendous baseball fan. "I dream every night about baseball!" The psychiatrist asked, "What about girls? Do you ever dream of them?"

"What? And miss my turn at bat?"

1512 Bible Baseball. The game was first mentioned in the words, "In the big inning . . ."

1513 Slide! A baseball fan went to the races, picked a 50–1 horse, which came right down the stretch, neck and neck with the favorite. As they neared the finish line the fan shouted, "Slide, you bum—slide!"

1514 What He's For. The rabid baseball fan took his wife to see the big game. Bases filled and two out, the opposition lifted a fly ball to left center, and the center fielder made an impossible circus catch, rolling over on the ground. So did the fans in the stands, including the husband. "What's the matter with you, John?" wifie asked. "Didn't you see him catch that ball?"

John replied, when he could talk at all.

"Well," said the disgusted wife. "Isn't that what he's there for?"

1515 Needs Life.
"That team needs life!"
"Oh, no, I think thirty days would be sufficient!"

1516 That Figures. The teacher was having trouble getting the boys to work on decimals until she pointed out that they were necessary to figure batting averages for baseball.

1517 Protects Players. Wifey: "Why does that man wear the mask, dear?"

Hubby: "It keeps him from biting the players."

1518 That's Right!

"I can tell you the score of the game before it starts!"

"Oh, yeah? Then what is the score?"

"Nothing to nothing."

1519 Attention! Just released from military service, Ken Hicks was pitching for Los Angeles. He was ready to deliver when the public address system called out, "Attention!" The pitcher froze in position. The umpire called a balk and advanced the runner a base.*

1520 Like the Pros. A young hopeful wandered into baseball training camp.

"What do you play?"

"In field."

"I mean, what position?"

"Stooped over, like the pros," said the lad.*

1521 Another Alibi. Larry Gilbert, when managing the Nashville Vols, collected alibis of players. Muffing the ball on a cloudy afternoon, the player insisted that he got a drop of rain in his eye.*

1522 Weak Athlete. An athlete on a professional baseball team insisted that as a child he was so weak he had to suck his thumb through a straw!*

1523 Get the Hitter. A scout reported to Casey Stengel about a young pitcher who tossed a no-hitter. The only solid blow off him was a foul. "Sign the guy that hit the foul," Casey replied. "It's hitters we need, not pitchers!"†

1524 Washington Note: Some wag reported that the Washington Senators of his day played like they were on Civil Service.†

---

* From Fred Russell, *I'll Go Quietly* (Nashville, Tenn.: *Nashville Banner*, 1944).

† From Fred Russell, *Funny Thing About Sports* (Nashville, Tenn.: *Nashville Banner*, 1948).

1525 Don't Know 'Em. A sports editor wired to a player for an out-of-town contest: "Send me 200 words on the game."

The player replied: "Sorry. Don't know 200 words!"†

1526 Best Alibi. Fred Russell gives Al Brancato, former Toronto infielder, credit for one of the best alibis of baseball. Al came to practice limping. "Bruised my knee," he said.

"How?"

"Kneeling in church!"†

1527 Tie Ball. There was a North Carolina semipro game with the home team a run behind, three on and two out, and the count three balls and two strikes on the batter, and an umpire frightened of home-team fans. The next pitch came streaking through and the umpire called out, "Tie ball."

"How you get it?"

He explained that it was so perfectly between that it was neither ball nor strike. Both sides accepted, and on the next pitch the batter popped out for the last out.†

1528 Triple Play. When Dizzy Trout was a Detroit Tiger, he used to claim that he pulled a triple play without pitching to a batter, using a little trickery. He took an extra ball from his shirt and, being ambidextrious, threw one to first and third, catching both runners off base. In the confusion the batter swung for his third strike and was out.†

1529 Insect Baseball. They have it all worked out. They put spiders into the outfield to catch the flies.

1530 Tough Choice. "We're trying to do what you said, teacher," said the two boys at recess. "Pick the nine greatest Americans. But we can't decide who to put on first base."

1531 Baseball in the Bible. There are several references to baseball in the Bible, as when Eve stole first and Adam stole second. Gideon rattled the pitchers, Goliath was put out by David, and the Prodigal Son made a home run.

---

† From Fred Russell, *Funny Thing About Sports* (Nashville, Tenn.: *Nashville Banner*, 1948).

Football

1532 Not from Here. Everybody but one man in the Green Bay stadium removed hats for the national anthem. Someone nearby asked him why. "I'm not from Green Bay," he answered.

1533 Coach: One who will gladly lay down your life for the school!

1534 In Color! The dad took his kid to the football game. "Look, Dad!" he shouted. "It's in color!"

1535 Perfect Losers. His team were such good losers—in fact, perfect!

1536 Generally Speaking, a rolling football gathers no score.

1537 Saturday Bowl. Bob Hope was doing the role of a broadcaster. "Here we are at the Broken Nose Bowl," he said. "The crowd is filled to capacity."

1538 Call All! The coach lost another game. He asked a friend, "Got a dime? Want to call a friend."

"Here's two dimes," said the other. "Call all your friends."

1539 Take One. The coach called the weatherman on the telephone. "Whaddya say? Shower tonight?"

The weatherman replied evenly, "Sure—if you need one, take one!"

1540 Man's Game. The coach gave his team final instructions. "Now, men, remember—football makes men of you. It develops initiative, leadership, and individuality. Now get in there and do exactly what I told you!"

1541 Not So Far. "How far out are the dollar-fifty seats?"

"From the game they're some distance. But you're very close to the radio shop that carries the broadcast on loudspeakers."

1542 Tough Game. It was a local football game in the mountains. "What are all of those grapes doing on the field?" asked a visitor.

"Grapes nothin'," replied the native. "Them's eyeballs!"

1543 Mightier? We want to see Sing Sing play West Point to tell whether pen is mightier than the sword!

1544 Shaped Nose. Did you hear about the ex-football player who went to have his nose changed to a Grecian nose. They asked him why. "Going to be on the stage?"

"No," he replied. "I've got a good chance for a restaurant job."

1545 Highest Score. Years ago Georgia Tech beat Cumberland University, a small law school of 178 students, by a score of 222–0. Late in the game Ed Edwards, a back for Cumberland, fumbled the snap. "Pick it up!" he screamed to his teammates.

One of them called back, "Pick it up yourself! You dropped it!"‡

1546 Let's Go, Girls! Knute Rockne's Notre Dame team was behind Wisconsin 7–0 at the half. He said not a word to the guys in the dressing room until a minute before time to go back on the field. Then he let loose with one sentence, "All right, girls, let's go!"‡

1547 Yes, Why? Why does football, played in all kinds of weather, have no covered stands, where baseball, never played in the rain, usually has the stands covered!‡

1548 Ivy Idea. Bill Cunningham in the **Boston Herald** tells of a handsome young football player from Harvard whose marriage to a beautiful New England gal was the talk of the social season. Everybody who was anybody was there, and the wedding went along uneventfully until the groom knelt. There plainly on the soles of his two shoes were the words, "To hell—with Yale."§

1549 Everyman's Best. Bob Higgins says there are three things all men think they can do better than any other: build a fire, run a hotel, and coach football.§

1550 Scrub Idea. The coach, testing a forlorn substitute who hadn't played all year, asked him, "What would you do if we were on their ten-yard line and they intercepted our pass?"

The sub thought a minute. "Move up the bench so I could see better," he said.§

---

‡ From Fred Russell, *I'll Try Anything Twice* (Nashville, Tenn.: *Nashville Banner*, 1945).

§ From Fred Russell, *Funny Thing About Sports.*

1551 Leahy Fundamentals. The team had done so poorly at Notre Dame that Leahy insisted on going back to fundamentals. "This is a football," he said. "It . . ."

He claimed that a tackle spoke up and said, "Please, coach, not so fast!"§

1552 Not Nawth, Suh! In a Kentucky-Ole Miss game, they announced on the loud speaker that Ole Miss had chosen to defend the north goal. A Mississippi supporter rose unsteadily to his feet and responded. "Mississippi will never defend the North goal, suh!"§

Fishing

1553 Both Here. Two business partners were out fishing. One snapped his fingers and looked startled. "We forgot to lock the safe!" he said.

"That's all right," soothed the other. "We're both here."

1554 Fish Biting.
"Are the fish biting today?"
"If they are, they're biting each other."

1555 Just One? He had really made a catch—the biggest fish in the lake, no doubt. He met another fisherman with twelve little ones. The multiple fisherman looked at the big fish and said, "Just caught the one, eh?"

1556 Good Bait. The stranger watched the old man fishing. Hours went by without a word. Finally he asked, "I see you're using fish bait for lobsters. You think it's good?"

There was a silence. "Nope," said the old fisherman, "but the lobsters do."

1557 Swimming Lessons. The old man was on the bank fishing out of season. He felt a presence behind him, looked to see a man behind him. There was a pause. "You the game warden?" he asked.

"Yep!" Another pause.

The old man nodded to the minnow on the line he had just lifted from the water. "Just teaching him to swim," he asserted.

---

§ From Fred Russell, *Funny Thing About Sports.*

1558 This Is Fishing. Uncle Nabob says that fishing is a jerk at at one end of the line waiting for a jerk at the other end.

1559 Big Fish Angles: A man caught a fish one time so big that just a picture of it weighed 3½ pounds! He had a relative who had some special fisherman's scales. The neighbors weighed their new baby on those scales and the infant weighed 46½ pounds! Another relative caught a fish that, he said, weighed 298 pounds! Someone asked if it weren't really 300 pounds. "Do you think I'd lie over two pounds?" he asked, indignantly.

1560 "Throw It Back." A Texan caught a fish that weighed six pounds. Texas style, he told his Arkansas guide that in Texas they used that kind for bait. The guide nodded, threw it back into the water.

1561 Trading-Stamp Bait. We've been told that, running out of worms, a California fisherman used trading stamps and caught a trout, seven bass and two bluegills.

1562 Fishing Wisdom. There is probably no better way to loaf, without attracting criticism and unfavorable attention, than to go fishing!

1563 You Can't Win. There were two worms. One was lazy, stayed out late. The other was up and about his business, very early. The early bird got the early worm. A fisherman with a flashlight got the night crawler. The moral is: You can't win!

1564 Fish Lady. At the marriage license bureau, the clerk asked the husband-to-be, "Is this young lady a minor?"

"No," he replied. "She works in the fish market."

THE ARTS

Music

1565 Get Married. The daughter of a Rubinstein admirer played the piano for the great man, then asked anxiously, "What should I do now?"

"Get married," replied Rubinstein.

1566 An Opera: The only place where a man stabbed in the back, instead of bleeding, sings.

1567 Virginian. The local orchestra was playing with great feeling, "Carry Me Back to Old Virginia." A man at a table in the corner was weeping. Touched, the leader went over to console him. "Are you a Virginian?" asked he.

"No—I'm a musician," replied the weeper.

1568 Gave Up.
"Why did you stop going to choir at church?"
"Well, I was absent one Sunday, and the people thought that the organ had been repaired."

1569 Built for Job. Some people are just built for the job. For instance, the cellist with bowlegs . . .

1570 Long Way. The big-city symphony had played the small New England town. Next day there was conversation galore. One older inhabitant said, "All I got to say is that it was a long way to bring that there big drum just to beat it wunst!"

1571 Mercy! "The choir will now sing. 'O Lord, Be Merciful.' "

1572 How's That? There's a hymn which says, "Grant us courage for the facing of this hour!"

Art and Artists

1573 Tit for Tat. Whistler is said to have sent his dog to a throat specialist. The doctor retaliated by asking him to paint his door.

1574 Whistler's Father. Talk about neglected people—how would you liked to have been Whistler's father?

1575 Art Appreciator. Picasso's summer relief postman was invited into the house. He looked at the paintings on the wall, patted Picasso's young daughter on the head, and said, "So the little one paints, too!"

1576 Period Furniture. At the exclusive shop Mrs. Newrich was getting some furniture. "That's a lovely chair," said she.
"Yes, that's a Louis XIV," replied the salesman.
"It's a little small. I like it, but I think I'll take a Louis XVI."

1577 If You'd Practiced.   Fritz Kreisler very much disliked to practice. They had a banquet for him—"the world's greatest violinist."
He beamed to his wife after the eulogy, "Well?"
She was unimpressed. "Just think of what you'd have been," she said, "if you'd practiced!"

1578 Finished Musician.   He was really a finished musician. (The neighbors attended to that.)

1579 Artist's Model.   There was one who made a bare living.

Writers and Books

1580 Great Reader.
"I'd like a book, please."
"Something light?"
"It doesn't matter. I have my car with me."

1581 Fiery Poetry.
"Shall I put more fire into my poetry [or 'sermons' or 'books']?"
"No, I should say quite the reverse."

1582 New Books:
Turkey in the Oven—Browning.
On Top of Old Smokey—Coleridge.
I Walked Across a Continent—Bunyan.

1583 Really Up!
Auctioneer: "Now what am I offered for this beautiful bust of Robert Browning?"
From the audience: "That's not Browning. That's Shakespeare."
Auctioneer: "Well, folks, the joke's on me. Just goes to show how much I know about the Bible."

Theater

1584 Leg In Cast.   While he hadn't been in a play before, it is true that his leg had been in a cast.

1585 An Actor Is . . .
"What is an actor, Daddy?"
"An actor, son, is one who can walk to one side of the stage, peer into the wings filled with theatrical props, dirt, dust, other actors, stagehands, old clothes and old sets, and say, 'What a lovely view from this window.'"

1586 Can't Lose. Did you hear about the actress who figured it all out and married a rich man, then an actor, then a preacher, and finally an undertaker—one for the money, two for the show, three to make ready, and four to go!

1587 Tiers With Audience.
"Are you looking for a good strong play, true to life, that will fill the audience with tears?"
"No. As a matter of fact, I'm looking for any kind of a play that will fill the tiers with audience."

1588 Best Hissing. In the old days of touring dramatic companies, if they could be called that, the performance was so miserable that the audience of nine people began to hiss. The manager gathered all his company onstage, and together they out-hissed the audience.

1589 You're It. In a rather ordinary production in England, Hamlet said dramatically, "Something is rotten in the state of Denmark."
From the balcony came the reply, "Right, and you're it, old chap!"

1590 Short, Short Play. Act 1. Lion, two hunters. Act. 2. Lion, one hunter. Act 3. Lion.

1591 Small Theater. The manager of a touring theatrical company wired ahead to a small town: "Rehearsal Monday afternoon three. Have stage manager, carpenter, prop man, electrician, stagehands present."
The reply came back by telegraph: "I'll be there."

COMEDY SCENES:
You remember some of them from movies and TV. Jot down notes, and use them in speeches.

1592 The Inimitable Charlie. For instance, mistaken identity in a Charlie Chaplin film: A truck with long pipes dropped its red flag. Charlie picked it up and was trying to restore it to his owner when a group of protesters swung around the corner marching, placing him in the front of them, and he was arrested as a Red.

1593 Or Harry. Or take a Harry Langdon scene in a film where he had a dual role of a dimwit and a tough gangster, with men out to get him. He jumped out from the corner of a building, hand in the air defiantly, and said, "Give me liberty or give me death!" There was a tat-tat-tat-tat-tat sound, and his hat flew off. He jumped back to safety behind the building and said, "Gimme liberty!"

1594 How Long? The little boy asked the ticket taker at the movie while his mother waited in the car at the curb, "What time is the picture over three times?"

1595 Great Actress. The reviewer said that she ran the gamut of human emotion, from A to B.

Movies

1596 Fair Enough. A church bulletin said of the Ten Commandments: "You've seen the film. Now read the book."

1597 Opportunity. You've got talent. You ought to be in the movies. If you hurry, the night prices are not on yet.

1598 Unverified Rumor: We heard that there was a movie so old on TV the other day that the cowboy was riding a dinosaur.

1599 Nosebleed. The usher took the customer up into the vastness of the balcony of a very large movie house and stopped. "You'll find a seat up there," he said. "When I go past here, my nose bleeds!"

1600 Movie Location. This is funny, but serious. An experienced theatre man said, "Pick a good popcorn location, and build a theater around it."

1601 Interpreter. "I don't know what to think," said a movie- and church-goer. "The Bible says. . . . But Cecil B. DeMille says. . . ."

1602 Jerks. The movies maintain their illusion by a series of jerks.

1603 Smells.
"The movies had moved right along during the past few years," said one moviegoer to another as they left the theater.
"How's that?"
"Well, the early ones were silent. Then they added sound. Now this one smells!"

1604 Clever Manager. Troubled with popcorn boxes in his movie house, the theater owner numbered each box of popcorn and gave a prize to the lucky number. Kids brought out their boxes, got their prize (if any), and deposited boxes in a receptacle outside.

1605 Modern Western. When the authors' daughter was two, she gave a fine brief description of a western movie with singing star. She said simply, "Man sing song. Bang! Bang! Bang!"

RURAL LIFE

1606 Rural Optimist. Farmer: "That drought cost me five thousand bushels of wheat."
Wife: "But there's some good in everything. We can get the salt out of the shakers better."

1607 Cow's Nest. The city kid found a pile of empty milk bottles. He rushed to his mother and said, "Come quick. I've found a cow's nest."

1608 Building a Horse. A city kid, seeing a horse being shod, rushed to see his friends. "Today I saw a man building a horse. When I was there, he was nailing on the feet!"

1609 Correct Answer. In the rural school the teacher was trying to give the kids a practical problem. "If your father sold two thousand bushels of wheat at three dollars a bushel, what would he get?"
The boy thought a minute and replied with confidence, "A new car!"

1610 Cruel Farmer. Did you hear about the cruel farmer who stalked through the corn, pulling off the ears?

1611 No Drought. We knew that a dry season was coming, but we licked the problem on our farm by planting onions and potatoes in alternate rows. The onions made the eyes of the potatoes water, and that got us through.

1612 Good Meat. On their way to the nearest railroad station the lumberjacks talked a housewife in a lonely cabin into cooking a meal for them. They liked the porkchops very much. She was pleased. "Ought to be good," she said. "None of this butchered stuff —this hog died a nacheral death!"

WEATHER

1613 Complete Dope. The radio announcement said, "Now hear the weatherman. The complete dope on the weather!"

1614 Still Sunny. A weatherman was overheard to say over the telephone, "Yes, ma'am, my corn is hurting too, but I still say fair and warmer."

1615 Shortest Month? Did you realize that March is really the shortest month of the year? It's because the wind blows two days out of every week, in March.

1616 Cave Weatherman. Two cavemen were talking. One said to the other, "Say what you want to—I say the weather has changed since they brought in those bows and arrows!"

1617 Cold Alaska. In some parts of Alaska it gets so cold that they have to thaw out the telephone lines to see what people said during the cold season.

1618 Oregon Rain. In Oregon they just have one rain, reported a visitor, but that's all winter!

11

Institutions and Ideas

THE WORLD OF BUSINESS

1619 Motto: "All work and no play makes jack."

1620 Running the Business. A friend asked a businessman if he and the son were carrying on the business together.

"Fifty-fifty," he said. "I run the business and my son does the carrying on."

1621 Creative. "Do it yourself," advertises a paperhanger, "and then send for us."

1622 Picketed. There was a strike where the pickets were picketed. Their signs were from a non-union shop.

1623 Know How. A small-businessman had to call a locksmith to open his safe. The locksmith gave him a bill for fifty dollars.

"I want it itemized," insisted the businessman.

"OK," said the locksmith, and wrote out: "Opening safe, $5.00. Knowing how, $45.00."

1624 Earthquake? Out here they call them "real estate adjustments."

1625 Got the Job! A young man applied at the factory for a job.
"What can you do?" asked the foreman.
"Anything," he said.
"Can you file smoke?"
"Yes, sir, if you'll screw it in the vise for me."
They hired him on the spot.

1626 Tough Times. A butcher of questionable reputation was answering the charge of putting sawdust in bologna. "Cattle are so high these days," he explained, "that it's hard to make both ends meat."

1627 Heavenly Ad. The advertising executive asked his little girl what she had brought home from Sunday school.
"Oh, just an ad about heaven," she replied.

1628 Put It Back! At the supermarket, one girl was helping another shop. Her friend picked up a package. "Put it back," said the first one. "You have to cook that!"

1629 Irate Customer. He answered a letter asking for payment with these words: "Another letter from you like this one and I'll take my debts elsewhere!"

1630 Going Concern.
"You know the store you sold me as a going concern?"
"Sure. Why?"
"Well, it's gone."

1631 Saved to Hilt. The home freezer salesman insisted that the housewife could save enough on food bills to pay for it.
"Yes," she replied. "but we are buying a car on the bus fare we save, paying for the washer on laundry bills we save, and paying for the house on the rent we save. We just can't afford to save any more right now."

1632 Hair Testimonial. The inventor wasn't sure whether to use this testimonial sent in. It said, "Before I used your restorer I had three bald patches. Now I have only one."

1633 Things Dull!
"How's business?" asked the housewife of the scissors grinder.
"Marvelous!" he said. "Never saw things so dull!"

1634 Rehearse. "We'll have to rehearse this one," said the under-taker as the casket rolled out of his vehicle.

1635 Won't Pay. A customer wrote to a publisher: "I never ordered the blasted book. If I did, you didn't send it. If you sent it, I never got it. If I got it, I paid for it. If I didn't, I won't."

1636 Spill That Much. An oil man was asking a department store executive in Dallas what their net profit was. "Oh, we make one and a half to three per cent," was the answer.

The oil man was surprised. "Why, we spill that much," he said.

1637 Atomic Talk? "What have you been making at the atomic plant, Tony?"

"I don't know," he replied, "but some fella said we were making the front end of horses, and they were going to send them to Washington to be assembled."

1638 Self-Operating. The visitor asked the custodian if he could see the president.

"He's gone."

"What about the vice-president?"

"He's in Chicago."

"The treasurer?"

"Home, sick."

"Well, then, who's running this business?"

"Guess it's running itself!"

The Boss

1639 Definitely. The boss, leaving the office, said to his secre-tary, "I'll be back either at noon, at four thirty, or tomorrow morn-ing—and that's definite!"

1640 You Get the Idea. A wrought-up businessman dictated this letter: "Sir, my stenographer, being a lady, cannot type what I think of you. I, being a gentleman, won't dictate it. But you, being neither, will know what I mean."

1641 Your Choice. To solve an office water problem, the boss had two water bottles plainly marked "Fluorided" and "Plain."

1642 Sign: "When everything else fails, why not try what the boss suggested?"

1643 Count Out. The irate employee came to see the boss and said, "I want a raise or count me out."

To which the boss replied, "One, two, three, four, five, six, seven, eight, nine, ten."

1644 Remarkable Letter. The boss told his tenographer that she was not to revise his letters. "Take it the way I tell you," he said. So the next day Mr. O. J. Squizz, of Squizz Soap Company read this letter:

"Mr. O. K. or A. J. or something, look it up, Squizz, what a name! Squizz Soap Company, Detroit, that's in Michigan, isn't it. Dear. Mr. Squizz: Hm-m-m-m. The last shipment of soap you sent us was terrible and I want you to understand—no, scratch that out. I want you to understand unless you can ship . . . furnish . . . ship . . . no, furnish us with your regular soap, you needn't ship us no more, period, or whatever the grammar is.

"Where was I? Paragraph. Them bums tried to put one over on us. Whaddya you want to paint yer faces up for like Indians on the warpath? We're sending the shipment back tomorrow. I'd like to ram it down their throats—the bums. Now, read the letter over—no, don't read it over, we've wasted enough time on them crooks. Fix it up and sign my name. Let's go to lunch!"
                                                        —Sunshine Magazine

1645 Locating the Boss. During the day, the secretary will give out information like this:

"He hasn't come in yet."
"I expect him any minute."
"He called to say he'd be a little late."
"He came in, but had to leave."
"He's already gone to lunch."
"He should be back from lunch by now."
"He's not back yet. May I take a message?"
"He's in the building. His hat is here."
"I'm not sure whether he'll be back or not."
"Sorry. He's gone for the day."
                                                        —The Lookout

1646 Lunch Date. "This is Perkins, Potter, Parker and Potts. Good morning."

"Is Mr. Potter there?"

"May I ask who is calling?"

"This is Sullivan, Chadwick, Bicknell and Hale. Mr. Sullivan calling."

"Just a moment. I'll connect you."

"Mr. Potter's office."

"Mr. Potter, please. Mr. Sullivan wants him."

"Will you put Mr. Sullivan on the line, please?"

"Mr. Sullivan? Ready with Mr. Potter."

"Hi, Pete—Joe. OK for lunch? Fine—see you." —**Sunshine Magazet**

1647 The Ones. At the end of the day a life insurance salesman was finally admitted to see the big boss. "You should feel highly honored," said the boss. "Do you know that I have refused to see seven insurance men today?"

"I know," said the agent. "I'm them!"

Secretaries, Stenographers, and Other Workers

1648 Secretary? Said one, a secretary looks like a woman, thinks like a man, and works like a dog.

1649 Throw Them Away. A secretary asked another if she filed her nails. "No," she said, "I cut them off and throw them away."

1650 In the Elevator. A cute little secretary spoke to the dignified-looking executive. "Hello, Cutie Pie."

His wife responded immediately. "And I'm Mrs. Pie," she said.

1651 What Happened? An angry boss accosted his stenographer, "You should have been here at eight o'clock!"

"Why? What happened?" she asked.

1652 "That's What They All Say." A big businessman told his secretary that he didn't want any visitors. "If anybody says that their business is important, just say, 'That's what they all say.'"

That afternoon a woman called and insisted on seeing the boss. "I am his wife," she said.

"That's what they all say," replied the secretary.

1653 Compensation's Set In. A man was talking with the son of a workman. "When will your daddy be able to work again?"

"Not for a long time," said the little boy. "Compensation's set in."

1654 Signal. There was the eager stenographer who thought that when the typewriter bell rang it was time for coffee break.

1655 Blank Check. Through error, the employee's pay envelope contained a blank check. He took it to his wife. "Just as I thought," he said, "my deductions have finally caught up with my salary."

1656 Don't Discuss. The company printed a note requesting employees not to discuss salary with others, since it was personal business.

"Don't worry," said one employee. "I'm as ashamed of it as you are."

1657 Talented. The office manager asked if the new girl were good at addition. "Not very, but she's top at distraction," said the treasurer.

1658 Hate to Work. The receptionist said to the filing clerk, "I know I should quit and get married. But I hate to quit this job and go to work."

1659 Jealous! "The foreman fired me. You know what a foreman does—stands around and watches others work? Well, he got jealous. People thought I was the foreman."

1660 Coffee Break. A ten-minute coffee break each day amounts to forty-three and a third hours a year—a week of vacation!

1661 Office Clock. A clock is in an office to tell you how late you wish you weren't, when to go out for lunch and coffee breaks before, and come back after, and how long before you can start stopping working by stalling until.

1662 "Congratulations!" said the boss to his stenographer. "This is the earliest that you have been late!"

1663 A Whole Hour? Elmer arrived at the office at nine o'clock black and blue, his clothes in tatters. His boss was livid with rage. "You should have been here at eight!"

"I fell out of a tenth-story window," said Elmer.

"It took you a whole hour?" sneered the boss.

1664 Wrong Spelling. The boss said to the custodian, "Ebenezer, I can write your name in the dust on my desk this morning."

"Yeah," replied Ebenezer. "And you spelled it wrong."

1665 Overlooked Seniority. His seniority was overlooked by the boss, who finally explained, "You haven't had twenty years of experience—you've had one year of experience twenty times."

1666 The Picture Postcard. It contained this message to the boys back at the shop: "Having a wonderful time and a half."

1667 Which Partner Is First? The office boy explained to a visitor: "At first Mr. Jones was always last, but later he began to get earlier till at last he was first, though before he had always been behind. He soon got later again, though of late he has been sooner, and at last he got behind as before. But I expect that he'll be earlier sooner or later."

—Sunshine Magazet

1668 Work Break. A notice to employees of a Texas firm suggested: "We are asking that somewhere between starting and quitting time—without infringing on lunch time, coffee breaks, rest periods, ticket selling and vacation planning—each employee find some time that can be used for what is known as Work Break. We believe this will be an aid to steady employment and regular paychecks, and we hope that each employee will give it a fair trial."

1669 Satisfied. Asking for a recommendation, a worker received this note, "Jack Jones worked for us for a week. We're satisfied."

Sales

1670 Spel or Sel? The president was horrified to discover that the new salesman, Bell, was virtually illiterate. Ready to let him go, he received a note, "Dat Cleveland company that ain't bot from us. Wel, I sold them $200,000. Now I go to Chicago." Next day another note same: "I sole them half a million."

The notes went up on the bulletin board with these words from the president: "We ben spending too much time trying to spel instead of trying to sel. Bell, who is on the rode, is doing a grate job for us. You shud go out and do like he dun."

1671 Good Yarn. The salesman held up a woolen garment and said, "It's just the thing, latest design, fast color, long wearing, and won't shrink. It's a very good yarn."

"Yes," replied the customer, "and well told, too."

1672 Two Orders. "On my first day out as a salesman I got two orders—'Get out' and 'Stay out.'"

1673 System of Charging. The old hand was telling the new clerk how to price spectacles.

"When the customer asks, 'What is the charge?' you say, 'Ten dollars.' If he doesn't flinch, say, 'That's for the frames. The lenses will be another ten dollars.' Then you pause again very slightly and if he doesn't flinch say, 'each.'"

1674 Higher Is Better. For an experiment a shoe store put a display of women's shoes in the window, half of them priced at $6.95 and half at $12.95. "These are identical shoes," said the sign. But most of the women still insisted on getting the "more expensive."

1675 Sales Psychology. In a wallpaper department the salesman, when a customer seemed about to make a choice, would say, "Let me see if it's in stock." This usually closed the sale.

1676 Expense Account: Sometimes called "land of the spree." One firm is said to have offered to buy fiction rights from one of its salesmen.

1677 Sales Device. In a small store with a window on the street the proprietor fed a cat in a priceless antique saucer. Antique lovers would come in, buy the cat, and ask for the saucer, casually, thinking that the owner didn't know its value. "Couldn't let that go," he told one customer. "I've sold nineteen cats from that saucer!"

1678 Wonder! The customer asked the storekeeper, "How do you sell your eggs?"

"I've often wondered," replied the man.

1679 Complete! Tired of seeing "specials" run by competitors, a car dealer in the Cincinnati area once ran this ad: "PLYMOUTH—

New. Heater, undercoat, mirror glaze, directional signals, visors, arm rests, front seat, steering wheel, rear seat, floor mats, 5 tires, 5 wheels, jack, lug wrench, gear shift handle, hub caps, engine, air cleaner, air in tires, oil in crankcase, battery, spark plugs and wires, electric starter (no old-fashioned crank), emergency brake, hydraulic brakes (no old-fashioned mechanical brakes), upholstery."

1680 Job Lost. "How did you lose your job at the dress shop?"

"Well, after trying on about twenty-five dresses, the customer said, 'I think I'd look nicer in something flowing,' so I suggested the river."

The Bank

1681 Same Handwriting. The bank clerk reminded the customer that he forgot to dot the "*i*" in his signature.

"Could you do that for me?" asked the customer.

"Sorry," said the teller, "but it must be in the same handwriting."

1682 Kindlier Eye. About to refuse a loan, a bank manager who had a glass eye said he would lend the money if the lady could tell which was the glass one. "The left eye," said the woman promptly.

"How can you tell?" asked the banker.

"By the kindlier look in it," said the customer.

1683 "Beaten to the Draw." That's what the bank teller told the husband that his wife had just done to his account.

1684 Your Name? The banker asked, "What is your name, sir?"

"Didn't you see my signature?" growled the customer.

"Indeed, sir." The banker was polite. "That is what aroused my curiosity."

1685 Wrong Number? A woman called up the First National Bank, asking some information about bonds.

"Conversion or redemption?" asked the bank clerk. There was a pause.

"Pardon me," she said. "Do I have the First National Bank or the First Presbyterian Church?"

1686 That Covers It! The bank sent a notice to a young housewife about an overdraft in their joint bank account. She wrote a note of apology and sent them a check.

1687 Full-Service Banking. A man borrowed five dollars, paid the interest of thirty cents and offered the security: ten thousand dollars in government bonds. He indicated to the astonished banker that they wanted ten dollars at the bank across the street just for a safety deposit box to put them in.

What They Say (Signs and Voices of the Daily World)

1688 Furniture Store: "Bedroom problems solved here. We stand behind our beds."

1689 Laundromat: "Ladies, why not leave your clothes with us and go out and have a good time?"

1690 Movie: "Young children must have parents."

1691 Store: "Farmers, bring in your eggs. We want 'em bad!"

1692 City Hall: "To Marriage License Bureau. Watch your step."

1693 Hotel Ad Near Cemetery: "For the rest of your life."

1694 Radio: "Five minutes of the latest news, followed by a Moment of Truth!"

1695 Boarding House: "Attractive room. Everything furnished. Venetian blonds."

The Barber

1696 Sign: "Twenty barbers—Continuous Conversation."

1697 Barber Wisdom: A hair on the head is worth two in the brush.

1698 Flame Thrower! Two kids were watching the barber work with a torch, doing a singe job for a customer. "Look, Bill," said one, "He's searching for them with a flame thrower!"

1699 Barbaric Magazines.
  Customer: "Why do you have only horror, detective, and mystery stories in your magazines?"
  Barber: "Simple. It's easier to cut hair that is standing on end!"

1700 Sign: "During alterations patrons will be shaved in the back."

1701 Tie Red?
Barber (giving patron a shave): "Are you wearing a red tie?"
Customer: "Why, no!"
Barber: "Uh-oh!"

The Plumber

1702 Two Aspirins. The doctor called the plumber after midnight. "I have an emergency at my house. My plumbing is leaking badly. Do hurry over."

"Let me tell you what to do," said the plumber. "Take two aspirins every four hours, and drop them down the pipe. If the leak hasn't cleared up by morning, call me at the office."

The Mechanic

1703 Short Circuit. The mechanic told the lady that he had found the trouble. It was a short circuit.

"Well," she said, "go ahead and lengthen it."

1704 Mechanical Charge. A cartoon showed a mechanic with his foot on the bumper of a car, facing the owner. "Well, you drove in here. That'll be five dollars," said the mechanic, starting his estimate.

The Contractor

1705 Exceeded Estimate.
Nurse: "Congratulations. You have triplets."
Contractor: "Confound it. Exceeded estimate again!"

1706 Like Lightning.
Carpenter boss: "You hammer nails like lightning!"
Apprentice: "You mean I'm fast?"
Carpenter: "No. I mean you never strike twice in the same place!"

1707 Thanks, Dad.

"When I was your age," said Dad, "I carried water for a gang of bricklayers."

"I'm proud of you, Dad," said Son. "If it hadn't been for your courageous boyhood activities, I might have had to do something like that myself!"

THE WORLD OF MEDICINE AND HEALTH

1708 Good Medicine. With modern medicine doing so well at increasing our life expectancy, we may have to pay the national debt ourselves instead of passing it on!

1709 Genius. The fellow who invented pills was clever, but the guy who put the sugar coat on them was a genius.

1710 Hypochondriac's Prayer: "I will lift up mine eyes unto the pills . . ."

1711 Transfusionist: This is one who works in vein.

1712 Real Thing. They ordered artificial respiration for him, but his wealthy family said, "We got money. Give him the real thing."

1713 No Complaints.

"I've been selling this medicine for fifteen years and have had no complaints. What does this prove?" asked a medicine man.

"Dead men tell no tales," was his answer.

1714 Broken Leg. Did you hear about my friend who broke his leg in two places: New York and Chicago.

1715 Claimant. He wrote to his insurance company: "My leg is still in a cast, but I have hopes that possibly next Thursday it will be removed."

1716 Doctoring.

"Daddy, does a doctor ever doctor another doctor?"

"Yes, I suppose so."

"Well, does the doctor doctor a doctor the way the doctored doctor wants to be doctored, or does the doctor doing the doctoring doctor the other doctor the way he wants to?"

1717 Prescription. In the fraternity house a brother paced madly, then dropped, exhausted, into a chair. "I'm taking my medicine," he explained.

"Medicine?"

"Yes. The doctor said I was to take it two nights running, and skip the third night."

1718 Too Late. In a medical school oral test a student prescribed five grains of a certain powerful medicine. A minute later he said to the professors, "I'd like to change my diagnosis."

"Too late," said the prof. "Your patient has now been dead for thirty seconds."

1719 Important Message. When the visitor was ready to go in to see a seriously ill patient, they warned him that the man would probably try to write a note, but not to bother with him. The patient at first looked pleased with his visitor, then he began to make violent motions toward him, and finally wrote a note. The visitor put it in his pocket. Soon the patient died. The visitor had time to read the note: "You're sitting on my oxygen tube."

1720 "Bumper Crop." That's what the clinic called their auto pedestrian victims.

1721 Smart Boy. In the old days an "Indian doctor" would do something to attract attention. This one auctioned off a silver dollar. His only bid was from a youngster—a nickel. There being no other bids, he said to the boy, "Hand up your nickel."

The boy replied, "Take it out of the dollar."

1722 Kick the Bucket? The late George Colman, even in his last illness, showed a sense of humor. The doctor had stopped on the way to see George to attend a patient who had fallen down a well. "And did he kick the bucket?" asked George.

1723 Ulcers: What you get from mountain-climbing over molehills.

1724 Smart Idea.

"Liniment makes your arm smart."

"Here, give me some on my head."

1725 Got It. An easterner came to Arizona for asthma. In less than a week he got it.

1726 Death Rate.
"What's the death rate out here?" asked a tourist at the filling station.
The old man paused a minute. "Same as it is back at your place I reckon," he said, "one to a person."

1721 Compound Fracture? Blondie said that she simply couldn't understand a compound fracture—she never was good at arithmetic.

1728 Powerful Stuff. "For ten years I was nearly deaf. Now after taking your medicine for only ten days I heard from my brother in New Mexico."

1729 Vast Improvement. "A few weeks ago I was so run down I could hardly spank the baby. After taking four bottles of your wonderful medicine I can now thrash my husband in addition to my regular housework."

The Doctor

1730 A Doctor: The only man with his appendix and tonsils intact.

1731 Wrong House. The doctor stopped at the house. The woman came to the door and said, "Doctor, this is the wrong house, but come in anyway. I feel terrible."

1732 Bells Ringing.
"Doctor, there is a constant ringing in my ears. I can't stand it."
"What is your occupation?"
"Bellhop."

1733 Certainly.
"Tell me, Doctor, was my life really in danger?"
"Certainly. Didn't I visit you twice a day?"

1734 Brain Food.
"Doctor, is it true that eating fish stimulates the brain?"
"Maybe," replied the doctor. "One thing is sure—fishing stimulates the imagination."

1735 Your Choice.
"Oh, Doctor," said the pert miss after an operation, "do you think the scar will show?"
"That is entirely up to you," he replied.

1736 Myself Again. The patient said, "Thank you, Doctor. I now feel myself again."
"In that case you'll need more treatment," said the doctor.

1737 That's Rough.
"The thing for you to do is to bury yourself in your work," the doctor prescribed.
"But Doctor," protested the patient, "I'm a concrete mixer."

1738 Operation Angle. In summer camp the kids have a stunt in which they do an operation behind a sheet in silhouette, using a coiled hose or sausage for intestines, etc. At one point a "guest surgeon" makes his appearance and says, "May I cut in?"

1739 Dry Humor. For my rheumatism the doctor told me to keep away from dampness. But really, I'll feel funny sitting in an empty tub, going over myself with a vacuum cleaner!

1740 Medical Progress. The patient with stomach trouble was advised by his doctor to eat a good meal before going to bed.
"But, Doctor," he said, "on my last visit you told me not to eat anything before going to bed."
"Did I indeed?" asked the doctor. "That just goes to show what progress has been made in medicine since I saw you last."

1741 Cheery Thought. "The other doctor and I have disagreed on your case," said a doctor, "But I'm sure the autopsy will prove that I'm right!"

1742 Why, Doc? A picture postcard said, "Dear Doctor, Having a wonderful time. Wish you were here to tell me why."

1743 Hardly! The patient wondered if the operation he was to undergo was dangerous. The doctor was incredulous. "A dangerous operation for forty dollars?" he asked.

1744 Caution Helps. A doctor friend warns that vigorous exercise after the age of fifty can be quite harmful, especially if it is with a knife and fork.

1745 Too Short. Heavy lady: "Doctor, don't you tell me that I am overweight."

Doctor: "No, madam. It is just that, according to my height and weight chart, you're about five inches too short."

1746 Practice? A doctor friend reports that, although medicine has made great progress, you can still say it is "the practice of medicine."

1747 Don't Want It. After telling the mountaineer what to do to regain his health, the doctor said to him, "That'll be five dollars."

"Fer what?" asked the patient.

"For my professional advice," replied the doctor.

"No siree. Made up my mind not to take it," said the customer, who walked firmly out the door.

1748 Specialized. At a party a woman addressed a doctor. "What kind of a doctor are you?" she asked.

"A naval surgeon," he replied.

"My, how you doctors specialize," she said.

1749 Reduced. "I want three fourths of you back for a checkup in six months," said the doctor to an overweight patient.

1750 How Was It? The doctor said to his patient, "Let me know if this prescription works. I'm having the same trouble myself."

1751 No Complaint. The patient thought his bill was quite too much. The doctor had an answer: "If you knew how strongly I was tempted to let your case go to a postmortem, you wouldn't grumble at three times the bill!"

1752 Musical Doctor. "Doctor, you're so musical. I wonder why?"

"Perhaps it's just that I've listened to so many organ recitals," replied the weary medico.

1753 Other Blessings. After examining a woman patient, the doctor said to the husband, "I don't like your wife's looks."

"To tell the truth, neither do I, but she takes good care of the kids and me."

1754 Not So Hot. "What's my trouble, Doc?" the patient wanted to know.

"Let's say it this way—if you were a building, you'd be condemned," replied the cheery doctor.

1755 Only a Man. The little girl went along when the dog was taken to the veterinarian, to see the "dog doctor." She came home very disappointed. "He wasn't a dog at all—just a man," she explained to her mother.

1756 Pain Reliever. The doctor relieved the man's terrible back pain almost instantly. "What was it, Doc—rheumatism?"
"No," replied the doctor. "Your suspenders were twisted."

1757 New Look. The doctor prescribed long walks for the patient.
"But Doctor," he said, "I'm a letter carrier in the post office."
"Let's see that tongue again," said the doctor.

1758 Not That Good. Doctor: "How do you feel—sort of listless?"
Patient: "Listless? If I felt that good, I wouldn't even be here."

1759 No Flattery. The doctor said to the young woman patient, "I believe you have acute appendicitis."
"Listen, Doc," she said. "I came here to be examined, not admired."

1760 Thoughtful. As he came slowly out of the anesthetic in his room the patient asked, "Why are the blinds drawn, Doctor?"
"There's a fire across the street, and we didn't want you to think the operation was a failure."

1761 Loyal Citizen. The doctor wanted to know whether the patient preferred gas, chloroform, or ether.
"I believe in patronizing home industry," said the Chamber of Commerce secretary. "Just give me a local anesthetic."

1762 Repeat! Doctor to patient with an odd skin disease: "Have you had this before?"
Patient: "Yes, Doctor, I have."
Doctor: "Well, you've got it again!"

1763 Medical Help. The surgeon warned the patient, "This is a very serious operation and I feel that I must tell you this. Four out of every five patients don't make it. Now—is there anything I can do for you before the operation?"
"Certainly," said the patient. "Will you kindly help me on with my shoes and pants?"

1764 Yes, Who?   The mother was a nervous woman. She brought Bobby to the doctor, who prescribed for him and then suggested that Mother use a tranquilizer for the next month.

On the next visit the mother was very calm indeed, and the doctor was pleased. He inquired, "How's Bobby getting along?"

"Who cares?" replied the tranquilized mama.

1765 Heart Repair.   The man went to the doctor with an odd ailment. "Doctor," he said, "I've never had this before—my heart squeaks."

"Lie on the table here," said the doctor, who made a quick examination, then went for an oddly familiar tool. The squeak stopped.

"What was it, Doc?" asked the patient.

"I just oiled your suspenders," replied the doctor.

1766 Shaky Too.   Nick Cullop, former major league baseball player, was taken by his son-in-law to an aging doctor. Nick was shaky and scared.

"How old are you?" asked the doctor.

"I'm seventy-two," said Nick, shaking.

"That needn't worry you," said the doctor, also shaking, "I'm eighty-five."

1767 Improved!   After sitting for about an hour in a reception room, an old man walked over to the desk to ask if E. S. Jones could have visitors. "No," he was told.

"How is he?" he asked. The volunteer consulted the records and said that he was doing nicely.

"That's what I wanted to know," he said. "I couldn't get anything out of that doctor for ten days, so I dressed and came down here. I'm E. S. Jones."

1768 Bit Me!   The three-year-old came out of the doctor's office with her little hand on her hip, where she had had a shot. "Mama," she said tearfully, "I think that man bit me." (Another, about the same age, once said, "He sharped my bottom!")

The Nurse

1769 It's Murder. The patient was nearly two hours late being wheeled toward the operating room. He overheard two aides discussing the situation in the operating room. "Man," said one, "it's been **murder** in there this morning!"

1770 On Nursing Exam: "Food should be picked up, not with the hands but with the tongues."

1771 Modest Nurse. There was a nurse so conscious of her charms for men that when she took a male patient's pulse she deducted five beats for her sex appeal.

1772 Coming Back. One nurse said to another of a male patient, "He's regaining consciousness. He tried to blow the foam off his medicine."

1773 Don't Worry! The nurse told the patient, "There's absolutely no cause for worry. The doctor has seen an operation exactly like yours on TV."

1774 Operation Operation? The attractive young gal was lying on the cart, sheet over her, ready to go for an operation.
  One at a time, three young men in white smocks walked by, raised up the sheet and peeked under, and walked on without a word. To the third one she said, "Is this operation or observation?"
  "I don't know, lady?" said the third. "I'm painting the room down the hall."

The Pharmacist

1775 Sweet Revenge. The soda jerk heard the druggist jumping up and down with glee. "What gives?" he called.
  "Remember that plumber who charged so much for fixing our water pipes last winter? He's coming over to have a prescription filled."

The Dentist

1776 Tooth Fairy. Someone was asking a dentist why he took home a little bag of teeth each night. "I put them under my pillow," he answered, "and the tooth fairy comes and leaves nice gifts."

1777 Leave Magazines. Sign in a dentist's office: "Don't remove magazines, please. The nurse will tell you the end of the story."

1778 Say Ah-h-h! The mother said to her darling, "Now, Junior, be a good boy and say 'Ah-h-h' so the dentist can get his finger out of your mouth."

1779 Do You Promise . . . ? The man said to his dentist, "Do you promise to pull the tooth, the whole tooth, and nothing but the tooth?"

1780 May Hurt! When the editor returned a manuscript to a dentist, he wrote: "This may hurt a little . . . "

1781 Down in Mouth. When a dentist feels dejected but keeps on working, he really is "down in the mouth."

1782 No Dentist. At a banquet a man complained that his false teeth were hurting him. The diner to his left reached in his pocket and brought out a dental plate. "Try these!" he said.

"No, they're too tight," responded the other.

"Well then, try these!"

They fitted perfectly. After the meal, when he returned the teeth, he said to his benefactor, "Those teeth fit beautifully. You a dentist?"

"Nope!" was the answer. "Undertaker."

THE WORLD OF PSYCHIATRY

1783 Others Insecure. The mother of a hyperactive small boy said to the child psychologist, "I don't know whether he feels insecure or not, but everybody else in the neighborhood does."

1784 We Cure Him. The visiting psychiatrist who lectured the college course in abnormal psychology was open for questions.

"You've told us about the abnormal person and how you deal with him," queried a student. "What about the normal person?"

"When we find him," said the great psychiatrist, "we cure him."

1785 Prescription. Jack Jackson says that anybody who goes to a psychiatrist ought to have his head examined!

1786 Psychiatry: Cracker-barrel philosophy in modern dress, at a price.

1787 What About Mine? He told the psychiatrist that he had lost all desire to live. Life was too hectic. After asking some preliminary questions, the doctor said, "I understand your situation. You'll need a year of treatment at fifty dollars a week."

The patient blinked and paused, "Now, that solves your problem, Doc. What about mine?"

1788 Still Not Normal. A woman was seeking psychological help for her son, talking with the psychologist on the telephone. "My son makes mud pies," she said.

"That's not so bad," said the doctor. "Lots of sons make mud pies."

"Well, I don't like it," she insisted, "and neither does his wife."

1789 Ate My Half. The little boy, judged impossible by his parents, was taken to the psychiatrist, in the hope that he could get the child to eat.

"What would you like to eat?" asked the psychiatrist.

"Worms," the kid said. Not baffled at all, the psychiatrist sent for some worms.

"Fried," said the kid. They fried them.

"Just one." The psychiatrist got one.

"You eat half," ordered the boy. Not to be outdone, the psychiatrist broke it in two, managed to get the half-worm down. The boy began to cry.

"What's the matter?" asked the infuriated doctor.

"You ate my half," said the kid.

1790 A Dog's Predicament. Have you heard about the dog who couldn't go to the psychiatrist because he was not allowed on couches?

1791 Why I'm Here. Outside the psychiatrist's office were a caterpillar and a worm. "Sometimes," said the caterpillar, "I can't tell whether you're coming or going."

"What do you think I'm doing here?" asked the worm.

244 • *The Public Speaker's Handbook of Humor*

1792 Answers Good Enough? Rogerian counselors laugh about the patient who went to two or three different nondirective counselors, and changed to still another one. (Counselors using this system usually reflect back to the client what they hear him saying, using his own words largely.) The patient said, "Doctor, I've been to some other counselors but I'm not straightened out yet."

"You're not straightened out yet?" replied the doc.

"I still feel baffled, confused."

"You're still confused."

"Yes, I felt it was best to change doctors."

"You weren't satisfied with the others."

"Aren't my words good enough?"

1793 Not My Department. A friend said to a college psychologist, "Isn't it a good morning?"

"I'm sorry," replied the psychologist. "Meteorology is not my department."

1794 You're Crazy! A man on a couch looked up at the psychiatrist with baleful glance and delivered his opinion: "The trouble with you, my friend, is that you're loco."

1795 What Meaning? Two college psychologists were walking across the campus. They were met by another who said as they passed, "Nice day, isn't it?"

When he had gone, one of the pair said to the other, "I wonder what he meant by that?"

1796 Not On Me. The client told the psychiatrist that he had illusions.

"What illusions?" asked the doctor.

"That bugs are crawling on me," he said, brushing his arms vigorously as if to get them off.

"Well, don't get 'em on me!" cried the alarmed psychiatrist.

1797 From the Wall? The worried man was telling the psychiatrist's receptionist his problem.

"All day I want to eat grapes," he said.

"I imagine most people want to eat grapes," she said.

"Off the wallpaper?"

1798 You Are Inferior. They tested him for his inferiority complex and reported the results. "No complex—you **are** inferior."

1799 He Was Lying. They gave a mental patient a lie detector test. One of the questions was, "Are you Napoleon?"

His answer was, "No."

The machine showed that he was lying.

1800 Mistaken Identity. A prominent official of the city was in the mental institution on business. In trying to leave he was stopped by a guard who thought him a patient. "Do you know who I am?" he asked, indignantly.

"No," replied the guard. "But I know where you are."

1801 Who's Playing? Two morons were playing a game. One had both hands cupped, peeking in. "What's in here?" he asked.

"Subway train?"

First one looked, said, "Nope."

"U. N. Building?"

"Nope."

"Major league ball game?"

He looked in again, and with a sly glance said, "OK, but who's playing?"

1802 Texas Crisis. In Dallas the other day a psychiatrist was startled to have a native Texan walk in admitting that he had an inferiority complex!

1803 Not Stupid. Helen's mother loves to tell of the man who had a flat tire near the mental institution, as an inmate looked on. He put the nuts in the hubcap while changing the tire, accidentally tipped the cap and the nuts rolled down the drain. He was completely perplexed. The mental patient said, "Why not take a nut off each of the other three wheels and use them? That'll get you to a filling station."

"That's a great idea," said the motorist. "How could you think of that?"

"I may be crazy, but I'm not stupid," replied the mental patient.

1804 What's It About? A man showed up at the office of "Believe-it-or-Not Ripley." He removed his hat politely, revealing a tulip growing from his head.

"I want to see Mr. Ripley," he told the receptionist.

"What's it about, please?" she asked.

1805 You're the Ninth. A visitor to a mental institution saw a patient fishing in a little ornamental pond where there could be nothing but goldfish, if that. Thinking he would humor the man, he asked, "How many have you caught?"

"You're the ninth," replied the fisherman.

1806 Cream Or . . . ? To occupy the time with a mental patient a visitor was exchanging small talk. It developed that they both liked strawberries, and the visitor grew them. "What do you put on yours?" asked the patient.

"I like to use manure," said the visitor.

"Here we use cream on ours," said the mental patient.

1807 Rooster. He had been going to the psychiatrist for ten weeks because he heard a rooster crowing. Then there was a fire in his apartment house, and he saw, rushing down the hall, a fellow dweller with a rooster under his arm!

1808 Sure Winner. One psychologist says that any girl in the world can marry any man in the world by repeating to him over and over four words, "You are so wonderful!"

1809 Psychological Division of Labor:
> Neurotics build air castles.
> Psychotics live in them.
> Psychiatrists collect the rent.

1810 Getting Mileage. Psychologists use the term "grief work," borrowed from bereavement, to apply to any loss. In a class a girl told of having had a traveling bag stolen five months before. "Got another one?" asked the prof.

"Not yet," she replied.

"Getting a lot of mileage out of the old one, eh?" he wanted to know.

1811 What Trouble? An older man went to the psychiatrist. "I'm having trouble with my memory," he said. "Doc, I need help."

"Give me an example of this difficulty," the doctor requested.

"What difficulty, Doc?" asked the patient.

PSYCHOLOGICAL EXPERIMENTS:

1812 Caffein in Milk. They took two groups. The first was to report how they slept after drinking milk at night and the second, after coffee. The milk actually had had caffein added and the coffee drinkers drank decaffeinized coffee. Most of the milk drinkers slept soundly; most of the coffee drinkers reported tossing and turning!

1813 Last Chance. A psychology class inserted an ad in a publication, "Last chance to send in your dollar," and gave their address. Several dollars were sent in without any knowledge of what it was for.

1814 Hang Yourself. Another psychology group tested the reading of petitions by the general public. They typed up a long one; the leading words implied that the signer supported some such issue as a school lunch program, but in the middle it asked that the petitioners below be "hanged by the neck until dead." Without reading it, many people signed willingly.

THE WORLD OF JUSTICE

Crime

1815 Ignorance No Excuse. If you could learn ten a day of the two million laws in the United States and remember them, you'd be all set in six thousand years! Ignorance of the law is no excuse.

1816 Kleptomania.

"What is this kleptomania that you read about so much? Is it catching?"

"No. I'd say it's taking."

1817 Reaping. She was speaking to various prisoners in the garment shop. To one she said, "Sewing?"

He looked up, "No, reaping!"

1818 Coining Money!
Visitor: "Did poverty bring you to this prison?"
Prisoner: "No, ma'am. As a matter of fact, I was really making money!"

1819 Explanation. A jury is twelve men chosen to decide who has the best lawyer.

1820 No Cop!
"Have you seen a policeman around?"
"Sorry, but I haven't."
"Then give me your watch and wallet!"

1821 Bailiff What? The stylebook said not to write "bailiff of court." What else could there be a bailiff of?
"Hay."

1822 Overshoe Back? The community was aghast when the jury brought the verdict, "Not Guilty." When the judge freed the prisoner, he said, "If you don't need my overshoe [the chief evidence], may I have it back?"

The Judge

1823 Not Blaming. Judge: "We're not blaming you—we're just fining you."

1824 Chicken! The judge handled the fresh guy who called a girl "chicken." He got her weight and set the fine at the going rate per pound for chickens.

1825 Drunk? Judge: "Just because a man was on his hands and knees in the road doesn't prove that he was drunk."
Policeman: "Even when he was trying to roll up the white line?"

1826 Justice! Two Supreme Court justices were on a ship together, one seasick.
"Can I do anything for you?" asked the other.
"Yes," replied the sick one, with a gasp. "Overrule the motion!"

1827 Smart Guy!
Judge: "Do you know any members of the jury?"

Witness: "Some."
Judge: "Half of them?"
Witness: "I know more than all of them put together!"

1828 Smart Judge. Several housewives were really in a heated argument in the court. The judge solved it all by saying, "I'll hear the oldest first."

1829 What Time?
Judge: "Have you ever been up before me?"
Accused: "I don't know. What time do you get up?"

1830 Fair Trial. Two parties in a lawsuit tried to bribe the judge, who had a reputation for rough and ready justice. He announced in court, "I have a check for one thousand dollars from the plaintiff and one for two thousand dollars from the defendant. The court is going to return one thousand to the defendant and try the case strictly on its own merits."

1831 Forlorn Effort. The judge asked the defendant how he could be so callous as to marry six wives at the same time. "Please," said the defendant, "I was just trying to get a good one!"

1832 You Decide. The judge, hoping to make quick work of it, asked the defendant whether he were guilty or not guilty. "And what," said the defendant, "are you put there for but to find that out?"

1833 Very Little. It was a warm case, a dull day. The rights of the river regulators were being debated and the judge went into a doze.
"But we must have **water!**" insisted one, loud enough to bring the judge to his senses.
"All right," agreed the judge. "But very little in mine!"

1834 Clever Dodge. When they were giving the new juror the oath, he said, "I can't hear what you say!"
"Are you deaf?" asked the judge.
"In one ear," said the juror.
"Then you must be replaced," said the judge. "The jury must hear both sides."

The Lawyer

1835 Face a Mirror? An overbearing lawyer, trying to browbeat a witness, told him that he could see a rogue in his face. "Till now," said the witness, "I never knew that my face was a mirror!"

1836 Never Alone.

Lawyer: "Did the defendant talk with himself when alone?"

Witness: "I never was with him when he was alone!"

1837 Ever Walk a Dog? The prosecutor was firm. "While you were taking the dog for a walk, did you stop anywhere?"

"Sir," said she, "did you ever take a dog for a walk?"

1838 Twenty-four Hogs. The rather inexperienced lawyer on his first case was helping a farmer prosecute a railroad for killing twenty-four hogs. "Twenty-four hogs, gentlemen," he said. "Think of it—twenty-four. Twice the number that are there in the jury box!"

1839 How Far? The browbeating prosecutor asked a witness, "How far were you from those front steps?"

"Fourteen feet, seven inches," replied the witness.

"How came you to be so exact, pray tell?"

"I knew some fool or other would ask me, so I measured it," replied the witness.

1840 Worthless? The prosecutor was rough. "Do you ever work?" he asked a slow witness.

"Not much."

"Ever earn as much as ten dollars a week?"

"A few times."

"Your father regularly employed?"

"Nope."

"Isn't it true . . . that he's a worthless good-for-nothing too?"

"Ask him. He's sittin' right there in the jury box!"

1841 Beardless Youth? When Clarence Darrow was young, another attorney accused him of being "a beardless youth." Darrow replied that the king of Spain once sent a youthful ambassador to the court of a neighbor, who protested that he was a beardless boy.

The young ambassador replied, "Sire, if my king had supposed that you imputed wisdom to a beard, he would have sent a goat." Apparently that won the case for Darrow.

1842 Nobody's Thinking. Two bright young lawyers were working in shifts for the defense, but the plaintiff had only one lawyer. Plaintiff wanted another.

"Why?" asked his lawyer.

"Well," said the plaintiff, "when one of them other fellers is up speakin', the other is settin' there thinkin', but when you're speakin', they ain't nobody thinkin'."

1843 Would Have Scared Me! One lawyer made such a loud summation of his case in court that his opponent had to do something. So he told this story: "You know the fable of the lion and the ass? The ass was to scare the animals out and the lion would catch them. The ass practiced, and asked the lion what he thought of it. Would that scare them? 'Scare them!' responded the lion. 'You'd have scared the daylights out of me if I hadn't known that you were a jackass!'" The story won the case.

The Police

1844 Pinched. He looked pinched as he rode down the street. That was appropriate. He was in the patrol wagon.

1845 Mile Away. The stout lady said to the policeman, "Could you see me across the street?"

"Lady," he said, "I could see you a mile away!"

1846 Police Shoes. He called his shoes "police shoes" because they had a tendency to pinch his feet.

1847 Impatient. One testy citizen refers to the police as "a never-present help in time of trouble."

1848 Exit.

Sheriff: "Did he get away? Why didn't you guard all the exits?"

Deputy: "We did. He must have gotten away through one of the entrances."

1849 Clubbed Again. A solid citizen excitedly called the police. "As I stepped out the back door in the dark, a man rushed up and hit me with a club."

A young policeman was sent over to investigate. He returned with a knot on his head.

"Wonderfully fast work!" said the boss. "How did you do it?"

"I stepped on the rake too," said the young copper.

1850 Faith in Human Nature. It was dull at the police station, but one of the men in waiting said to the rest, "I think things will pick up later. I still have faith in human nature."

1851 Flew Away. The sheriff was scolding his deputies. "Did you catch the car thief?"

"Was he lucky!" exclaimed the deputy. "We were chasing him and almost had him, when the thousand miles were up on the car and we had to have the oil changed!"

The Nation's Highways

1852 Limit. "Let's hit one more pedestrian, and then go home."

1853 Safety Slogan. Drive as if a police car were ahead of you.

1854 Too Young.
"You're letting your son drive the car?"
"Sure. He's still too young to be trusted as a pedestrian."

1855 Limited Driver. The Texan said that his son didn't have a driver's license, so he just let him drive his Cadillac around in the house.

1856 No Centipede! The pedestrian loudly demanded compensation from the driver when the car went over his foot. "I want one thousand dollars!" he said.

"A thousand dollars?" screamed the driver. "I'm not a millionaire!"

"Yeah," said the victim, "and I ain't no centipede, neither!"

1857 Coming Back. An elderly motorist who couldn't see too well was going the wrong way down a one-way street.

"Do you know where you're going?" asked a policeman.

"No," he admitted, "but I must surely be late. Everybody else is coming back!"

1858 Where's My Trailer? The policeman waved a driver over to the side, insisting that he had no taillight. The man went around to look, and cried out in anguish.

"It's not as bad as that," said the officer.

"It's not the taillight I'm worried about," said the man. "What's become of my trailer?"

1859 Not More Than Twenty. A policeman overhauled a woman speeder.

"I couldn't have been over thirty-five at the most," she said. "In fact, officer, I think I was not going more than twenty."

"All right, lady, I'll tear up this ticket and give you one for parking."

1860 Fainted. Policeman: "How did you come to knock him down?"

Motorist: "I didn't. I just stopped to let him by, and he fainted."

1861 Hearing Tomorrow. "Didn't you hear me whistle?" asked the policeman.

"Sorry, I'm sort of deaf, officer."

"That's all right. You'll get your hearing tomorrow."

1862 Too Good.

"Officer, what was I doing wrong in my driving?"

"Nothing. You were doing so well that I thought you might not have your license."

1863 Like Any Other. Policeman to cute little thing: "Let me see your license."

"Well, I don't have it with me, but it's just like any other little old driver's license."

1864 Warning. Sign at a New Jersey intersection: "CROSS ROAD—Better Humor It."

1865 Window Open. A New York cop asserts that you are sure of one thing when a woman driver puts out her hand—the window's open.

1866 Know His Laugh. Policeman to pedestrian just struck by a hit-and-run driver: "Did you get his number?"

Victim: "No, but I'd know his laugh anywhere."

1867 Crook! He's not only a bad driver, he's a crook. We had a collision at Main and Broad and he gave me a drink to steady my nerves—then called the police.

THE WORLD OF POLITICS

1868 Mud Loses. Did you hear of the politician who refused to join in mudslinging, saying, "He who slings mud loses ground."

1869 Political Art. Sir Winston Churchill said that a politician must be able to foretell what will happen tomorrow, next month, or next year—and then explain why it didn't happen.

1870 Which One? When Hall Lusk was approached about possibly finishing out Senator Neuberger's Senate term, he called his wife. "How'd you like to be the wife of a U. S. Senator?" he asked.

She thought a moment on the other end of the wire. "Which one?" she wanted to know.

1871 Who Else? The pollster interviewing a man on the street was outlining the candidates and asking which one he would support. The man thought a minute and then asked, "Who else you got?"

1872 United States. The United States is a land with a President for a head, a Supreme Court for backbone, and Congress for lungs.

1873 Trust You. Years ago a farmer drove his team to town. He said to a well-dressed stranger, "Would you hold my horses for jest a minute?"

"Sir!" replied the stranger. "I'm a member of the Legislature!"

"That's all right," said the farmer. "I trust you!"

1874 Saint Peter? Said a voter, "I wouldn't vote for you if you were Saint Peter!"

"If I were Saint Peter," replied the politician coolly, "you wouldn't be in my precinct!"

1875 Time-Saver. Two candidates were speaking from the same platform. One spoke eloquently, promising great things. The other rose simply and said, to the approval of the audience, "Voters—all that he said, I will do!"

1876 Rain Better. Politician to farmer: "What did you think of my speech on the agricultural problem?"

Farmer: "Not bad, but a good day's rain would probably have helped more."

1877 Females Prohibited. A girl who applied for a position as a Senate page was told by Senator Joseph S. Clark that the reason the job is for males only is that sometimes pages must round up Senators from places where females are not permitted.

1878 Thankful. A voter listened to two candidates. "How do you feel about it?" he was asked.

"Thankful."

"What do you mean?"

"Thankful that at least they can't both get elected!"

1879 Washington Then. Everybody has not always admired "The Father of the Country." A prayer after George Washington's death frankly said: "We thank Thee that Thou hast taken the tyrant of the Potomac and given us our freedom back!"

1880 Bologna Sandwich. Did you hear about the cannibal who was hoping to capture a politician so that he could have a bologna sandwich?

AROUND THE WORLD

1881 Language Problem. "I hope I don't protrude," said the foreign gentleman as he crashed the party.

1882 Memory Work. They're still chuckling in one country about a group of Americans trying to learn the language. The instructor was working hard with vocabulary. "Hand. Elbow. Shoulder," he would say, pointing to each place. None of the pupils seemed to be able to do it, but finally one stood up and slowly said "Hand. Elbow. Shoulder," pointing correctly.

"Wonderful!" exclaimed the instructor. "How did you remember?"

The pupil pointed to his head proudly. "Good kidneys," he said.

1883 Forreigner? The folk dance expert Dave Rosenberg was on the subway in New York strap-hanging, his Tyrolian hat and leather pants making him conspicuous. A passenger eyed him carefully for quite a time, then leaned forward and said one word, "Forrrreigner?"

1884 Check This Pole. Sometimes people of other nationalities work in British mines. The first Pole was said to be Mr. Skrzpczak. His previous employment was as the bottom line of an optometrist's sight-testing chart.

1885 Age Space. "If the Russians get to Venus, they will find it boiling hot. If they get to Mars, they will find it freezing cold. On neither planet will they be able to breathe. The best of luck to them."—Astronomer Royal

1886 Two-Two. In the early days on the West Coast a Chinese passenger wanted to know the next train to San Francisco. "Two-two," said the agent. "Not **how** he go, but **when** he go," the passenger insisted.

1887 Sears Affluence. Examining a Sears Roebuck catalog, a Russian delegate to the U. N. asked, "Are these things all available to the masses?"

"Available!" exclaimed the American. "We have to **beg** people to buy them!"

1888 Truly American. After the couple's long study for their naturalization as United States citizens, the husband rushed home with the papers. "Maria! Maria!" he shouted. "We're Americans! We're Americans!"

"Good" responded Maria. "Now **you** wash the dishes!"

1889 More Intelligent? Is the man blowing his horn in a traffic jam more intelligent than the African drumming to keep spirits away? Or can we laugh at an African wearing a wool overcoat in hot weather when we wear hot suits for Oklahoma summer weddings. Or should we smile at the African chief who wears proudly a badge given by a colonial official when the American scholar decorates his watch chain with his Phi Beta Kappa key.

1890 Seeing? Westerners do not fully understand Middle Eastern, African, and Oriental minds. One learns not to "see" his host, even though he views him, until the host is properly dressed. At the Mandelbaum Gate between Jordan and Israel tours sometimes cross from Israel to Jordan, which is said to be impossible, because under certain conditions they are not "seen" doing it.

1891 Thoughtful Care. Knowing how Caucasians feel about eating from a common pot, some primitive folk provided their visitors spoons, while they themselves continued to use their fingers as always.

1892 Gesture Only. Polite Filipinos wipe their chairs with their handkerchiefs, and even give the silver a going-over with the napkin. This is no insult to the hostess, but only custom. In some parts of Africa the people sit to honor a guest (making him taller) instead of standing.

1893 Secret Ballot. At the polls the Russian peasant was about to open the envelope which had been given him to drop into the ballot box. He wanted to see who he was voting for. "Certainly not," said the official. "This is a secret ballot."

1894 Women Over Men. They never place women on the second floor of the Thai hospitals. That would be taboo—to place women over men!

Customs and Cultures*

1895 See a Psychiatrist. Tradition says the Mar Thoma Church of India was established by St. Thomas. A student from that church roomed in a United States college with an American boy who had no religious background. When the Mar Thoma youth knelt by his bed to pray, his roommate thought he was crazy and recommended a psychiatrist.

---

* This and other information about culture from *Customs and Cultures*, by Dr. Eugene Nida (New York: Harper & Row, 1954), used by permission.

1896 Laughing on the Outside. The Chols of Mexico laugh at tragedy. When they heard the story of the beheading of John the Baptist, they laughed to keep from crying.

1897 Alphabet Soup? The Marshall Islanders, watching how Europeans seemed to cherish the mail, thought it was good to eat. Once they got hold of the mail packet, tore letters to bits, and cooked them.

1898 All Floors Dirty. An American in Mexico was trying to help the people learn sanitation. "Please don't spit on the floor," she said. "It's dirty. You should go outside to spit!"

"But Senorita," complained one of the men, "it's dirty outside too!"

1899 Four Reincarnations. Asked how he had enjoyed his reading of the four Gospels, a Buddhist said he had found them wonderful. Jesus had "made it" in four reincarnations. He lived, died; lived, died; lived, died; lived, died, and arrived in Nirvana!

1900 Sacred to Americans. To many peoples of the world there are three big sacred things to Americans: Turkey, Christmas Tree, and Santa Claus.

1901 Strange Medicine. Two single women missionaries to the Pame-Chichimec Indians, in Central Mexico, drank lime juice as a health measure, for breakfast. The Indian folk were sure that they had secret lovers, and that actually they were using it as abortion medicine. In the language lime juice is called "baby killer."

1902 You Missionary! A South Indian teaching in Ethiopia so incurred the wrath of a student that he first denounced him, and then called him the worst term he could think of: "Missionary."

1903 Heavenly Spanish! South Americans like to make people happy. A visitor to South America overheard the maid tell his wife that she spoke "beautiful Spanish." Actually, she spoke terrible Spanish.

"Where do people who tell such things go when they die?" he asked the maid.

"To heaven, of course," answered the maid, "for making people happy!"

1904 Included All, Said Nothing. An Oriental politician was doing a document to deal with some touchy problems. Finishing, he said, "We have included all and said nothing."

1905 Where Do You Love? The heart is not the only place where love is felt. The Karre people in French Equatorial Africa say it's in the liver. The Conobs in Guatemala say it's in the abdomen. The Marshall Islanders say it's in the throat.

1906 What Is Sorrow? The Habbe in French West Africa say, "My liver is sick." The Bambara, for sorrow, say, "My eye is black." The Mossi people say, "The heart is spoiled." The Uduks, on the Ethiopian border of Sudan says, "Sorrow is heavy stomach."

1907 "Empty-Headed": This is a high compliment in New Caledonia, because this compares you to a hollow tree which serves as an aqueduct to bring needed cool water to the people.

1908 Language Problems. Americans in foreign lands frequently make errors in using the native tongue. One told the servant to pray when he meant to order him to serve dessert. Another at the table called for "horse manure" when he meant "peanut butter."

One missionary answered the "call" to come to the altar for prayer, but she had misunderstood the invitation. It had been given for those who admitted being adulterers.

1909 Direction. Underground is the term used in England for the subway. An Englishman asked in New York how to get underground. "Drop dead!" was the uncourteous answer.

1910 Prime Insult. During World War II a British sailor walked over to a German prisoner and beat him unmercifully. His superior officers wanted to know why. "I didn't mind it so much when he called me names," said the sailor. "I didn't even get mad when he insulted our queen. But when he spat in our ocean. . . ."

1911 Tongue Twister! The English spelling of "aluminum" has one more "i" than the American, making it "aluminium."

In a British pot factory once a visitor asked, "Are you aluminium-ing 'um?"

"No," was the answer. "We're copper-bottoming 'um, mum!"

1912 Prisoner Source. Modern Australia still jokes about its population origin. A young lad asked his father, "What about England? What kind of a place is it?"

"Oh, lad," said the father. "It's a **terrible** place! That's where all the **prisoners** came from!"

1913 Mind Yer Business. At a football game an unknown fan was giving out with considerable noise. One of the locals went over to question him. "Are thee Yorkshire?"

"No."

"Are thee Lancashire?"

"No."

"Then mind thee own bloody business!" he said in the name of all.

1914 A Gift. All Scotsmen have a sense of humor. It's a gift.

1915 Remove Glasses. Going on a business trip, a Scotsman told his wife, "Dinna forget to take little Donald's glasses off when he isn't looking at anything!"

1916 Moose? A Canadian was showing his Scotch friend a mounted head—a moose. "A moose!" exclaimed the Scot. "Man, what are your rats like over here?"

—**Tid-Bits** (London)

1917 Greatest Country? In London the Scot and the American met. The American said he was from the greatest country in the world. "Mon, so dae I," replied the Scot, "but you dinna speak like a Scotsman."

1918 Help Later. When the Scot farmer fell into a well his wife offered to call a workman from his field to help. "What's the time?" asked the farmer. "Eleven thirty-five," said she. "Bide a wee, and I'll swim roon till their dinnertime," he said.

1919 Real Quiet! The Scot was marching around and playing his bagpipes enthusiastically in the tiny cottage when his wife asked him mildly if he could be a bit more quiet. He took off his shoes and marched around in stocking feet, still playing his pipes.

1920 Clever Metering. An African photographer friend of the authors has a clever way of using his light meter. When he is photographing white people, he meters the palm of his hand; for Africans, the back. It works out beautifully.

1921 Mazoe Dam Snake. Into Mazoe Dam in the citrus area of Rhodesia, a farmer had a big black hose, siphoning water to the fields. An African saw the hose there when he went to work and when he returned to his village. Excitedly he told the village, "Come over to Mazoe Dam and see the biggest snake you ever saw. It was crawling into Mazoe Dam when I went to work and hadn't finished when I came home!"

1922 That Is Right. Americans, mortgaged to the hilt for things they don't need, smile at Africans who for effect wear squeaky shoes and unneeded glasses.

1923 Can Be Civilized. A long-time resident of Africa from Britain was asked if he thought Africans could be civilized. "Certainly so," he replied. "I have known many who thought as little of a lie or an oath as any civilized European."

1924 Rough! An African who owned a car used to drive it over the rough reserve roads. When he'd hit an unusually rough bump, he'd pat the dash and say, "Sorry!"

1925 Like Your Ways! Chief Albert Luthuli of South Africa, who won the Nobel Prize for his book **Let My People Go,** says, "We Africans like your western ways. You just won't let us have them!"

1926 Tricky Language. Writing to the music specialist to invite him to come to a special village celebration, an African forgot that he had not invited the wife, so for a postscript he added, "And don't forget your wife's behind!"

1927 African Wisdom. At Kampala, Uganda, an Anglican priest told of teaching classes in Scripture to sons of chiefs on the West Coast of Africa. Once he gave them the problem of King Herod, who in pleasure offered up to half his kingdom for the dancing of the daughter of Herodius.

"Now, you boys have watched your fathers solve problems," he said. "What if you had this problem, and you made the offer of anything she wanted, and the girl came to you asking for the head of John the Baptist, but you didn't want to give her the head of John the Baptist. What would you do?"

Soon a hand was raised.

"I'd tell her," said the young blue blood, "that the head of John the Baptist was not in the half of the kingdom I was offering to her."

1928   Petrol? Essence?   A brash young European pilot came winging into a Congo airport and ordered his plane filled with "petrol." This is the term for gasoline in Britain, but in Congo it means kerosene.

"Don't you mean 'essence'?" asked the African.

"No," replied the pilot with self-assurance. "When I say 'petrol' I mean 'petrol.'" The African did as he was told. It took a full day to get the plane straightened out.

1929   Chameleon Story.   Why are the hands and feet of an African much lighter in color than the rest of him? There is a folk tale that the chameleon was sent up the mountain to ask the god what Africans should do to become white like the white man. The answer was, "Wash in the spring." But the chameleon was so slow that he didn't get back until the dry season. There was just enough water for the soles of the feet and the palms of the hands!

1930   Scandinavian Fun.   The Norwegians, Swedes, and Danes for centuries have had a kind of rivalry, but they also recognize their own characteristics. They say that if two each of Danes, Norwegians, and Swedes should land on a desert island the Danes would form a cooperative, the Norwegians would be fighting, and the Swedes would be waiting to be introduced.

Or, to say it another way, the Norwegian invents a product, the Swede patents it, and the Dane heads the sales force.

1931   Ingenuity.   In Iran a Volkswagen owner, finding two hubcaps missing, asked a boy selling lottery chances to get him two more. The boy showed up at his office with two shiny ones, and collected $4.75. When the man went out to his car he was shocked to see that now the other two caps were missing—he's bought back his own. Missing also was the boy.

American Indians

1932 Full Blooded?   At the blood donor's station the tourist eyed the Apache across from him. Finally he said, "Are you a full-blooded Indian?"

"No," replied the Apache. "I'm a pint short."

1933 Hopi Family.   "Do you ever have fights and trouble?" the tourist asked an Indian.

"Oh no," replied the Indian. "We are just a big Hopi family."

1934 DC 9.   The white visitor met the Indian chief, Brave Eagle, his son, Fighting Bird, and his grandson, DC 9.

1935 Ever Win?   As the Indian father and son were coming from the movie, the boy said, "Dad, don't we **ever** win?"

1936 Safe Here.   The white visitor on the reservation asked if it would be safe to leave his things in the wigwam. "Oh yes," assured his Indian friend. "There's not a white man in a hundred and fifty miles!"

1937 Space-Age Wisdom.   The old Indian, with his son, was looking from a height to a lovely valley below. The old one said, "My son, some day this will all belong to Indians once more. Palefaces go to moon."

1938 Ugh!   A solemn-faced Indian friend in Oklahoma asked, "What did Indian say when he first saw white man on bicycle?"

"I don't know; what?"

"Ugh!"

THE MILITARY

1939 Field Marshal Electric.   Now that everything is going up, we have heard that they're considering making General Electric, "Field Marshal Electric."

1940 Things In General.   The day after Thanksgiving the doctor was called to the home of the general. "What do you think is wrong?" he asked the officer's wife.

"Oh," replied the wife, "things in general."

1941 Right At Home. Sergeant: "All right—straighten up your stance, throw your shoulders back, button your coat."

Married recruit: "Yes, dear."

1942 Marine Admiral. Have you heard about the young admiral in the Marine Corps? He was in charge of all the vessels in the kitchen.

1943 All Day, Sir. The tough sergeant was getting tired of the raw recruits he was training. One dropped his gun, and that really set him off. "Step out of formation," he ordered. "Now, tell me . . . how long have you been in this man's Army?"

The recruit looked completely defeated. "All day, sir!"

1944 Help, Sir. The recruit was in the water over his head when he saw an officer coming by. He called out, "Help! sir!"

1945 Army Computer. The programmer put the word "yes" into the Army computer. It asked right back, "Yes, what?"

The programmer knew what to do. He replied, "Yes, sir!"

1946 Like to Jump! "Why are you in the paratroopers?"

"I like to be with people that like to jump!"

1947 Sure It Works! At a naval postgraduate school they were feeding material into a computer, and it would immediately give the solution. Once, just for fun, they fed the same material a second time. The machine gave them the answer right away, "Sure it works, Buster!"

1948 You Tell Them. Drilling a batch of raw recruits, the sergeant saw one constantly out of step. "Do you know they're all out of step except you?" he asked the offender.

"What?" asked the offender.

"I said they're all out of step except you."

"Well, you'd better tell 'em. You're in charge."

1949 Major Shirts. President Theodore Roosevelt prided himself on remembering names and faces. In a long reception line his tailor of former years came through and explained, "I'm the man that made your shirts."

"Major Shirts!" exclaimed Teddy. "How are things back at the old outfit?"

1950 Surprise Daddy. Daddy had been in the service for fourteen months, overseas. Little Bobby said to Mommy, "Let's surprise Daddy and get us a baby brother!"

1951 Who Said That? The recruits were absolutely exhausted after several hours of drilling. When they were at ease, a recruit muttered, "How wonderful is death!"
"Who said that?" demanded the sarge.
"I believe it was Shelley," answered the recruit, grinning weakly.

1952 Sharp Sentry. "Halt! Who goes there?"
"Nobody."
"Are you alone?"

1953 Sort of Ran.
"When they started shooting, did you run?"
"Not exactly—but I passed some that were running!"

1954 No Heart!
"The bullet went in me chest and came out me back," said the old soldier, describing a lively battle.
"If it did that," the friend reminded him, "it would have gone through your heart and killed you!"
The vet thought quickly. "Me heart was in me mouth at the time," he said.

1955 Freak at Home! The soldier was reading a letter to his buddies. He wasn't pleased. "Trouble at home?" asked one.
"No. But my wife wrote me that I wouldn't know Willie when I get home because he's grown another foot. Looks like we've got a freak in our family!"

1956 Being Helped. The chaplan walked up to one of the men sitting in the military chapel. "May I help you?" he asked.
"No, thanks," replied the young man. "I'm being helped!"

1957 No Relish. To the complaint that the bread wasn't too good, the commanding officer snapped, "If Napoleon had had that bread in Russia, he would have eaten it with relish."
"Yes sir," replied the representative, "but we haven't any relish!"

1958 Forever! Upon listening to an unending military speech, Irving Cobb once said, "Now I know why it is 'Stars and Stripes Forever.'"

1959 Swell Wedding. The military wedding was such a swell affair that they used puffed rice. And when the groom kissed the bride, a kid from one of the post families said aloud, "Is he putting the pollen on now, mama?"

1960 Unified Services. In a certain installation there was rivalry between two different branches until they sent in a shapely young gal to work in the top office. She quickly unified the services.

1961 Lose Bet.
"What must a man be to have a burial with military honors?"
"I think he has to be at least a captain."
"I lose my bet. I said he must be dead!"

1962 Large Order. The sign on the movie said "Service Men 50¢." A lady came up with a five-dollar bill and asked for six paratroopers and four marines.

1963 Admits It. The sergeant called out "Squads right."
A recruit muttered under his breath, "So now he admits it!"

1964 Honest Man. "What were you in the war?"
"A private," said the soldier. So Diogenes cheerfully blew out his lamp and headed for home.

1965 Targets. On a bulletin board for nurses in a military installation under "Targets for Tonight" were listed the men scheduled for shots.

1966 Army Salesman. Did you hear about the salesman who entered the Army and got a lot of orders? When he left, they asked if he got a commission. "No," he replied, "Straight salary."

1967 Forever. You ask what are the Army and Navy for? They are for ever!

1968 West Pointer? There was an ex-cadet who turned against West Point and was rotten to the corps! He said he was a West Pointer, but to tell the truth there was more resemblance to an Irish Setter!

1969 Marine Sweetheart. "You're the nicest soldier I've ever met," she said.

He was skeptical.

"Tell it to the Marines," he said.

"I have," she replied. "Lots of 'em!"

1970 Dirty Salt. A woman was fascinated with the tattooing on the Navy veteran. She asked the old salt, "I wonder if these tattoo marks would wash off!"

He replied, "Sorry—I couldn't say, lady!"

1971 Off His Chest. The chaplain offered to help the serviceman get his troubles off his chest. "I need to," said the caller. "I have the name of the wrong girl tattooed there!"

1972 Gobs of 'Em.

"How many sailors are around Norfolk?"

"Oh, gobs of 'em!"

1973 Sign Here! A young man of draft age went into the recruiting station. "How is the quickest way to get to Vietnam?" he asked.

"Well, you first will have to sign up."

"I'm ready. Do I have to have an examination?"

"Sure."

"Can't skip it?"

"No."

"Then what?"

"You'll have to have basic training."

"That'll slow me up."

"Yes, but it's necessary."

"Do they send you on a boat?"

"Usually."

"I want to fly. I want to get over there and into the action."

"You sound anxious."

"Yes, I want to be in the thick of the fighting. I want to be where the danger is."

"You sound like you're crazy!" the recruiter said.

The boy extended a paper quickly and said, "Sign here."

268 · *The Public Speaker's Handbook of Humor*

1974 Military Furlong. The mountaineer explained that his boy in the Army was being subjected to some disciplinary action. "He took a furlong!" he explained.

"Don't you mean a furlough?"

"Naw, he went too fur and stayed too long."

1975 Platoonic Love. That's what the girl called it, said Fred Russell, when she was in love with fourteen soldiers at the same time.

MODERN LIFE

1976 Modern Life: Spending money you don't have for things you don't want to impress people you can't stand the sight of.

1977 Snack: The pause that re-fleshes.

1978 Remember: These will be the good old days in 1988.

1979 Reindeer: Horse with TV antenna.

1980 Child: Creature standing halfway between an adult and a TV set.

1981 Racetrack: The only place where **windows** clean **people.**

1982 A Thought: "Nothing exceeds like excess!"

1983 Life's Meaning? A woman looked to heaven as she did her housework and intoned, "There must be more to life than having the whitest wash in the block, week after week!"

1984 Machine Age. Not too long ago a store in New York received an order. It was for an abacus. What's odd about that? It came from IBM!

1985 Contemporary Church. The woman said she didn't know whether to pray in it, at it, or for it.

1986 Perfume: "This perfume is so good it was banned in our Boston store."

1987 Terrible Day. "How was it at the office, dear?"

"Terrible. The computer stopped, and we all had to think!"

1988 Even Drinks It! Recently a friend put a dime into one of those coke dispensers that use cups. Only no cup fell, and the coke went right on through the grill, of course. He looked on in wonder. "Isn't it marvelous?" he said. "It even drinks it for you!"

1989 You Look Hungry. At the supermarket a woman crowded ahead of another. "I hope you don't mind," said she, carrying a can. "All I wanted was this catfood."

"Not at all," replied the other coolly. "You look hungry."

1990 Smart Man. The soap factory was afire, but a worker on the top floor was not really worried. He just waited for the foam to reach his floor, and then went down the lather!

1991 Modern Middle Age: When a man's favorite nightspot is in front of a TV set.

1992 Surrender! An unattended addressing machine in the Chicago firm that mails the **National Geographic** went haywire and sent to a sheepherder in the West 9,374 notices requesting renewal. The man walked ten miles to the post office and sent in his money, saying, "I give up. Renew."

1993 What Would You Do? A deputy sheriff in Michigan was called to the home of a woman who was getting police shortwave signals on her hearing aid.

1994 With Earplugs. There is said to be a new cigarette package containing earplugs for those who don't want to hear reasons that they should quit smoking.

1995 Stopped! A man who read that smoking was bad for the health gave up—reading.

1996 Want Cigarettes! A Michigan telephone operator heard money dropping into a public telephone. "What number, please?"

"Number!" called a horrified voice. "I thought this was a cigarette machine!"

1997 Modern Girls! "He's a cad, but he drives one!"

1998 Modern Parent: "I said perhaps, and that's final!"

1999   Modern Executive: Talks golf around the office all morning, and business around the course all afternoon.

2000   Modern Traveler: Flying East, he said, "I hate these locals. Denver, Chicago, and now Pittsburgh!"

2001   Modern Kid Superiority: "My father is more insecure than your father!"

2002   Modern Animals: The mouse in the experiment said, "When I press this thing, I make him give me a pellet."

2003   Modern School Singing: "O beautiful for Space-Age skies . . ."

2004   Modern Indians: One of the authors saw two little Indian boys with improvised bows and arrows chasing each other, playing Indian.

2005   Modern Oldster:
"Doctor, I'm worried about my eyesight. I keep seeing red and green lights, like traffic lights."
Doctor: "Have you seen an oculist yet?"
Patient: "Nope. Only red and green lights!"

2006   Modern Child-Sex Prediction.   A young doctor when he examines a pregnant patient, says to her, "It will be a boy." Then he writes, "girl" on a slip of paper, in the presence of the prospective mother, and drops it in the file. If it proves to be a boy, he says, "See, I told you." If she chides him about a wrong prediction, he says, "Remember that we wrote it down. Let's see what we wrote." The file, of course, shows "girl." "Ah, you just didn't remember," he says. And the poor mother is diverted.

2007   Modern Education: The teacher wrote that Billy excels in initiative, group integration, and responsiveness. "Now," she added, "if he can only learn to read and write . . ."

2008   Modern World-Traveler: In a land where he knew not the language, he showed the cab driver the picture of his hotel on a match cover. The driver nodded and smiled—and took him to the match factory.

2009 Modern Reader: One of them went to a bookstore to inquire, "Are any more of Mr. Gunther's 'Insides' out?"

2010 Modern Church Competition: "Our chimes have more wattage than your chimes!"

2011 Modern Father (to daughter): "I want you home by eleven."
"But, Daddy, I'm not a child anymore."
"That's why I want you home by eleven."

2012 Modern Insurance Problem: The wife said, "Double indemnity is not fair. In case of his natural death, you mean I only get half as much?"

2013 Modern Entertainment: Offered an airplane ride, the old lady said, "No sir! I'm gonna stay here and watch TV, like the Lord intended!"

2014 Modern Elevator Operator (muttering to self): "I'm not a man—I'm a yo-yo!"

2015 Modern Benediction. At a mythical conference bringing together the late Paul Tillich and Billy Graham, an ingenious diplomat was said to have given this blend benediction. "May the Ground of All Being bless you real good!"

2016 Modern-Day Theology. To understand it, and other theology, approach like an umpire at a ballgame:
Liberal: "I call 'em as I see 'em."
Fundamentalist: "I call them as they are."
Existentialist: "It's either a ball or a strike, but neither until I call it."

2017 Churchy Sign Language:
"Thou Shalt Not Smoke."
"This machine taketh. It giveth not."

2018 A Choice Churchy Knock-Knock: "Goliath down—thou lookest tired."

2019 Visited Regularly. A charity case gal wrote in to the office, "I have had no clothing for a year and have been visited regularly by the clergy."

2020 Wise and Foolish Versions. To some the Bible now comes in these.

2021 Vanished Ghost. In England a clergyman visited a home having a family ghost, who came to his bedside. The clergyman dispatched the fellow quickly by asking him for a contribution.

2022 Answer to Prayer. The new young preacher, unmarried, was doing a great job rounding up members. He was pleased to see a young widow among the worshipers one morning. "I want to welcome you," he said. "I prayed for you the other night for a whole hour."

"Why didn't you give me a buzz?" she asked. "I could have been over in ten minutes!"

2023 Analogy: As effective as an existentialist teaching Sunday school.

2024 Unusual Experience. Dr. James Doty tells of speaking in a home for the aged on the subject "My name is Joseph, father of Jesus." At the conclusion an old man came to him and said, "Young man, you've had an unusual experience!"

Drunks

2025 Who Would Walk? The motorist said to the policeman: "Shertainly I indend to drive. Can't you shee I'm in no condishun to walk?"

2026 Intoxication: To feel sophisticated and not to be able to pronounce it.—**Columbus Reporter**

2027 Nobody Driving. The judge asked, "Who was driving when you hit the other car?"

"Nobody," said the drunk triumphantly. "We were all in the back seat!"

2028 Fiddle Dee Dee! Caught driving right down the railroad track, a drunk was stopped by police. "Do you know where you are?" they asked.

"No," he said slowly.

"You're driving down the railroad track," they said.

He looked incredulous, then grinned. "Well, fiddle dee dee!" he said.

2029 Good-Bye. Intoxicated man, stopping a bus: "Does thish bus go to Forty-Shecond Street?"

"Yes," said the driver.

"Well, g'bye, an' God blesh you!"

2030 Not Even Indians. The drunk was going the wrong way down a one-way street.

"Didn't you see the arrows?" asked the policeman.

"No," he said slowly. "Ash a matter of fac', I didn' even shee the Indians!"

2031 At Cocktail Party: "Henry," said the wife, "don't take another cocktail. Your fash is getting blurred."

2032 Real Car. The intoxicated guest at a ritzy place said to the attendant, "Ish my car the one on the lef' or on the right?"

"Yours is the car on the left, sir," said the man. "The car on the right is a subjective phenomenon!"

2033 Yes, Why? The drunk got into the crowded elevator so that he was facing a jam-packed crowd. As they expressed up in the building he cleared his throat to say: "I s'pose you all wonder why I called thish meeting . . ."

2034 Monkey Cooked. In suburbia a drunk stopped to watch a backyard chef, with radio nearby, turning a chicken on his outdoor grill. Finally the inebriated one said, "I like your mushic, but your monkey is cooked!"

2035 Lost Cork. There was a drunk who told the judge that he had to drink what was in the bottle because he had lost the cork.

2036 Lost Fifty Pounds! A drunk put a dime in a parking meter and watched the arrow go over to 120 minutes. "Gosh," he said, "I've lost fifty pounds!"

2037 "How Flime Tyes," said Miss Gadabout at the cocktail party.

2038 Long Stairway. The drunk tried several times to get from the curb up onto the sidewalk. "Long stairway," he muttered to himself.

2039 Lousy TV. The drunk staggered into a Launderette, sat down, and watched the clothes tumbling for several minutes. He got up, shuffled out, and muttered, "That televishion wasn't so hot!"

THE NEWSPAPERS

2040 Not a New. When he was a New York editor, Horace Greeley insisted that the word **news** was plural. Once he wired a reporter on the job in Miami: "Are there any news?"

The reporter wired right back: "Not a new!"

2041 Small-Town Newspaper. The reason the circulation stays steady, said one small-town editor, is that everybody knows everybody else's business. It's just that they want to see if they got caught at it!

2042 First In Everything! A newspaper in Kansas advertises itself as "First with the news. First with the corrections." A California intermittent sheet in a resort town said it had "most of the news, some of the time!"

2043 Newspaper? A little boy said it tells you who won, and who's been murdered. Another called it, "Same things happening to different people."

2044 Don't Read 'Em. The customer said to the small boy selling papers, "Son, don't they make you tired?"

"Naw," replied the boy. "I don't read 'em!"

2045 Thanks, Subscriber! Sometimes the editor of the weekly newspaper was given farm produce. He acknowledged it in the paper. "We have received some fine grapes from our friend, B. D., for which he will please accept our thanks, some of which are nearly two inches in diameter!"

2046 Apology Demanded. The politician was raging at the editor. "You have insulted me. I demand an apology in the paper," he said.

"Now wait a minute," said the editor. "Didn't I run the story of your resignation as city treasurer just as you gave it to us?"

"Yes. But you put it in the column for 'Public Improvements.'"

2047 Communication Note. For delivering news, the "femail has been found more rapid than the mail or the newspaper.

2048 Correction. The musicians objected strenuously to an article stating that "half of the musicians are screwballs." The paper printed its retraction: "Half of the musicians are not screwballs!"

2049 Editor-In-Chief. In cannibal territory a managing editor was captured. "What was your business before you were captured?" he was asked.

"I was a managing editor of a paper!"

"Cheer up. Promotion is near. After dinner you will be editor-in-chief!"

2050 Wonderful Paper. "Dear Sir. I want to thank you for your fine paper. I lost my watch, and put an ad in your paper. I went home and found the watch in the pocket of another suit. You've got a wonderful paper!"

2051 Better Paper. In London two men were walking down the street, one saying, "The **Times** is better," and the other, "The **News of the World** is better."

A man broke into their conversation to say, "I happen to be an editor of the **Times**." To the **Times** defender, "Why do you like the **Times** better?"

The man was apologetic. "We're fish and chips dealers," he said. "My friend says the **News of the World** holds the vinegar better, and I say the **Times** does!"

THE WORLD OF RELIGION
(See also "Kids in Church," 956–989)

2052 Speak Loudly. A visiting clergyman in an English church asked advice of the custodian.

"Speak loudly," he advised. "The agnostics hear poorly."

2053 Ain't Goin'. When his kids were young, W. R. Rollins said, one of them asked if there were services that evening.

"Yes," he replied.

"Who's preaching?"

"I am," he said.

"Then we ain't goin'," the kid said.

2054 Whither? At a conference center a speaker mentioned his new book, **Whither Shall I Go?** Later, a woman delegate went to the bookstore, leaned over the counter, and said to the new clerk, "Whither Shall I Go?"

The clerk looked up. "Right down the hall, second door to the left!" she said.

2055 Conscience: Defined by an Indian as "a triangular piece in my insides that is active when I do wrong."

2056 Christian? A visiting revivalist in a Virginia church was going up and down the aisles. In the community was a family named Christian. "Are you a Christian?" he asked a teen-aged boy.

"Yes," replied the boy.

To the boy's companion he said, "Are **you** a Christian?"

"No," said the boy, "I'm a Gollehon."

2057 Lily of the Field. The census taker asked the lady of the house what was her occupation. In a mood of poetry the lady answered, "I toil not, neither do I spin." Unabashed, the census taker wrote, "Lily of the field."

2058 Better Work. The kid said, "Dad, did God make you?"

"Yes."

"Did he make me?"

"Yes."

"Doing better work lately, eh?"

2059 Sufferer.

"There's a woman who suffers for her convictions."

"How's that?"

"She has the conviction that she can wear a size five shoe on a size seven foot!"

2060 Delayed Conversion. What is the use of anticipating an eleventh-hour conversion when you may die at ten thirty?

2061 Choosing Hymns. The minister gave a spinster the opportunity to choose the hymns as they stood near the front of the church. Grinning and pointing, she said, "I'll take him . . . and him . . . and him!" Then she said that actually she'd like "Blest Be the Tie That Binds."

2062 Faith: It's sort of like a bath. Nobody else can do it for you.

2063 No Grandchildren. God has many children, but no grandchildren.

2064 Resisting. The average number of times people say "No" to temptation is once weakly.

2065 Lost? In a rural community a revivalist asked a dweller if he were lost.
   "No," replied the man, "I live right up the road, three houses."

2066 Eternal Question: Why is it that the same people who won't sit in the front seats in church do nothing else when riding the bus?

2067 Two Kinds. There are two kinds of people—the good and the bad. The classifying is always done by the good.

2068 Kind of Life. On the elevator a nervous shopper asked the operator, "If the cable broke, would we go up or down?"
   "That, madam," replied the operator, "depends entirely upon the kind of life you've lived."

2069 Trademark. An apple is the trademark of a Milwaukee tailor. He explains it simply. "If it weren't for the apple, where would the tailoring business be today?"

2070 Great Faith! A woman asked her clergyman to visit her husband in the hospital to pray for his healing. Afterward, outside the room, she said to the cleric, "I do hope you'll be able to have my husband's funeral."

2071 His Hobby? In a discussion some youngsters were asked, "Why did God make us?"

The answer bears some thought. "Maybe it's his hobby," one replied.

2072 The Trouble about dying and going below is, when you get mad at your friends, where do you tell them to go?

2073 Wonderful? In the days before electric pumps, a boy was usually hired to pump the organ. After a great concert the boy said to the famous organist, "Aren't we wonderful?"

2074 Powerful Man! He had the power of the Lord vibrating in his hand. Yes, he was the church bell-ringer.

2075 Boil. In the boarding house it was customary to have grace at the table. One boarder didn't bow his head.

"Atheism?" asked the mistress.

"Boil," he told her.

2076 Keeping Lent.

"Are you keeping Lent?"

"Certainly."

"Of what are you denying yourself?"

"Coffee. But to tell the truth, I like hot chocolate better anyway!"

Preachers and Preaching

2077 Modern Preaching. A fiery dissenter called modern preaching "a mild-mannered man, in a mild manner, trying to persuade mild-mannered people to be more mild-mannered."

2078 Reduced Heat. A preacher said, "I used to put a lot of hell in my sermons, but the congregation got to fanning so I had to ease up."

2079 Try Five Hundred. The young, inexperienced preacher was trying to lead the singing in the rural church, without the piano. He pitched "O, For a Thousand Tongues to Sing" too high. "Try for five hundred, son," advised a farmer from the pew.

2080 Safety in Exodus. The unmarried young preacher was trying to manage his matrimonial affairs by himself. Finally he moved to another post.

"Did you find safety in Numbers?" quipped a friend.

"Oh no," he answered, "in Exodus."

2081 Worth It. The former seminarians were bragging to each other. "When I leave my pulpit, my men say it costs them two hundred dollars," one said.

"Yes," countered the other, "and they tell me it's worth every cent!"

2082 The Winner. Two friends in Britain, where trainmen wear fancy uniforms and bishops wear cassocks, met after years of separation. One was now a bishop. He walked over to the other, a high-ranking military man, and said (as if he didn't recognize him at all), "Pardon me, guard, is this the train to Oxford?"

The other was ready for him instantly. "Certainly, madam," he said, "but do you think you should be traveling in your condition?"

2083 Save the Seeds. The hotel was serving watermelon to two gatherings, one of preachers and one of salesmen. The order for the salesman was for spiked melon, but the kitchen got it mixed and gave that to the preachers. Upon investigation, the manager found the salesmen disgusted with their plain melon, but the preachers picking out the seeds and putting them in their pockets.

ADDRESSING THE DEITY:

2084 "**Paradoxically** as it may seem to thee, O Lord . . ."

2085 "**As our Lord** says in the Sermon on the Mount—and he's right—"

2086 "**O Lord,** as you saw in **The New York Times** this morning . . ."

2087 **A minister,** in the pulpit just after his first book was published, said, "O Lord, who hath also written a book . . ."

2088 But Be Quiet. A drunk sitting by a collared clergyman on a bus, said, "There ain't no heaven."

After the drunk had made three tries, the man of the cloth turned calmly to him and said, "Well, go to hell, then, but please be quiet about it!"

2089 Inadequate Pastor. They were taking a special collection to supplement the inadequate salary of pastors in small churches. On one check was written, "For some inadequate pastor."

2090 Ministerial Call. One clergyman-with-collar says to another, "I've got a call to St. Dunstan's-in-the-Meadow. Twelve thousand smackers a year!"

2091 Approval. The minister asked his son, "Do you think the congregation reacted favorably to my message of the morning?"

"I'm sure of it, Dad," said the son. "I saw several of them nodding all through the service."

2092 Fire! John Wesley, preaching to a drowsy congregation, once called out suddenly, "Fire! Fire!"

"Where?" asked a startled listener, awakening.

"In hell, for those who sleep before the message," warned Wesley.

2093 Tweedle Something. A minister named Tweedle reluctantly refused a Doctor of Divinity degree. He said that he'd rather be "Tweedle dumb" than "Tweedle, D. D."

2094 Meddlin'. A rural preacher was really letting 'em have it on dancing, card-playing, smoking, tobacco-chewing. The old lady in the front was encouraging him along, "Preach it, brother!" Then he got onto snuff-dipping. "Now you've stopped preachin' and gone to meddlin'," she said, disgusted.

2095 Where? "Where would we be without sin?" asked one preacher of another.

2096 Preaching. "A good text should be the gate leading to green pastures, and beside still waters, and to restored souls. Most of us just swing on the gate," said a pastor.

2097 Spiritual Test: "If you arrived, where would you be?"

2098 All Provided. The preacher was waxing warm indeed. "There will be weeping and wailing and gnashing of teeth," he shouted.

"I have no teeth," called out one of the congregation.

"Teeth will be provided," he answered quickly.

2099 Revealing. "Dr. _____, it has been so good to have you with us. We just didn't know what sin was until you came."

2100 Embarrassing Moment. Going down the home stretch of his sermon on the wise and foolish virgins, the late Dr. Eiselen, then president at Garrett Seminary, said earnestly: "Young men, would you rather be in the **light** with the wise virgins . . . or in the **dark** with the foolish virgins?" (The young men made their choice right away. Soon chapel was dismissed.)

2101 Object of Prayer.

"Preacher, will you pray for something for me?"

"Certainly. What is it?"

"Last week you prayed for the loose-livers. I have a floating kidney."

2102 Okey Dokey. At the altar with a penitent woman whose mouth was filled with chewing gum was a Kentucky mountain preacher, seeking to help her.

"What do you want the Lord to do for you?" he asked.

She shifted her wad of gum and said, "Save me!" in a loud voice.

"What're you doing about it?"

"I ast him."

"And what did He say?"

"He . . . said . . . 'OKEY DOKEY!'"

2103 Changed Subject. An eccentric clergyman knew how to get an audience. He announced that he was going to preach on sex. The church was crowded. "I've changed my mind," he told his packed crowd. "I'm gonna preach on **tithing!**" And he did.

2104 Can't Win. Going along the road, the farmer with a Sabbath load of hay met his pastor, to his embarrassment. He explained it, "Don't know whether it's better to be in church thinking of this hay, or to be with the hay thinking of church."

2105 Kiss Me! The nephew of an ultra-dignified minister gave his uncle as a Christmas present a beautiful dark blue tie overprinted with phosphorescent letters, "Kiss me!"

2106 Poor Preacher. Trying to get a price reduction, the clergyman said to a merchant, "Remember—I'm just a poor preacher."

"Yes," said the merchant, "I know. I heard you last week."

2107 His Congregation. He was a shoestore salesman during the week and a volunteer preacher on weekends. "I have about seventy-five soles and the same number of heels," he said, describing his membership.

2108 Hunting Money. The priest, hearing a sound at night, discovered a burglar. "I'm hunting money," said the thug.

"Just a minute until I get a light," said the priest. "I'll join you."

2109 Monastery Wisdom. Refused his request to smoke while praying, a monk was corrected by another. "You should have done as I did," he said. "I asked if it was all right if I prayed while smoking!"

2110 Leaf Between. At a banquet, seated between a minister and a rabbi, a woman quipped, "I feel like a leaf between the Old and New Testaments."

To which the rabbi replied, "That page, madam, is usually blank!"

2111 Halo's Too Tight. A young man to a doctor with a headache.

"Do you smoke, drink?"

"No."

"Chase women?"

"No."

"Stay out late?"

"No."

"I have it—maybe your halo's too tight!"

2112 Yes, Surely! The receptionist was trying to keep the clergyman from her boss's office. The parson was not to be outdone. "I talk with God daily," he said. "Surely I can have a few minutes with your boss."

2113 Substitute Spirit. A clergyman, given to drama in worship, had a dove in the high gallery, to be thrown down on the cue "The Holy Spirit descended like a dove" by the janitor. At the proper time he gave the cue words, three times. After the third, the voice of the janitor was heard, "The cat ate the Holy Spirit. Do you want me to throw the cat down?"

Denominations

2114 Lifelong Member. "I'm a lifelong member of that church," said a "member."

"How's that? I never see you in church."

"I was baptized there!"

2115 Dog Funeral. They came to the minister for a dog funeral.

"Dogs don't have souls," said he.

"Certainly not, but there was five hundred dollars in the will of his owner for his burial when the dog died," said the attorney.

The preacher shifted gears quickly. "Why didn't you tell me that Old Shep was a Baptist," he said.

2116 No Place for That. In a stiffly liturgical church the preaching was warm and a Methodist let go with an "Amen." A white-gloved usher came to his seat and waved a cautioning finger at him. The sermon waxed stronger, and he responded again, louder. The usher was at his side in an instant, warning him, and shushing him.

"But I've got religion," cried the Methodist.

"This is no place for that!" said the liturgical usher.

2117 No, Not One. Two churches on opposite corners had their singing at the same time. One sang, "Will There Be Any Stars in My Crown?" And the other was singing, "No, Not One!"

2118 Thriller. The Anglican Bishop of the Johannesburg Diocese was having a meeting of priests and their wives. The stern, frightening bishop suddenly accosted a timid wife. "What are you going to do this afternoon?" (The women were not meeting with their husbands.)

"I guess I'll . . . go to bed . . . with a thriller!" she said hesitatingly.

"And . . ." thundered the bishop, "which one of us might that be?"

2119 Dry Cleaned. The Baptists and Methodists were discussing their churches. "Your problem is, you've been dry-cleaned," said the Baptist.

2120 Singer. Her singing was the kind that was used to augment grief at funerals.

2121 Rest In Peace. The lodge brothers ordered the finest floral pieces with "Rest in Peace" on one side. They said on the telephone to the florist, "And put on the other side, 'We shall meet in heaven,' if there is room." They were shocked to see the end result, a display saying, "Rest in Peace on one side. We shall meet in heaven if there is room."

2122 Safe Arrival? There were two men of the same name, and one had just died. The other wired home from a trip, but the message was given to the widow by mistake. "Just arrived. Heat terrific."

2123 "Cousin." They rushed the visiting clergyman into the little church where the funeral was ready to begin, without telling him at all who was dead. Already the mourners were singing.

He leaned over to a weeping relative, thinking at least to get the sex straight. "Brother or sister?" he asked.

The reply was brief. "Cousin!"

2124 Corpse. "This corpse has been a member of this church for thirty-two years."

2125 True Baptist. Baptist loyalty is often envied by other churches. One Baptist preacher was letting go with all stops out. "If Jesus could walk sixty miles to be baptized by a Baptist preacher . . ." he began.

2126 In My Seat. It was a terribly cold day in the little rural community in Pennsylvania. A stranger to the community went to the Quaker meeting house and found himself completely alone. He took a seat and meditated. At about the normal time for the service to end, he heard the front door creak open, and in walked a gentle Quaker who came to his side and said softly, "Friend, thee is sitting in my seat!"

2127 Plain Doctrine! The Mennonite lady asked her missionary if she taught the doctrine of plain clothes on the mission field. "Plain clothes, indeed," cried the missionary. "We're lucky if we get them to wear anything at all!"

2128 Pretty Warm. A little boy said, "It was so warm that I felt the Presbyterians running down my back!"

2129 No Difference. Kermit Long quotes a little boy as saying, "It don't make any difference what abomination you belong to . . ."

2130 Predestined? The Presbyterian was quite outdone with Methodist looseness. "I'd rather be a Presbyterian, predestined to go to hell," he said with feeling, "than to be a Methodist and not know where the hell I was going."

2131 Episcopalians Around? Taking a survey in a remote area, the question was asked, "Any Episcopalians around here?"

Ma thought a minute. "Pa has shot and skinned just about anything. You might find some of them over at the barn."

2132 Acoustics. "And what do you think of the acoustics?" asked the minister of the visitor who had just been shown the new sanctuary.

"I believe in letting everybody worship as they please," was the answer.

2133 Where We Baptize. A Methodist and a Baptist were arguing the virtues of their baptisms. The Methodist said, "All right, if I take a man and lead him in the water to his ankles, is he baptized?"

"Nope!"

"Till just the top of his head is showing above the water. Is he baptized?"

"No," said the Baptist.

"All right, then," asserted the Methodist, "that's where we baptize."

2134 That's Why! A Colorado Episcopalian once was accounting for the greater number of denominations other than his own. "In pioneer days, one denomination forded icy streams and came out with the wagons," he said. "When the trains carried day coaches, the second one came. When they put on the pullmans, we came."

2135 Heaven! A story of heaven says that people were doing things there that they couldn't do on earth. Methodists were playing cards, Baptists were dancing, Church of Christ was singing with instruments, but one group were just sitting with hands folded, doing nothing. Why? They were from a denomination that could do **anything on earth!**

2136 Irrigated. A Mormon told this story at a meeting. A man died, went below. There things were so far different from what he had expected. "I had expected it to be hot, dry, barren, and here are little rivulets running around, green grass everywhere."

"It used to be like you say," said an old inmate, "until those Mormons came down and just irrigated the hell out of it!"

2137 That'll Do It. A Quaker is said to have threatened his cow, "If thee does that again, cow, I'll sell thee to a Lutheran, who will know what to do with thee."

2138 Unbaptized. Larry claims to be one of the few "unbaptized" people alive. He went to an American Baptist meeting at Green Lake, Wisconsin. They insisted on "baptizing" him by tossing him into the swimming pool. Then, as he was ready to go back to the Methodist, they used a toy sprinkling can to "sprinkle" him in a public ceremony, thus "unbaptizing" him.

2139 Used All Three. Rev. Joe Baker said he's had sprinklings, pouring, immersion, all. Once a man who "wanted immersion" would not go under. Joe cupped his hand and poured water onto the man's head. Joe said, "Are you satisfied?"
"Yes."
"I am too," said Baker. That was it!

2140 Ecumenical. "It's nice to have these different kinds of people in the Bible," said the youngster. "There was John the Baptist, and Jesus the Presbyterian."

2141 Seating for Eight. A denomination, supposedly very narrow, sought through its office to get tickets to a big football game between SMU and Notre Dame. They needed eight seats. Two tickets were sent. When a check was made by telephone, the voice said, "We figured that you were narrow enough to sit in the space normally occupied by two."

2142 Keep Away. A Baptist friend reports that fifteen drops of rain can often keep away from church twenty-five water-minded Baptists. It could do the same to about fifty sprinkled Methodists.

2143 Cold Church. The church was said to be so cold that they used ice skates for their ushers.

2144 Walk This Way. To a woman worshiper the bowlegged usher said, "Walk this way, madam."

"I don't know," she said uncertainly, "but I'll try."

CHURCH SIGNS:

2145 In Arizona, during a heat wave of 105 degrees: "So you think it's hot here!"

2146 Seen Elsewhere. "This church is prayer-conditioned."

2147 Hallelujah! One bookie was correcting the other as they left church. "The word is 'hallelujah,'" he said, "not 'Hialeah.'"

2148 Favorite Indoor Sport: In churches it's confessing the sins of others.

2149 Risk One Eye. One Sunday when the church service was moving along smoothly, a young woman in the balcony leaned too far forward and toppled over the railing; fortunately her dress caught in the chandelier, and she was suspended in midair over the congregation. The clergyman pronounced solemnly as help was coming, "Any person turning to look will be struck blind."

A man whispered to his companion, "I'm gonna risk one eye."

2150 No Good Either. "Pop, when you were a boy, did you go to Sunday school?"

"Never missed a Sunday."

"Bet it won't do me any good, either."

2151 Who'll Teach His Class? The church treasurer stole twenty thousand dollars and ran off with the wife of the choir director. "Heavens!" said one of the members. "How awful! Who'll teach his Sunday school class?"

2152 Better Than Lot! The pupils learned about Lot's wife, who looked back and turned into a pillar of salt—which reminded Sammy of the time when his mother looked back while driving the car and turned into a telephone pole.

2153 Hold My Quarter! Two little boys came to the swimming pool in Louisville. One walked up to a strange woman and asked if she went to Sunday school.

"Yes," she replied.

"Then will you take care of my quarter while I'm swimming?"

2154 Sodom and Gomorrah. Sunday school teacher: "What was Dan and Beersheba?"

Pupil: "I think they were husband and wife almost like Sodom and Gomorrah."

2155 Amorite! Two theological seminarians liked to pun to each other. One said, "Habiru this morning?"

The other replied, "Amorite."

2156 Remember: It wasn't raining when Noah built the ark.

2157 Deserves Printing. A young priest, eager to please the congregation, memorized the "Sermon on the Mount" to give for his Sunday message. One of the congregation was tremendously impressed, and said, "Father, that's the best sermon I ever heard. And if you'll have it printed and distributed in this church, I'll foot the bill."

2158 First Base Man. It was Cain, who hated his brother as long as he was able.

2159 Boa! Adam and Eve were naming the animals. "That's a boa constrictor," said Adam.

"How do you know?" asked Eve.

"Because it looks more like a boa than anything we've seen so far."

2160 St. James' Bible. Many are confused about the origin of the King James translation, done in 1611. One loyal lady said, "If the St. James Bible was good enough for James, the brother of Jesus, it's good enough for me."

Prayer

2161 Pardon Me. A little girl interrupted her nightly prayer, "Pardon me, God, while I kick my brother."

2162 With Clothes On? A three-year-old, on the promise of being good, got to go to the church service for the first time. At a point in the service, all knelt. "What are they doing?" she whispered to her mother.

"They're going to say their prayers!"

"What! With all their clothes on?"

2163 Moment of Prayer. He was sleeping on the job when the boss caught him, but his imagination went to work quickly. "Can't a man have a few moments of prayer?" he asked.

2164 Take the Money. Their talk got to religion, and they bet each other that neither could pray. "I can," one announced. "I know the Lord's Prayer."

"Here's ten that says you don't," said the other.

The first one began, "Now I lay me down to sleep, I pray thee, Lord, my soul to keep . . . "

The other looked on in amazement. "Take the money," he said, "I didn't know you knew it."

2165 Be Reasonable. "We know we prayed for rain a few weeks ago, Lord," said a faithful one after a period of incessant rain, "But Lord, do be **reasonable!**"

2166 Keep You From Falling. Hearing the underpinnings of the temporary choir structure cracking, the harried parson grasped for a hurried benediction, which proved to be, "The Lord keep you from falling." He may be the same one who asked to "forgive us our falling shorts."

THE WORLD OF EDUCATION

2167 Teacher Wisdom: Most children are basically sound.

2168 Sign: Over a clock in school: "Time will pass. Will you?"

2169 Deep Thinking. Jack Waldrum said he fell into a well in the schoolyard in third grade, and did some of the deepest thinking of his life.

2170 Correspondence Hookey. My brother plays hookey from correspondence school. He mails in empty envelopes.

2171 Education. Mistress to maid: "Sarah, just look at this table. I can write my name in the dust."

"Yes, ma'am. There's nothing like education."

2172 Bee. A chrysanthemum by any other name would be—easier to spell.

2173 College Scene. "You must look at Oxford as a whole; and what a hole it is!"

2174 Students? In a school of about a thousand a visitor asked the principal how many students were there. He thought a minute and replied, "About two hundred."

2175 Entertainment. A visitor to a very small town wanted to know if there were a movie or any other entertainment in town. "No," said an oldtimer, "but come on to the drugstore. We've got a freshman home from college."

2176 Weightier. At its twentieth reunion, a Princeton class discovered that it had gained two and a half **tons** of weight!

2177 Wolf Antics. At the University of Alabama an enterprising student, acting as if he were a part of registration procedure, got from the blank of every pretty girl her name, age, address, and telephone number.

2178 Improvement Needed. What's the difference between a mental institution and a college? In the mental institution you must show improvement to get out.

2179 Often!

"At college here how much do they ask for your tuition?"

"Oh, about twice a day."

2180 Educated. "Whom are you," he asked, for he had been to night school.

2181 Graduation. The commencement speaker at Yale was using the letters in the school name for points. "Thank goodness," said a weary listener, "We're not at Massachusetts Institute of Technology."

2182 Automation. Men go to college to learn about automation, which makes man's work so easy that woman can do it all.

2183 No Excuse.
"But, officer, I'm a college student."
"You get the ticket. Ignorance is no excuse."

2184 Fortnight.
"I've been trying to think of a word for two weeks."
"What about 'fortnight'?"

2185 Electric Effect. The TV announcer said, "He swang at it." Whereupon seventeen sets in Boston burned out.

2186 Big Word. A movie producer wanted to see the sheepskin of the job applicant. Lacking that, he said, "Well, then, say a big word."

2187 Youth: Such a wonderful gift to waste on the young.

2188 Ought To.
Dean, to wife: "I'm going to stop this necking on this college campus."
Wife: "A man of your age ought to."

2189 Hirsute. In college he wore an installment moustache: a little down, a little more each week.

2190 Terms.
Student, to local boarding-house owner: "What are your terms for students?"
She: "I usually call them bums, loafers, and deadbeats."

2191 Cheaper.
Coed: "Daddy, the girl who sits next to me has a dress just like mine."
Dad: "So you want a new dress?"
Coed: "I think it would be cheaper than changing colleges."

2192 Slightly Confused. A student made 98 on a course, attending one lecture. When asked how, he said, "I'd have made a hundred, but the one lecture got me slightly confused."

2193 Logical. The instructor was scornful. "You say an effect can go before a cause. Would you kindly give me an example?"

"Sure," said the student. "A man rolling a wheelbarrow."

2194 Two Words. Said the professor, "There are two words that I want you never to use. One is 'swell' and the other is 'lousy.'"

"Good, prof," said the student. "What are they?"

2195 Not the Same.

Secretary: "Professor, isn't this the same exam you gave last year?"

Prof: "Yes, but I've changed the answers."

2196 Just Early.

Student: "Sorry, I'm late, prof. I'll be bright and early tomorrow."

Prof: "Don't promise too much. Just be here early."

THAT ABSENT-MINDED PROF . . .

2197 Sitting beside bed, shoe in hand. "Am I going to sleep or waking up?"

2198 With his wife, visiting another faculty member. The hour got later and later. Finally his host said, "It's quite late and you have a long way to go home . . . "

"My goodness," cried the visiting prof. "I thought I **was** home."

2199 Out West, he looked at the rope in his hand. "Either I've found a rope or lost a horse," he said to himself.

2200 Hoodla. The wife of a Latin professor, reading from the paper, said, "They were attacked by a gang of hoodlums."

"'Hoodla,' dear," gently corrected the prof.

2201 Thermometer. They called the prof "Thermometer" because of his many degrees. They called a friend of his "Sanka" because 97 per cent of the active ingredients had been removed.

2202 Sorry About That. Sophomore: "We modern students can tell exactly what a person is thinking."

Prof: "In that case, I humbly beg your pardon."

2203 Study Time. The father visited his son at college. The boy was sitting in a chair that had a note to his roommate pinned to its back: "If you come in and find me studying, wake me up."

2204 Sure Knowledge.
"My son is home from college."
"How do you know?"
"I haven't heard from him in three weeks!"

2205 Germless. The teller at the bank apologized for the dirty bills he gave the teacher for her salary check. "That's all right," she said. "No germs could live on my salary, anyway!"

2206 Father looking over son's report card: "One thing is certain —with grades like this, you couldn't be cheating."

2207 There was a father who signed his son's report card X. He didn't want the school to know that with grades so horrible, the kid had a literate father.

TEACHER AND PUPIL

2208 Good Work! Kid: "Dad, I was almost at the top of the list of those that failed."

2209 Warning! Eight-year-old to teacher: "I don't want to scare you, but my daddy says if I don't get better grades, somebody's gonna get spanked."

2210 With Options? A TV star's kid was asked if he were promoted. "Better than that, Dad. I've been held over for another twenty-six weeks."

2211 No Passing.
"That must be my teacher in the car up there ahead."
"Why?"
"He won't let me pass."

2212 Star Spangled What? The teacher played "The Star Spangled Banner," and asked the children what it was.

"That's easy," said one. "It's what they play on TV on Friday nights just before the fight."

2213 How's That? The first-grade teacher, after long years of repeated words, came out to her car with a friend to drive to school. Seeing a flat tire she said, "Oh, oh, oh. Look, look, look. Damn, damn, damn!"

2214 Nice Day. A little girl came to school one day with a note saying, "Candy just had to have a note. Nice day, isn't it?"

2215 Mixed Feelings. The school board gave leave of absence to a teacher who was "expecting," but also told her that they took a dim view of her contribution to the already overcrowded conditions.

2216 Casey Jones! Mother: "What did you sing at school?"

Son: "I don't know what the rest of 'em sang, but I sang 'Casey Jones.'"

2217 Clock Says. The teacher asked, "If the short hand of the clock is on six and the long hand on twelve, what does the clock say?"

One bright pupil answered: "Tick-tock!"

2218 She Likes Him. The teacher asked a little girl on the first day of school what was her father's name.

"Daddy."

"But what does your mother call him?"

"Nothing. She likes him."

2219 Don't Blame You. The teacher asked, "Do you know how matches are made?"

"No'm," said Henry, "but I don't blame you for asking."

2220 Revised Version. In a junior high school a teacher was amazed to hear the students singing lustily in "Battle Hymn of the Republic" these words: "He has trampled out the vineyards where the grapes are wrapped and stored."

2221 Kid Advice. One suggested to another, "Play dumb for the first few weeks of school, then they'll think you're making real progress afterwards."

2222 What's the Use? Coming home from school, dejected, a little boy said that he wasn't going back. "I can't read or write and they won't let me talk," he explained to his mother.

2223 Exciting! The teacher asked the class to write an exciting short story with suspense. The entire essay of one pupil was "Help! Help!"

2224 Very Important. In an old-fashioned school with fireplace, the teacher said: "Before you speak, think. Count ten before you say anything important, and twenty before you say something very important. Suddenly he saw the lips of the children moving in unison. ". . . Eighteen-nineteen-twenty. Your coattails are on fire, sir!"

2225 Which End? The new and inexperienced school nurse wrote a note to the home: "This child is underweight and too tall for her age."
   The answer said: "We're feeding her what the doctor ordered. About her being too tall—which end should we cut off?"

2226 Sure I Know! A policeman said to a teacher who had not obeyed his signal, "Don't you know what I mean when I hold up my hand?"
   "Sure," said Miss Smith. "I've been teaching school for years."

2227 A Kid Definition. "The spine is a long, limber bone. Your head sets on one end, and you set on the other."

2228 School Teacher: One who takes a lot of live wires and tries to see that they are well-grounded.

2229 Crooked. The teacher asked the class whether the world were round or square. "Neither," was one reply. "It's crooked!"

2230 Nothing. One child said that "nothing" is "a balloon with its skin off."

2231 Lost Coin. The kid was sobbing: "I l-lost the d-dime the t-teacher gave for being the best boy in class." The sympathetic adult quickly replaced the dime and asked how he lost it.

"I-I wasn't the best b-boy in class," he answered.

2232 Impossible Parents. A little girl wrote in her essay, "We get our parents when they are so old that it is hard to change their habits."

2233 Get a Friend. The teacher in grammar study wrote on the board, "I didn't have no fun at the beach" and asked a boy to correct it. He suggested that she get a boyfriend.

2234 Memory. One student defined it as "the thing I forget with."

2235 Officiate. Putting the word into a sentence, a pupil said, "A man got sick from 'a fish he ate.' "

2236 Posture. Rural teacher: "How do you get good posture?"
  Kid: "Keep the cows off and let the grass grow awhile."

2237 Value of Education. Weary of homework, a boy wanted to know what was the use of education. His father said, "There's nothing like it. With it you can worry about conditions all over the world."

2238 More Important. The teacher asked which is more important—the moon or the sun. Johnny insisted that it is the moon.
  "Why?"
  "The moon gives us light at night when we need it. The sun gives light only in the daytime when we don't need it."

2239 Class Hatred: Why kids stay out of school.

2240 Poison! A pupil insisted that a poisonous substance was "aviation" because "one drop, and you're dead!"

SPELLING:

2241 A "B"? One child wrote a friend, "We're having a spelling B and I'm in the finalls."

2242 "Rat." A Texas pupil asked another to spell "rat." The answer was "R-A-T."

"No," he said. "You know—like 'rat now.'"

2243 Problems. A youngster came home and told his mother that he couldn't learn to spell. "The teacher keeps changing the words on me," he said.

"Spell 'Mississippi.'"

"The river or the state?"

2244 "Wet"! "Dad, is 'water works' all one word, or do you spell it with a hydrant?"

2245 Worse Next Week. Daddy was helping daughter with arithmetic.

"It's going to be even worse next week," she said.

"Why?"

"Next week we start the dismal system."

TRAVEL AND TRANSPORATION

2246 Never Do It. A Cape Kennedy resident was in Washington, seeing the Washington monument for the first time. "They'll never get it off the ground," he remarked.

2247 For Bicycles. They were from the back country, seeing a marked highway for the first time.

"What's the white line for?"

"Think it's fer bicycles."

Cars

2248 Not Ripe. The sports car owner, returning to his machine, saw a farmer eyeing it up and down. The farmer grinned and said, "Picked that 'un before it was ripe, eh?"

2249 Changing Tires. A motorist stopped to help a sports car owner who seemed to have had a wreck, since the car was on its side. "Thanks," answered the owner. "I'm just changing a tire."

2250 Can Too Much. A nearsighted man was almost knocked down by a huge dog. As he was trying to right himself a sports car bumped him from the other side. "Dog wasn't bad," he told it, "but the can on his tail almost finished me."

2251 A Curb! The friend said to the sports car driver as they rode along, "My, that's the longest wall I ever saw!"

"Wall?" exclaimed the sports car enthusiast. "That's a curb!"

2252 It's Not Right. Nothing works out right, it seems. In the part of town where you can park as long as you want to, you don't want to.

2253 Drive Right. If we'd all drive right, there would be more people left! In other words, if motorists would give more ground there'd be fewer in it!

2254 Improves. One of the ways to make your old car run better is to check the price on a new one!

2255 Leap Year. This is leap year for pedestrians.

2256 Tombstone. Many a tombstone is carved by chiseling in traffic.

2257 Needed Invention: Wall Street Journal calls for brakes that automatically get tight when the driver does.

2258 Caution! Sign on a 1950 automobile says: "Watch out for flying parts!"

2259 Live to Ninety? If you want to, don't look for it on your speedometer.

2260 Never. A utility pole never hits a car except in self-defense.

2261 Correct! A government pamphlet once observed that "Most accidental injuries do not result in death, but those that do are obviously of a serious nature."

2262 Troublesome: People who rush to the scene of an accident right after it happens. More troublesome: people who rush to the scene just before it happens.

2263 Not Far.
"How far is it to the next town?"
"Three miles as the crow flies."
"And what if the crow has to walk and carry a blasted gasoline can?"

2264 Directions: "Is this the second turn to the left?"

2265 Your Color? She sat at the traffic signal through a red, amber, green, amber, red, amber, green. A policeman wandeed over and said mildly, "Don't we have any color you like?"

2266 Think So. Policeman: "Say, you can't turn around here."
Motorist: "Just step back. I think I can make it."

2267 Innocent Accidents. An insurance investigator for auto claims indicates that he spends a large part of his time investigating collisions between cars, each of which was on its own side of the road, each of which had sounded the horn, and each of which was practically at a standstill at the point of impact.

Trains

2268 Fortunate Indeed.
"I'm lucky to be alive. Just stepped in front of a moving train!"
"And it didn't hit you?"
"No, it was backing up."

2269 Behind Before.
"Porter, do you know why the train is late?"
"The train in front is behind. We were behind before, besides!"

2270 Nervous Motorist. Did you hear of the one who raced a train to a rail crossing and flew all to pieces?

2271 Go Ahead! A sign at an auto graveyard near a rail crossing: "Go ahead and take a chance. We'll buy the car."

2272 Directions.
"The way to the Chicago train?"
"Just turn left and you'll be right."
"Don't be such a smart aleck!"
"All right, turn right and you'll be left!"

2273 Creeping Thing. Taking up the clergyman's ticket on a very local local train, the conductor quipped to the Bible-reading man, "What about the railroad is in the Book?"

"Right in the first chapter, where it says that the Lord made every creeping thing."

2274 The Time Again? The little boy kept asking the train agent when the train would be in.

"Four forty-four," said the agent. "I've told you a dozen times."

"When you say that," said the little one, "I just love to see your whiskers wobble!"

2275 Neat Trick! On a dark night the freight brakeman, signaling to the engineer, dropped his lantern from the top of the car. The switchman caught it and tossed it back up.

The engineer came back and said, "Do that again!"

"What?"

"Let's see you jump from the top of the boxcar and back up again!"

2276 Connection to Oshkosh. The old lady asked the train agent for a schedule to Oshkosh, Wisconsin, from Cairo, Illinois. He wrote it all down. She was back in a few minutes for the same information.

"But I just gave it to you," he said.

"I know," replied she, "but this is for my sister. She wants to go too."

2277 Warning! In the train coach the woman warned a nearby man passenger that her daughter had scarlet fever. "That's all right," he replied. "I'm committing suicide at the first tunnel."

Airplanes

2278 Zip Your Zipper! A woman with a little boy and a little girl took both to the rest room on a plane, putting the boy in one, and going in with the girl to the other. The boy left quickly, and a man went in, forgetting to lock the door. Coming out of the other lavatory the mother cracked the door of what she thought was the boy's a little and said in a whisper, "Don't forget your zipper!"

When the man returned to his seat, he said to his wife, "These stewardesses think of everything!"

2279 Not Too Fast. Two older women boarded the plane at the same time as their pilot. "Now don't go faster than sound," said one to the pilot. "We want to talk."

2280 Cautions.

"How did you enjoy your first plane ride, Grandma?"

"It was pretty good. I was scared. But then I didn't put my whole weight down."

2281 Gum Out. The hostess gave out chewing gum, explaining to first-flight passengers that it kept the ears from popping on descent. At the airport an older man told her that it worked all right, but would she please help him get it out of his ears?

2282 Fast Trucks Too! It was an older man's first plane ride. He observed the truck that refilled the tanks at each stop. A fellow passenger said, "These jets make good time, don't they?"

"Sure do," said the old man. "But that little red truck ain't doin' so bad either!"

2283 No Long Wait. The luggage-laden husband stared miserably out the giant picture window in the airport as their plane departed. "If you hadn't taken so long getting ready," he said, "we could have caught that plane."

"Yes," she replied sharply, "and if you hadn't hurried me so, we wouldn't have so long to wait for the next one."

2284 Your Passenger. A businessman, finding himself the only passenger on a jet, requested the stewardesses' mike and said, "Good morning. This is your passenger speaking."

Taxi

2285 Faster!

"Can't you go faster, driver?"

"Yes, sir, but I ain't allowed to leave the taxi."

2286 Correct? The passenger paid the cab driver the amount on the meter. "That's correct, isn't it?"

"It's correct," he admitted. "But it ain't right!"

2287 Already Settled. The lover, eloping with his adored, said to the cabbie, "Now how much is the fare?"

The driver replied, "That's all right, sir, the young lady's father already took care of that!"

2288 Look Out! Seeing the National Archives in Washington, a visitor asked the cab driver what the carved words—"What is past is prologue!"—meant. The driver thought a minute and said, "Lady, it's government talk for 'You ain't seen nothin' yet!' "

2289 Call Me!

"Would you call me a taxi?"

"All right. You're a taxi."

2290 I See. The passenger was wondering whether he could get his driver's license renewed. His cabbie encouraged him. "I'm sure you can," said he. "I did—and I'm nearly blind!"

Ships

2291 Helping. The master of the ship called below. "Who's below?"

"Will, sir!"

"What are you doing?"

"Nothing."

"Tom there?"

"Yes, sir!"

"What are you doing?"

"Helping Will."

2292 Try Again. Off the coast of Newfoundland there was a ship that hit a fishing boat, backed off, and hit again. Concerned, the captain called, "Can you stay afloat?"

"Think so," was the reply. "Want to try again?"

2293 Watch. The captain, seeing a passenger at the rail on the ocean liner, said, "Sorry, you can't be sick here!"

"Watch!" replied the passenger.

2294 Rescued! After being shipwrecked for three years on an island, he was overjoyed to see a ship in the distance and a small boat coming ashore. The naval officer handed him some newspapers and said, "The captain suggested that you see what's going on in the world and see if you want to be rescued!"

2295 No Better. The ocean was rough. The young bride was having it rough too. "Maurice," she said, "do you still love me?"

"Dearly," he replied.

There was a pause. Then she said, looking a little green, "I thought that would help, but it doesn't."

Trucks

2296 Not Scared. A frightened passenger said to the lady driver, "Not so fast, passing those big trucks. It frightens me."

"Do as I do," responded the driver. "Shut your eyes when you come to a truck."

2297 You're Nice Too. Two drivers of big trucks locked bumpers at a very busy crossing. One called out to the other, "Why don't you look where you're going, you great big pig-eyed, knock-kneed, bowlegged dumbbell!"

The other one smiled and said, "You're nice-looking too, buddy!"

2298 Load Lightener. A car trailed a big truck for miles. Every once in a while the truck driver would stop, bang on the side of the truck, and drive off. Finally the driver of the car pulled up to ask the truck driver what he was doing. "There's a load limit up ahead of two tons. I have four tons of canaries, but if I bang on the sides, it keeps them on the wing!"

Buses

2299 Very Kind. Woman passenger: "I waited and waited and waited for this bus."

Driver: "You were very kind!"

2300 Quite Different. An aggressive woman riding the bus poked the operator with her umbrella. "Is that the First National Bank?" she asked.

"No," replied the operator. "That's my stomach!"

2301 Passenger Check.   On a long-distance bus run the driver was seen checking for absent passengers at a rest stop by feeling the seats.

2302 Made It!

"Did you get home all right last night?" asked the bus operator of a regular passenger.

"Sure. Why?"

"Well, when you got up to give a lady a seat, there were only two passengers on the bus."

2303 How's That?   The tired little man got up to give a young woman a seat on the bus. There was a silence. "I beg your pardon?" asked the man.

"I didn't say anything," she said.

"Oh," he replied. "I thought you said, 'Thank you.'"

Selected Bibliography

HUMOR FOR SPEAKERS

Day, J. Edward (former Postmaster General). *Humor in Public Speaking*. New York: Prentice-Hall, 1965.

Friedman, Edward L. *Speechmaker's Complete Handbook*. New York: Harper & Row, 1966.

————. *Toastmaster's Treasury*. New York: Harper & Row, 1965.

Gerler, William R., ed. *Executive's Treasury of Humor for Every Occasion*. New York: Prentice-Hall, 1965.

Prochnow, Herbert V. *New Speaker's Treasury of Wit and Wisdom*. New York, Harper & Row, 1958.

————, and Prochnow, Herbert V., Jr. *The Successful Toastmaster*. New York: Harper & Row, 1966.

GENERAL HUMOR BOOKS

Arnold, Oren. *Wild West Joke Book*. New York: Frederick Fell, Inc., 1956.

Copeland, Lewis and Faye, eds. *10,000 Jokes, Toasts and Stories*. New York: Doubleday & Co., 1939.

Esar, Evan. *Comic Dictionary*. New York: Horizon Press, 1951.

————. *Dictionary of Humorous Quotations*. New York: Horizon Press, 1949.

————. *Humor of Humor*. New York: Horizon Press, 1952.

————. *Humorous English*. New York: Horizon Press, 1961.

Fuller, Edmund. *Thesaurus of Anecdotes*. New York: Crown Publishers, 1942.

Little Riddle Book, The. Mt. Vernon, N. Y.: Peter Pauper Press, 1954.

Meiers, Mildred, and Knapp, Jack. *Thesaurus of Humor*. New York: Crown Publishers, 1940.

SPECIALIZED BOOKS

Armour, Richard. *Going Around in Academic Circles: A Low View of Higher Education.* New York: McGraw-Hill Book Co., 1965.
This and other Armour books are good to read aloud for humorous purposes.

Ausubel, Nathan. *A Treasury of Jewish Folklore.* New York: Crown Publishers, 1948.
This classic, which has gone into more than twenty printings, gives 750 stories and 75 songs. Many are humorous; all are interesting. Usable for speakers.

Burke, Carl F. *God Is for Real, Man.* New York: Association Press, 1966.
Interpretations of Bible passages and stories by kids in the inner city.

Eisenberg, Helen and Larry. *Fun With Skits, Stunts and Stories.* New York: Association Press, 1955.
Contains a number of short humorous pieces to be read aloud, such as spoonerisms and boners; this is also a good source of group starters and of short skits that can be used as warm-ups at banquets.

————. *The Omnibus of Fun.* New York: Association Press, 1956.
This is 640 pages of humor for the toastmaster, group starters, spoonerisms, boners, and material to be read aloud from Richard Armour, Stephen Leacock, Bob Benchley, and Dave Morrah.
Contains helps for speakers, fun for socials and banquets.

Golden, Harry. *For 2¢ Plain.* New York: World Publishing Co., 1959.
Also published in Permabook edition by Pocket Books, New York.
Inimitable short essays by the famous Jewish editor of *The Carolina Israelite.* Useful for speakers.

————. *Only in America.* New York: World Publishing Co., 1958. Also in Permabook edition.
More of the same!

Harbin. E. O. *The Fun Encyclopedia.* Nashville: Abingdon Press, 1940.
Classic general fun book for humor, socials, and games.

Hudson, Virginia Cary. *O Ye Jigs and Juleps.* New York: The Macmillan Co., 1962. Published in paperback by Macfadden Bartell Corp. in 1964.
Clever writings of a precocious child. Read cuttings aloud to groups for fun; quote phrases.

Johnson, Lyndon Baines. *The Johnson Humor,* ed. Bill Adler. New York: Simon & Schuster, 1965.

Linkletter, Art. *Kids Say the Darndest Things!* New York: Prentice-Hall, 1957.

McKinney, Laurence. *People of Note,* illus. Gluyas Williams. New York: E. P. Dutton & Co., 1940.
Priceless, clever, realistic jingles about music and musicians. Good for reading aloud.

Morrah, Dave. *Cinderella Hassenpfeffer and Other Tales Mein Grossfader Told.* New York: Holt, Rinehart & Winston, 1948.
Very entertaining read-aloud stories in a German-English dialect, originally published in *The Saturday Evening Post.*

_____. *Fräulein Bo-Peepen and More Tales Mein Grossfader Told.* New York: Holt, Rinehart & Winston, 1953.
More of the same!

Nida, Eugene A. *Customs and Cultures.* New York: Harper & Row, 1954.
Contains humorous and serious material written by a warmly human anthropologist.

Russell, Fred. *Funny Thing About Sports.* Nashville, Tenn.: *Nashville Banner,* 1948.
Sports stories by a veteran *Saturday Evening Post* writer. Very usable for speakers.

_____. *I'll Go Quietly.* Nashville, Tenn.: *Nashville Banner,* 1944.
More of the same . . . !

_____. *I'll Try Anything Twice.* Nashville, Tenn.: *Nashville Banner,* 1945.
. . . And more!

Smith, H. Allen. *Don't Get Perconel With a Chicken.* Boston: Little, Brown & Co., 1959. Published as a Permabook in 1960.
Clever writings of children, as collected by Mr. Smith, who has written many other useful books.

Van Buren, Abigail. *Dear Abby.* New York: Prentice-Hall, 1958.
Those marvelous short, punchy answers to requests for advice. Good for reading aloud.

Webster, Gary. *Laughter in the Bible.* St. Louis: Bethany Press, 1960.
A study of humor in the Scriptures.

RECORDS

The availability of humor records changes, but you will find it a good idea to keep up with them if you make speeches frequently. See your record dealer.

Index*

* Numbers in this Index refer to the *joke* numbers, not *pages,* except where indicated by "p."